IRVING BERLIN

Irving Berlin

New York Genius

JAMES KAPLAN

Yale
UNIVERSITY
PRESS

New Haven and London

Yale University Press books may be purchased in quantity for educational, business, or promotional use. For information, please e-mail sales.press@yale.edu (U.S. office) or sales@yaleup.co.uk (U.K. office).

Set in Janson Oldstyle type by Integrated Publishing Solutions, Grand Rapids, Michigan.

Printed in the United States of America.

Library of Congress Control Number: 2019933153
ISBN 978-0-300-18048-0 (hardcover : alk. paper)

A catalogue record for this book is available from the British Library.

This paper meets the requirements of ANSI/NISO Z39.48-1992 (Permanence of Paper).

10 9 8 7 6 5 4 3 2 1

This book is for

Peter W. Kaplan
and
Peter Bogdanovich

Irvy writes a great song. He writes a song with a good lyric, a lyric that rhymes, good music, music you don't have to dress up to listen to, but it is good music. He is a wonderful little fellow, wonderful in lots of ways. He has become famous and wealthy, without wearing a lot of jewelry and falling for funny clothes. He is uptown, but he is there with the old downtown hardshell. And with all his success, you will find his watch and his handkerchief in his pockets where they belong.
—George M. Cohan

He doesn't attempt to stuff the public's ear with pseudo-original, ultra modernism, but he honestly absorbs the vibrations emanating from the people, manners, and life of his time, and in turn, gives these impressions back to the world—simplified—clarified—glorified.

In short, what I really want to say, my dear Woollcott, is that Irving Berlin has *no* place in American music. HE *IS* AMERICAN MUSIC.
—Jerome Kern, in a letter to Alexander Woollcott, 1925

It must be hell being Irving Berlin. The guy's his own toughest competition.
—Anonymous music publisher

CONTENTS

CONTENTS

A BORN NEW YORKER, I first discovered my fellow Manhattanite Irving Berlin during the sliver of time in which we both occupied the same city. It was during the mid-1970s, when, as a very young man, I worked as an editorial typist at the *New Yorker*, while that august institution was still ensconced in its ramshackle original offices, built in 1925 at 25 West 43rd Street. The city, too, had a ramshackle air about it then: it was, famously, a period when New York was broke, and Manhattan, in those days before it became a cold and glass-faced digital video game, was a gritty, graffitied place, a town that couldn't yet afford to efface its links to the past. Every morning, rain or shine, I walked the three-odd miles from my apartment at 106th and Riverside to Midtown, amid traces of an older and slower New York: ancient painted signs, faded but still visible, on the brick sides of buildings ("OMEGA OIL—STOPS PAIN—TRIAL BOTTLE 10¢"); a blind accordionist on a Broadway corner; a 1920s-vintage barber shop at the top of Sixth Avenue where it was still possible to get a straight-razor shave. It was a time when, strolling into the Hotel Algonquin or Brooks Brothers or Grand Central, you could squint and imagine yourself in a city of Elevated tracks and black automobiles and, of course, the blue nimbus of cigar and cigarette smoke hanging over the island like a low-lying front.

The ghosts of Manhattan past were even more palpable in the hushed linoleumed halls of the *New Yorker*, where the cream-colored walls themselves seemed to hold secrets of the magazine's early days—literally, in the case of James Thurber's old office on the eighteenth floor, which retained cartoons, penciled right onto the plaster, of leaping dogs and doughy, baffled-looking men. In warm weather, fans whirred throughout the non-air-conditioned offices; windows were thrown open to the sounds and smells of the city. In the halls one could spot dinosaurs like Rogers E. M. Whitaker and Geoffrey Hellman and S. J. Perelman drifting by; now and then there was even a glimpse of the small and flushed presiding eminence, William Shawn, flitting past like a rare ruby-throated vireo. Silently, of course. Silence was overarching at this great institution; the hard work of turning out a magazine every week proceeded in deep quietude, punctuated only by the faint clacking of type-writers.

As a rule the half dozen members of the typing pool barely spoke to one another, let alone socialized—it was assumed, though never said outright, that we were all jockeying for higher positions at the magazine, the true brass ring being publication. I usually ate lunch solo, sometimes taking a turn around the block afterward. Now and then, though, I got no farther than the small, sedate record shop adjoining the lobby of 25 West 43rd. Music Masters was its name.

This too was a hushed place, a temple to classical music and classic popular tunes, collected and reissued on Music Masters—

labeled LPs, which were sold in severe but elegant black album sleeves. Like record shops of old, the store had a glass-enclosed listening booth, and the proprietors, two bald middle-aged men with clever expressions, exuded a sense of high purpose, as did the browsing communicants. Though the place fascinated me, I felt like a rank outsider. I knew a little classical, a little more Broadway—I'd grown up with parents who listened to show tunes along with their Bach or Berlioz or Beethoven—but my musical tastes generally comported with my era and my hormones, running to rock, blues, and folk: Dylan, the Beatles, the Stones.

On the other hand, I felt the pull of the past, and had a young man's fascination with old age. I had a grandfather, still alive, who had been born in the late 1880s: I sometimes asked him about New York at the turn of the century; he preferred to talk about the Mets. The twenties—only fifty years past then, after all—were much in the air. As at the *New Yorker*, it was a time when great artistic figures of that decade still walked among us—Eubie Blake, George Burns, Nadia Boulanger, Henry Miller, and Josephine Baker; the pianists Arthur Rubinstein and Vladimir Horowitz. At the West End Café I attended a performance by a spry and smiling Papa Jo Jones, who had begun drumming with Walter Page's Blue Devils in Oklahoma City in the 1920s; at the Cookery I was enthralled by the regal Mary Lou Williams, who had played with Duke Ellington as a teenaged sensation in 1924. The continuance of these ancients blended with my own youthful sense of immortality to induce, in my spirit if not my intellect, a soaring hope of deathlessness.

As if to close the argument, there was Groucho Marx, in turtleneck and tam-o'-shanter, on the *Dick Cavett Show*—Groucho, who had begun his vaudeville career before World War I, who had starred with his brothers Chico, Harpo, and Zeppo in *The Cocoanuts*, a 1929 Paramount musical now and then shown on TV, a picture that, while primitive, still possessed the power to charm. The crackling, early-talkie soundtrack, the cheesy sets and creaky pace, the women in cloche hats, men in white flannels and boaters—the whole musty business (all shot in Queens, I later learned, the Astoria Studios standing in for land-rush Florida) was galvanized by Groucho, Chico, and Harpo's timeless sass, an irreverence that also possessed a secret subtext: no matter their characters' names, the Marxes were patently, transcendently Jews, and the movie's straight men and women, especially the majestically obtuse Margaret Dumont ("What in the *weld!*"), were patently, transcendently not. Speaking truth to power was the greatest in-joke of all, the greatest antidote to powerlessness, and Jews were scarcely more puissant in the Nixon years than they—we—had been during the Coolidge administration.

The Cocoanuts was buoyed by a lilting, effervescent score with a glittering handful of songs, including "Florida by the Sea," "When My Dreams Come True," and "The Monkey Doodle Doo"—all Jazz Age curios, to be sure, by turns corny-sweet and infused with a lyrical cheekiness commensurate with the Brothers' depredations:

> Let me take you by the hand
> On a trip to Monkey Land—
> If you're too old for dancing,
> Get yourself a monkey gland . . .

Both music and lyrics, I learned, were by Irving Berlin.

I knew little of Berlin—only, vaguely, that he had written "God Bless America" and "White Christmas," not to mention "What'll I Do?," the haunting waltz used as the theme song of the recently released, bad yet strangely compelling film adaptation of *The Great Gatsby*. And this: Berlin, the same age as my 1888-vintage grandfather, was still alive, somewhere on the Upper East Side.

I badly wanted the soundtrack of *The Cocoanuts*, if such a thing existed, but in that predigital age, I could think of no way to find it. Things were harder to find then.

Then I found it.

Part of it, anyway—the three songs mentioned above—during a postprandial Music Masters browse, on a house-brand double LP titled, piquantly, *Irving Berlin, 1909–1939*. The album contained Berlin songs by various artists from various Broadway shows and Hollywood musicals, a lot of it stuff I wasn't interested in at the time; but besides the *Cocoanuts* material, one thing stopped me in my tracks—that first date, 1909. Had phonograph records even *existed* then? Apparently so. Cut number 1 on side 1 of the album was from that year, and the artist was none other than Berlin himself, singing something called "Oh, How That German Could Love."

I listened to the song, then, carefully lifting my turntable's tonearm and setting the stylus back down, listened to it again. The sound, electronically mastered from an acoustically recorded disk, was predictably scratchy (singer and musicians of that era, I later learned, vocalized and played into a large funnel-shaped horn, at whose narrow end an isinglass diaphragm vibrated sympathetically with the sound, in turn vibrating a cutting stylus that engraved a wax master disk); the band, heavy on the brass, had a clumping, oom-pah beat; but the vocal was—there's no other way to put it—thrilling.

From the first time I heard the song, I have tried to analyze what has made me return to it again and again. Is it its sheer earliness? Not really. In the years since, I have listened to recordings by Enrico Caruso, the great Irish tenor John McCormack, and Billy Murray, "The Denver Nightingale," all of the same vintage or earlier—recordings that fascinate and delight, but don't compel in the same way. For one thing, Caruso, McCormack, and Murray didn't write the songs they sang, and here is the beginning of an explanation. What mainly remains startling about Irving Berlin's rendition of "Oh, How That German Could Love" is Berlin himself.

The singer-songwriter was all of twenty-one; the lyric and the performance were energetic, breathtakingly assured—and most strikingly, very funny. Unlike the songs of Caruso, McCormack, or Murray, "Oh, How That German Could Love" pierced the thick veil of time. Scratches and pops aside, the primitive recording sounded as though it could have been made yesterday. The young Berlin vocalized with verve and soaring confidence, selling the song, shifting into a beer-hall German accent when it suited him, and generally seeming to be having the time of his life:

> Once I got shtuck on a sweet little German,
> And oh what a German was she;
> The best what was walking,
> Well, what's the use talking,
> Was just made to order for me.
> So lovely, and witty, more yet she was pretty,
> You don't know until you have tried.
> She had such a figure, it couldn't be bigger,
> Und there was some more yet beside.

This was freshness (in all senses of the word) incarnate: conversational, superbly visual, borderline bawdy. Berlin swung into the chorus:

> Oh, how that German could love,
> With a feeling that came from the heart;
> She called me her honey,
> Her angel, her money,
> She pushed ev'ry word out so smart.
> She spoke like a speaker,
> And oh what a speech
> Like no other speaker could speak.

Ach, my, what a German,
When she kissed her Herman,
It shtood on a cheek for a week—
And more yet, too!

Mel Brooks could have done no better.

The lyrics, veering from Katzenjammer Kids humor to sentimentality, possessed a kind of wildness: even the sentiment contained extra fizz, like a shaken-up bottle of soda:

I bet all I'm worth that when she came on earth,
The angels went out on parade;
No other one turned up, I think that they burned up
The pattern from which she was made—they can't make no more!

And I kept coming back to the sheer chutzpah of that quadruple repetition in the first chorus:

She spoke like a speaker,
And oh what a speech
Like no other speaker could speak.

This (it dawned on me, slowly) was modernism on the hoof: startling formal innovation smuggled into a seemingly banal idiom. This, the song *itself*, was speech like no other speaker could speak. The more I learned about popular music at the turn of the century—almost all of it thick with schmaltz, or, when meant to be funny, merely old-fashioned and arch—the more I realized that it simply didn't *sound* like this.

Who was the prodigious twenty-one-year-old who had written—and sung—these words?

Page xvi is blank

IRVING BERLIN

Page xviii is blank

1

The Fugitive

A photograph survives of Irving Berlin at thirteen, a solemn, chubby-cheeked boy in a dark suit and tie—in all likelihood his bar mitzvah suit: on what other occasion in the year 1901 would an immigrant Jewish boy be thus photographed? Young Israel Baline (for this was still his name) sits carefully posed, hands folded, looking not at the camera but, in the style of the time, thoughtfully off to the side.[1] His eyes and thick brows are dark, his gaze intense. This boy seems to be watching something carefully, or appears, at the very least, intensely *aware*. His keen attention to whatever it is notwithstanding, his thin lips form a surprisingly relaxed expression: an almost-smile.

It is a remarkable face, though one impossible to take in without the knowledge of who and what the chubby-faced boy will become. And if indeed this is a bar mitzvah photograph, it marks a notable juncture in Israel Baline's life, well beyond the symbolic, for his childhood will soon, actually and quite abruptly, come to an end.

* * *

He was the baby of the family, the eighth and youngest child of Leah and Moses Beilin, recent immigrants from eastern Europe. Moses was an itinerant cantor who, for whatever reason, would have terrible trouble finding work in New York. Before the Beilins left the Old Country, they seem to have lived for a while in the city of Tyumen, in western Siberia—where Israel is said to have been born, on May 11, 1888. At some point the family moved to Tolochin, Belorussia. As is the case with so many eastern European Jews of that era, accounts are sketchy. This much, however, is known: late in the summer of 1893, Moses and Leah's family left Europe for good, part of the great Jewish exodus that had begun a decade earlier amid the vicious institutionalized antisemitism and widespread pogroms that characterized the reign of Czar Alexander III.[2] In later life Irving Berlin claimed that his earliest memory, at age three or four, was of lying on a blanket by the side of a road, watching his family's house burn down: a terrifying image of loss.[3]

After a long and arduous trip by foot and rail across Europe and then, even more gruelingly, in steerage over the Atlantic, the Beilins arrived at New York Harbor on September 14, 1893, on the Red Star Line's S.S. *Rhynland,* out of Antwerp.[4] The family spoke only Yiddish, and the surname as spelled on the ship's manifest is surely an Anglicization of what would previously have been written in Hebrew or Cyrillic characters. In any case, during processing at Ellis Island, an immigration clerk, probably from hearing Moses pronounce the name, changed the spelling once more, and Baline (pronounced, depending on whom you ask, either Bay-leen, a spondee, or Bah-*leen*) it stayed.[5] For the time being.

And then the family settled, like so many thousands of their ilk—like my father's father's family, for example, and perhaps like some of your ancestors too—in a Lower East Side tenement. At first, in the Balines' case, home was a basement apartment on Monroe Street. Eight people, fresh off the boat and disoriented, in a windowless three-room cellar with no running water, the privy in the courtyard—one wonders what dreams, if any, of the *goldeneh medina*, the golden land, survived this shock. The family had arrived in the teeth of a national financial crisis, the Panic of 1893. Banks, railroads, and farms were failing; factory and mill jobs vanished. Yet somehow the lower orders survived. A few years on, the Balines' situation had even improved slightly: The 1900 U.S. Census shows the family, now numbering only seven—twenty-year-old Sophie had married and left the nest—occupying the second floor of a tenement at 354 Cherry Street.[6]

Amid the teeming chaos of the Lower East Side, the Balines, like a hundred thousand other immigrant families, somehow managed to put together a living—in their case without much help from the nominal head of the household. In 1893, the ship's manifest of the *Rhynland* had listed the forty-four-year-old Moses Beilin's occupation as butcher—perhaps since he had worked as a *shomer*, an inspector of kosher chickens. Six and a half years on, the 1900 census lists his profession as painter, also noting that he has been out of work for nine months. Cantor or painter or chicken inspector, unemployed was unemployed.

As for Moses's wife, her name Americanized to Lena on the census form, no profession, trade, or occupation is listed. She is said to have contributed to the family income by assisting in the delivery of babies. Twenty-two-year-old Sarah Baline is listed as a wrapper maker (for cigars), employed, as is fifteen-year-old Augusta. On the other hand, the other two older children, nineteen-year-old Benjamin, a shirt-maker, and seventeen-year-old Rebeckah, also a wrapper maker, are declared out of work. Thirteen-year-old Israel's occupation is listed, simply, as "school."[7]

Of the theoretical breadwinner, next to nothing is known. Berlin, who adored his mother—he kept a photograph of her by his bedside long after her death in 1922—scarcely spoke of Moses, even to his own daughters. Perhaps he was ashamed. After a half dozen years scrounging for work in the New World, Moses Baline—whether through hard luck, illness, depression, or some combination thereof—had hit a dead end. On the other hand, he was apparently able to find a post, paid or not, during the High Holy Days, leading the choir in a Lower East Side temple. Oh, and he took along his youngest son, who could also sing a little.

* * *

At what age Irving Berlin began to vocalize in public is anybody's guess—accounts of his early years, especially his own, are hazy at best—but it seems plausible that he first became a sidewalk entertainer of sorts not long after he started working as a newsboy, at about age eight, hawking William Randolph Hearst's sensationalistic *New York Journal* on the hard streets of the Bowery. It was a business whose minuscule profit margins (half a cent per paper sold) rewarded only the most energetic and assertive—but then from childhood, Izzy Baline seems to have been what is called in Yiddish a *bren*. From the German word *brennen*, to burn. "Someone of great energy, vivacity, competence, and optimism," according to Leo Rosten; "a 'fireball.'"[8] Good-looking in a small and dark way; quick on his feet and quick-witted.

His first ambition was to be a cartoonist—a profession that had just become big business. In 1896, around the time the eight-year-old Izzy hit the streets as a newsboy, Hearst's *Journal* stole the nation's premier cartoonist, Richard F. Outcault, from Joseph Pulitzer's *New York World*. Outcault had created a national sensation with his comic *Hogan's Alley*, set in a fictional slum populated by children of various ethnicities, chief among them a shaved-headed boy known (for the color of the smock he wore) as the Yellow Kid.

Young Izzy, with a bundle of *Journals* in his bag, would certainly have had plenty of opportunity to look over Outcault's work, which often appeared on the front page, and no doubt he gazed with admiring recognition at the antics of the Kid and his pals, marveling at Outcault's ability to render the chaotic essence of tenement life with a few strokes of his pen. This was storytelling at its most economical, thoroughly American in style and substance. And the storyteller was, no doubt, a very rich man.

Izzy had seen boys and men make money by drawing caricatures in chalk on the sidewalk. He decided to give it a try himself—he had a lot of funny ideas—but discovered he wasn't much of a draftsman.

What he could do was sing.

A half-cent profit per paper wasn't much. But Izzy found that if he broke into song, the paper buyers might toss an extra penny or two his way.

He could keep a tune. "The boy had a clear, true soprano voice—a plaintive voice tuned to the grieving of the *schule* [*sic*]," Berlin's first biographer, Alexander Woollcott, wrote.[9]

To which one is tempted to say, Oy. But then, Woollcott, who was taking his close friend's measure in 1925, when Berlin was all of thirty-seven, was, in an era of unapologetic Waspocracy, a Wasp mandarin—the *New York Times*'s chief drama critic, a columnist for the *New Yorker*, and a charter member of the Algonquin Round Table (where Berlin occasionally sat in)—who wrote with affection and florid verve, not to mention a certain ham-handedness common to the age, when it came to matters Judaic. At any rate young Israel Baline, as a recent greenhorn eager to *oysgrinen zikh*—literally, de-green himself—would have been eager to get out of shul and onto the street.

The end of the nineteenth century was a time of rich cultural ferment in America: the young nation was casting off European influences and forging a brash, demotic personality of its own, in politics, literature, even popular music. And for music, New York City was the hot center of the action. Vaudeville had begun here in 1881, at Tony Pastor's theater on 14th Street near Third Avenue, when that impresario realized he could instantly double his audience for variety shows by cleaning up the material and banning the sale of alcohol on the premises, thereby bringing in women as well as men. Shows needed songs, and by the middle eighties, music publishers began to cluster in the Manhattan neighborhood just north of Madison Square that would soon come to be known as Tin Pan Alley. With the explosive growth of piano manufacturing in the late nineteenth century—suddenly every middle-class home had to have an upright—came huge growth in the market for sheet music: in 1892, Charles K. Harris's ballad "After the Ball" became the first popular song to sell a million copies.

In those preradio days, music was to be heard everywhere on the streets of the city—from street musicians, or buskers, who played the hurdy-gurdy, street piano, or spoons, or just stood there and sang; from the upright pianos found in every saloon and aspiring middle-class parlor.

Izzy Baline would have taken it all in, would have heard "After the Ball" and "Little Annie Rooney" and "The Sidewalks of New York" and "A Bird in a Gilded Cage," and "The Band Played On" and dozens of other tunes of the late nineties and early aughts: drippingly sentimental, most of them, as was the style of the day, and many of them in waltz time, a carryover from Europe. The schmaltziness of these songs made them highly susceptible to parody if one were of a satirical turn of mind, and Izzy Baline, who was, may have begun creating racy special lyrics as early as his newsboy days.

Then his life imploded.

In his accounts of his boyhood, Irving Berlin tended to polish up the same select bunch of chestnuts again and again: the getting-knocked-off-the-dock-by-the-crane story (he was fished out of the water still clutching the five pennies he'd made selling papers that day). The yarn of how he pawned, bit by brass bit, the samovar his family had brought over from the old country. The tale of how he learned about Christmas by going across the street to his poor Irish neighbors, the O'Haras, whose stumpy and scraggly Christmas tree, the ancestor of Charlie Brown's, nevertheless seemed to young Izzy to "tower to Heaven."

What he never discussed, with his three daughters or with his French son-in-law Edouard Emmet, with whom Berlin liked to reminisce as the two men strolled the sidewalks of Paris together in the 1960s, was the death of his father when Izzy was thirteen.

In later years, Irving Berlin spoke only obliquely, and with insistent nostalgia, about his early days. "Everyone should have a Lower East Side in their lives," he said. Close to sixty, he told the *New York Sun*:

> I never felt poverty because I'd never known anything else. We had an enormous family. Eight or nine in four rooms and in the summer some of us slept on the fire escape or on the roof. I was a boy with poor parents, but let's be realistic about it. I didn't starve. I wasn't cold or hungry. There was always bread and butter and hot tea. I slept better in tenement houses . . . than I do now in a nice bed.[10]

Speaking to his son-in-law, Berlin slightly fleshed out the story: "He said that in the summertime, the tenement became unbearable," Emmet recalled. "They were crowded—there was him and his brother, surrounded by his sisters and mother; his father quickly was no longer there."[11]

The only record we have of Moses Beilin's passing is a stark one: his New York City death certificate, dated July 19, 1901. The cause of death is listed as chronic bronchitis and arteriosclerosis. He was fifty-three.

And his youngest child was thirteen.

* * *

In all likelihood, Izzy made the decision that September, when he would have been about to enter the seventh or eighth grade at P.S. 147 on East Broadway.[12] A quick study, he had taken in all he felt he needed to know: grammar and penmanship and arithmetic, the fundamentals of civics. School—especially with just a few dollars a week coming into the household—was now quite superfluous.

But the household itself?

Woollcott describes young Izzy's leave-taking from 354 Cherry Street:

> As far as he knew, there was always enough to eat stewing away on the back of Mother Baline's stove. . . . But, he knew, too, that he contributed less than the least of his sisters and that skeptical eyes were being turned on him as his legs lengthened and his earning power remained the same. . . . Finally, in a miserable retreat from reproaches unspoken, he cleared out one evening after supper, vaguely bent on fending for himself or starving if he failed. In the idiom of his neighborhood, where the phenomenon was not uncommon, he went on the bum.[13]

Berlin told a rather different tale to his family, recalling, according to the eldest of his three daughters, Mary Ellin Barrett, his "uncomfortableness with a household of nothing but women—Ben had moved out—and a certain desire to get away from all the women."[14]

Izzy already knew the Bowery well. He had acquired a street education there, selling his papers along raucous sidewalks deeply shadowed by the Elevated tracks. The district was,

Berlin biographer Edward Jablonski writes, "the place to go for entertainment, inebriation, drugs, prostitutes, and colorful characters. In addition, it was the locus of fleecing, robbery, venereal diseases, and even murder."[15]

Now and then the newsboy would step into one of the saloons—where minors were of course expressly prohibited—to try moving a few *Journals*. Here he found a different kind of clamor than on the street: the pounding of an out-of-tune upright, drunken singing and bragging and joking and ragging. And once, perhaps, amid the din, a high voice, piping:

> She's only a bird in a gilded cage,
> A beautiful sight to see,
> You may think she's happy and free from care,
> She's not, though she seems to be . . .

Izzy would have watched the drunken men as the urchin sang: some ignoring him, some laughing scornfully; but not a few discreetly wiping away a tear at the memory (or the dream) of such innocence. Then a coin was thrown at the boy's feet, and then another and another—Indian-head pennies mostly, but here and there a buffalo nickel or Liberty dime. The kid scuttled to grab the loose change.

An instant later, the bouncer was grabbing the kid by the arm and slinging him out the door. But he had his dinner money.

And Izzy, looking on with fascination, had a plan.

2

◆▪◆▪◆

I Have Discovered a Great Kid

HE COULD SING. He could keep a tune; he could remember the words. He could, if the spirit or the audience moved him, fill in better, spicier, words of his own. It may not be overreaching to say that even then, barely into his teens, he felt a fascination for what a song said and how it said it. How it was put together, where the rhymes fell. Whether it was silly or moving, trivial or well made.

And so Izzy Baline joined the great corps of buskers on the streets of the Lower East Side—the sidewalks of New York, as the song so romantically put it. The real sidewalks of New York were, as we have seen, a little less than romantic, beginning with the ubiquitous horseshit (and, sometimes, horse carrion) that the lyrics failed to mention. Not to mention, if you happened to be a Jew, the Italian and Irish kids who would just as soon smash your head in as look at you.

But Izzy was nimble. Quick on his feet and quick with

words too, both in tight spots and in the saloons, where sometimes, as he raised his high voice in song (it grew huskier, but
not much deeper, as he matured), the words came out not *precisely* as the songwriter had written—

> She's only a bird in a gilded cage,
> A beautiful sight to see,
> Her hourglass figure is all the rage,
> Her charms can be yours for a fee . . .

—or something along those lines.

He would have noted, with his sharp eye, that these men in
their cups were suckers for sentimentality. But his quicksilver wit
proved equally appealing, if not more so. A slightly (or more
than slightly) ribald twist to the lyrics could surprise and delight,
almost as though he had performed an act of prestidigitation.

Working Bowery saloons like the Morgue, the Bucket of
Blood, the Flea Bag, and Suicide Hall—places named with swag-
gering, slightly self-conscious irony (for the Bowery was a mag-
net not just to drunks and the lower classes seeking amusement,
but to uptown slummers)—Izzy learned to be deft in all ways,
even with his feet: he could stamp on a coin, slide it toward his
hand, and pocket it in a flash, all without breaking the phrase of
the song.

If Leah had known where her youngest child was laying his
head at night, she would never have slept at all. There was, for
example, the Cobdock Hotel, "to which the gals would take
their sailors," as Berlin jauntily recalled years later. And the
Mascot, "a fifteen-cents-a-night joint," where he lived for a year
of his adolescence. "You got a cubby-hole to sleep in . . . open
at the top, and you were always scared that somebody would
reach over and steal your pants."[1]

Or worse. Berlin's recollections mostly tap-danced over the
problems of bedbugs, disease, and the sheer dangers inherent in
close and disreputable quarters. In one flophouse, Izzy got into

a fight with another boy that nearly turned deadly: "The kid stabbed me, and I was rushed to Bellevue," Berlin remembered.[2] What he didn't say was that the kid with the knife no doubt carried it for defensive purposes: God alone knew, in a world of boys and men on the bum together, who might be reaching over from the next cubbyhole, and not just for your pants.

Still, one way and another, he survived. For a while he worked as a seeing-eye boy to a busker named Blind Sol, who fiddled in saloons while his watchful young assistant sang along and monitored the take. Then Izzy took a fateful step up: just before his fourteenth birthday, in early 1902, he auditioned for and won a spot in the chorus of a musical called *The Show Girl*, with songs by H. L. Heartz and R. A. Barnet.

The show left Manhattan that spring for out-of-town try-outs. And chorus boy Baline must have had something on the ball, for he was assigned the "bit" of rushing out front during a lull in the action, climbing to one of the stage-side boxes, and breaking into a Heartz and Barnet number called "Sammie."

Even at the turn of the century, this bit, called the "singing stooge," had been around awhile. The surprise of hearing what seemed to be an audience member suddenly pipe up could galvanize a house and sell a song. But somehow either "Sammie" or Izzy failed to sell, and the chorus boy was given his walking papers in Binghamton, N.Y.

Nevertheless, the bug had bitten him. And Izzy Baline had faith in himself. In the crucible of the Bowery, under the toughest of conditions, he had learned how to put over a song, whether sentimental or ribald, and make a tough crowd eat out of his hand. A nervy kid, he knew he could do it again.

So he marched uptown to Tin Pan Alley—the block of 28th Street between Fifth and Sixth Avenues that got its name from the din of dozens of music publishers' pianos banging and clanging through open transoms and windows—and presented his credentials to none less than Harry Von Tilzer.

The already legendary songwriter with the mysterious, vaguely noble-sounding name had been born Aaron Gumbinsky in 1872 in Goshen, Indiana, the son of Polish-Jewish immigrants.[3] At fourteen he ran away with the circus and soon began writing songs. Once started, he seemed barely able to stop: Von Tilzer claimed to have written eight thousand tunes in his life. At least a dozen—numbers such as "A Bird in a Gilded Cage," "Wait Till the Sun Shines, Nellie," "I Want a Girl (Just Like the Girl That Married Dear Old Dad)"—became million sellers, when sales, tallied by copies of sheet music sold, were driven by nothing more than word of mouth or the sound of a song being played on a neighbor's parlor piano or in a music store.

Von Tilzer also made a substantial part of his living writing in a genre that flourished during the age of immigration: the ethnic number. He turned out Irish and German dialect tunes by the score, as well as dozens in black dialect, the variant then known, with unapologetic offensiveness, as "coon songs." (One of them, 1904's "Alexander, Don't You Love Your Baby No More?" got its comic lift from the contemporary convention that Alexander was a ridiculously pretentious name for a black man.)

Mere compositional volume wasn't enough, however. Von Tilzer had figured out early on that while it was all well and good to make a nickel a copy on a song he'd written—and that he could do very well indeed with a million seller, in the days when the average American income was something like six hundred dollars a year—it was even better to publish the music himself, assuming the downside risk but, knowing he had a cascade of hits in him, planning for a significant upside. After serving two years as the junior partner to the publishers Shapiro and Bernstein, in 1902 he opened the Harry Von Tilzer Music Publishing Company, at 37 West 28th Street.

And in walks this boy Izzy Baline, who has somehow managed to talk his way into an audience with the man himself. Von

Tilzer, not yet thirty but prematurely balding, with a long, sensitive face, took one look at this fourteen-year-old street kid—small, dark-eyed, full of beans—and felt some kind of pull. No doubt Izzy told him about "Sammie," and no doubt Von Tilzer asked him to sing a few bars. A cappella. Izzy, being the crackerjack he was, would have had the wit to throw in some of Von Tilzer's own stuff as well. As he sang, Izzy certainly would have glanced around the prosperous young songwriter/publisher's swell new office and taken it all in.

The great Harry Von Tilzer hired Israel Baline, on the spot, to be a song plugger, at the grand salary of five dollars a week. Young Baline's job, as a "boomer," was to use that sweet, hoarse voice of his to demonstrate Von Tilzer compositions to possible song buyers, in the public and in show business alike. And Von Tilzer had just the song for him. It was another of his specialties, a fallen-woman tearjerker, very much in the mold of "Bird in a Gilded Cage" (even the meter was identical), called "The Mansion of Aching Hearts." Once again, the lyricist was the Englishman Arthur J. Lamb:

> She lives in a mansion of aching hearts,
> She's one of a restless throng;
> The diamonds that glitter around her throat,
> They speak both of sorrow and song . . .

Few listeners, even in those supposedly more innocent times, would have failed to understand exactly what kind of house the mansion in question was. And, canny businessman that he was, Von Tilzer would have known how strangely moving the song would be when crooned by an adolescent boy. The coarsest possible subject matter in the sweetest possible package, and the songwriter/publisher had just the family-friendly venue in mind for the song's introduction.

Twenty years on, Tony Pastor's Music Hall, the cradle of vaudeville, was still going strong on East 14th Street. And one of Pastor's most popular attractions in 1902 was a family act that featured an actual family. As a review of the era put it: "For real rough-and-tumble fun, there is no act which equals that of the Three Keatons, father, mother and son. The latter, the inimitable 'Buster,' is one of the funniest little fellows on the stage . . ."[4]

The rough-and-tumble fun went as follows: Ma Keaton would stand to the side of the stage and play saxophone while Pa Keaton threw Buster around. Literally. The child—aged seven that autumn—had a handle sewn onto the back of his shirt so that his father could get a good grip. Little Buster, who'd learned early on how to break his fall with a covertly extended arm or leg, would fly across the stage, land in a heap, then stand up, dust himself off, and make droll stone-faced remarks, much to the audience's amusement. Then, at a crucial juncture in the merriment, the stage orchestra would segue into Von Tilzer's latest song, and young Izzy Baline would rise from his balcony seat and burst into a stirring tenor rendition of "The Mansion of Aching Hearts." This he did for two shows a day until the Keatons headed off to the next stop on the Keith-Albee circuit.

The chronology of Israel Baline's years on the bum, especially the period from his fourteenth to sixteenth years, is short on detail but long on pluck. After Pastor's Izzy returned to busking; he also worked as a "slide singer" at the primitive movie theaters known as nickelodeons, leading audience sing-alongs during the piano interludes that accompanied reel changes, as the lyrics (on slides) flashed onto the screen.

Most remarkably, during the formative years of his adolescence, without a parental hand to guide him, Izzy seems to have avoided the seamy pitfalls with which his stomping grounds were richly furnished. And he didn't just survive; he appears, somehow, to have thrived, finding occupation, amusement, friends.

Even father figures, of a sort. One was a tough-talking, derby-wearing mountebank named George Washington Connors, better known as Chuck. The former prizefighter, who dubbed himself the Mayor of Chinatown, made his living showing wide-eyed uptowners the colorful low life among that district's dark, crooked streets—opium dens, cockfighting pits, bordellos—all the while providing a running narrative in a singular Bowery Boy–Cockney patois. And at some point, no one knows where or how, Chuck Connors took a shine to the gutsy young Jewish busker and told him he could do better than singing on the street. Accordingly, one day in early 1904, Connors led Izzy Baline through the swinging doors of the Pelham Café, in the heart of Chinatown at 12 Pell Street, better known as—there is no other way to say it than to say it—Nigger Mike's.[5]

* * *

The Pelham—crudely nicknamed after its owner Mike Salter, a Russian Jew with olive skin, kinky hair, and a broad nose—was the liveliest stop on Chuck Connors's slummers' tour: a saloon and dance hall featuring singing waiters, a backroom piano player, and a whorehouse upstairs. Salter took one look at the runty fifteen-year-old with the unruly mop of hair and said he didn't need any more waiting help. But the irrepressible Izzy was hard of hearing when it came to the word *no*. "After the owner stepped out," Berlin biographer Philip Furia writes, "he began singing to the customers. When the other waiters tried to drown him out, he sang louder and finally won the crowd over just as Salter returned."[6]

And so, for the impressive sum of seven dollars a week—plus tips—Izzy landed his first steady job. One of his first tasks was running around the corner to Olliffe's Apothecary, at 6 Bowery (owned and operated by the brothers Joseph and Nicholas Schenck), to pick up supplies of the purgative with which Mike dosed the drinks of undesirable customers.[7]

Of which there were plenty. Both the Pelham and its rival around the corner, Callahan's Dance Saloon, sat in dangerous territory: the bend of Doyers Street, also known as the Bloody Angle, was the epicenter of the Chinese Tong wars, and Pell-Doyers was a kind of no-man's-land between the turfs of the rival (Irish-Italian) Five Points and (Jewish) Eastman gangs. Irving Berlin told a reporter many years later: "I got my musical education in the Bowery, but I never mingled with the real tough people, so-called gorillas, but attended strictly to business."[8]

Business itself was tough enough. The clientele was drunk and rowdy, and the hours were eight to six—eight P.M. to six A.M. (This flip-flopped circadian rhythm stayed with Izzy for the next eighty-five years of his life, contributing to his lifelong insomnia.) The patrons dispensed their tips by tossing coins onto the floor, partly, one guesses, for the sadistic pleasure of watching the waiters scurry for them. *Nickel-kickers*, the waiters were called. And the biggest tips would come, Izzy Baline found, when he deployed his subspecialty: improvising dirty lyrics to the schmaltzy hits of the day, especially yet another Von Tilzer composition, "Are You Coming Out Tonight, Mary Ann?"

Imagine the possibilities.

The quick-witted Izzy could, and did, to the raucous delight of the patrons. One impressed customer was a twenty-one-year-old Harry Von Tilzer song plugger and talent scout named Max Winslow. After hearing the young waiter's blue parody of "Mary Ann," Winslow came back to the Pelham again and again. At last, as Von Tilzer recalled in an unpublished autobiography, the talent scout could contain himself no longer: "Max Winslow came to me and said, 'I have discovered a great kid, I would like to see you write some songs with.' Max raved about him so much."[9] But for all Winslow's enthusiasm—and with plenty of songwriting talent already in house—Von Tilzer took a pass on Izzy Baline.

The following year there was a stir in the neighborhood when the house pianist at Callahan's, Al Piantadosi, wrote a song that, wonder of wonders, actually got published. Its name was "My Mariuccia Take a Steamboat," and its Italian-dialect lyric (written by Callahan's bouncer, Big Jerry) sounded like Chico Marx *avant la lettre:*

> My Mariuccia take a steamboat—woo woo!—she's-a gone away
> She make-a too much-a jealous for me—she fly away . . .

In the undemanding world of 1906 ethnic songs, "My Mariuccia" caught on and enjoyed a brief vogue—quite gallingly to Mike Salter, for the tune siphoned away customers from the Pelham to Callahan's, where they were eager to hear Al and Big Jerry themselves perform it while the drunk and delighted crowd chimed in on the steamboat-whistle *woo-woo*'s.

And so one day, Salter turned to *his* house pianist, Michael "Nick" Nicholson, and his wiseacre singing waiter Izzy, and said, You're so goddamn smart—why don't you write something like that? Or words to that effect.

*   *   *

It was one thing, Izzy Baline quickly found, to improvise dirty lyrics to a song someone else had written; it was quite another to invent brand-new words for a brand-new melody. As Irving Berlin told the Broadway columnist Ed Sullivan in the late 1930s, "I never wanted to be a songwriter. All I wanted in those days was a job in which I could earn $25.00 a week. That was my idea of heaven."[10]

Yet Izzy and Nick sat at the piano and, note by note, sweated out the song that became "Marie from Sunny Italy." All these years later, you can still smell the sweat. Irving Berlin himself was recorded singing the tune during a CBS Radio tribute on his fiftieth birthday in 1938. It's a winsome rendition, in Berlin's light, hoarse tenor—the sheer charm of it almost covers the song's sheer lousiness:

My sweet Marie from sunny Italy,
Oh, how I do love you,
Say that you'll love me, love me, too,
Forevermore I will be true . . .

No doubt someone, Baline or Nicholson, committed this deathless poetry to paper. But then—conceivably after a forehead-smacking double take—it occurred to the musically illiterate songwriters that they were going to have to find somebody to actually put the *notes* of the song down on paper.

The job was finally done by one Julius Saranoff, a fiddler and occasional entertainer at the Pelham. The next step was to get the thing published. The tunesmiths wound up at the firm of Jos. W. Stern & Co., which, as Edward Jablonski notes, was "actually not in Tin Pan Alley proper, but ten blocks north, at 102–104 West Thirty-eighth Street."[11]

Song publishing in the early 1900s was a land-rush business: by 1910, Tin Pan Alley was spewing out some twenty-five thousand titles a year. And with sheet music cheap to produce, and sales of more than five million units per annum, publishers could afford to take a chance on more than a few dogs.

In this undemanding context, Jos. W. Stern & Co. sent Julius Saranoff's lead sheet (the first handwritten rendition, on staff paper, of a song's music and lyrics) to a cover designer, an edition was printed, and soon Izzy Baline, no doubt very proud and probably also a little incredulous, was holding the sheet music for "Marie from Sunny Italy" in his hands.

Cover designs in these palmy days of sheet music were an art in themselves, and "Marie"'s cover was a nice-enough-looking example of the genre: a greenish one-tone illustration depicting a mandolin-playing swain serenading his lady love on a gondola crossing a Venetian lagoon. As was the common practice then, the cover also featured an inset photograph of a singer—in this case, for some reason, the pretty Yiddish-theater performer Leah Russell.

All nice enough, and conventional enough. But what jumps out, to the modern eye, are the names of the songwriters, lettered in dark green over the lagoon's gray-green waters, just beneath the gondola's prow: "Words by I. Berlin/Music by M. Nicholson."

* * *

According to Woollcott, who would have had it straight from Irving, people had started to call him Berlin sometime after he first arrived on the Bowery: "For some reason his really distinguished patronymic, Baline, proved difficult to his neighbors and Berlin represents an effort to spell out the sound of the thing everyone called him anyway."[12]

Bah-leen, Berlin. A plausible theory. But in all likelihood, only part of the truth. No doubt Izzy Baline still wished to *oysgrinen zikh:* to look American, sound American, *be* American, as quickly as possible. Berlin may have been the name of a foreign capital, but at least it was familiar. A word everybody knew, one that ended in a consonant rather than a vowel. Philip Furia maintains the name was a shrewd choice, "one that drew upon the reverence of Americans toward German composers."[13] Maybe. Most likely Berlin just looked good, and sounded good, to Baline.

But then there was that pesky first name. Woollcott says that young Izzy had "for some time" harbored a secret ambition to be known as Irving. He wasn't alone. Such (then) British-sounding, and therefore classy-sounding, given names as Irving, Murray, Milton, Seymour, and Sidney became wildly popular among Jews in the early 1900s—who little suspected how typically Jewish these names would come to sound in time. Yet, Woollcott tells us, Baline was shy at first about a complete transformation:

> When the time came to publish the first song, he itched to sign it Irving Berlin, but he knew a copy would always be left

casually on the piano rack at Nigger Mike's and he feared the derision of the gang. Still Israel was too solemn and Talmudic a name with which to depress a popular song. Izzy was too ornery. It smacked of Cherry Street and sweltering doorsteps. So, compromising between an old pride and a new embarrassment, he signed the first song "I. Berlin."[14]

He was still in the pupal stage of his metamorphosis. "Marie from Sunny Italy" may have made him a songwriter on paper, but not many people—including, in all likelihood, the lyricist himself—considered it much of a song. At least "My Mariuccia," for all its caricatured Italianness, had the virtue (those steamboat whistles!) of being fun. And fun went a long way in selling a song in those days. As did schmaltz. "Marie," earnest in the extreme, wasn't really either. Published on May 8, 1907, it earned its composers precisely 75 cents in royalties that year and $1.20 the next, meaning that if Jos. W. Stern & Co. had published ten thousand copies of the sheet music—a common print run—and sold them at ten cents each, the company had moved about two thousand units—taken a bath, in other words. Irving Berlin claimed in later years that his pharmacist pal Joe Schenck had bought the first copy—which, if true, showed early on what a good and loyal friend Joe Schenck was destined to be.

3

—◆·◆·◆—

You Can Never Tell Your Finish When You Start

OFFICIALLY, I. Berlin was a songwriter. But at this point he would have been hard pressed to prove to anyone, himself included, that he was anything but a nineteen-year-old singing waiter. And in very short order after the publication of "Marie from Sunny Italy," he was an unemployed one. The details of Izzy's firing from the Pelham Café are murky. One night in early 1907, apparently, Mike Salter left him in charge of the cash register, and after Izzy fell asleep at his post, twenty-five dollars—the equivalent of some six hundred dollars today—vanished from the till. No small matter. Yet some say Salter took the money himself—either drunkenly, forgetting about it afterward, or maliciously, to punish Izzy for his dereliction. Whatever the case, Nigger Mike, disappointed with his junior waiter, unceremoniously kicked him to the curb he'd come from.

But the enterprising and affable Berlin quickly found another job, with higher pay and better hours, uptown at a new saloon called Jimmy Kelly's Folly, on East 14th Street, just a stone's throw from Tony Pastor's Music Hall, not to mention much closer to Tin Pan Alley. Uptown meant a better class of barroom clientele: specifically, and significantly, the show-business types—"jugglers, comedians, tenors, and hoofers," in Woollcott's words—who appeared at Pastor's and the other nearby houses in what was then a vibrant theatrical district.[1] The show people were drawn to the whip-smart, entertaining young waiter, and he to them.

Max Winslow, the Von Tilzer talent scout who had been so impressed by Izzy at the Pelham, found him again at Kelly's; by and by, the two young men became friends. Friendship was something that Berlin, from the beginning, never took lightly: throughout his long life, he would have hundreds of acquaintances and correspondents, and perhaps a half dozen intimates. Though outwardly amiable, Berlin didn't let people in easily: he possessed a core of intense feeling, shadowed by early loss and deprivation. And as a genius in progress, he would, from the beginning, have been an observer above all.

Winslow and Izzy found a furnished room on East 18th Street, just off Union Square, and became roommates. Flophouses were a thing of the past. With a little more money coming in, the young waiter could get his unruly hair barbered regularly and begin to pay attention to his wardrobe.[2]

He could also start to think about his future rather than mere survival. On his free afternoons he walked the cacophonous sidewalks of Tin Pan Alley, soaking in the atmosphere, listening to words and music. One day at one of the music publishers—it was probably the fall of 1907—he encountered a live wire of a girl, a sixteen-year-old with a substantial nose, direct brown eyes, and a sly sense of humor. Within the first minute, Izzy knew two things about Fanny Borach, as she was then known: she was convinced she was going to make it in show business, and for the time being she was working—just as he had a few years earlier—as a slide singer in a nickelodeon. She was there looking for songs—as, in a way, he was, too.

The two hit it off immediately. Years later, Borach, who had long since become Fanny Brice, remembered "a brown-eyed, mild young man who generally came forward offering diffident suggestions" about what she might sing. Shy or not, though, he became "convulsed with laughter" when they piped up together on one of the publisher's more corn-syrupy offerings, something about "a moon, a girl, a boat, a float."[3]

He thought he could do better. But actually doing it was something else. Back to Kelly's he went and, with racking labors (and the help of the house pianist), Izzy sat down and wrote a song of his own, words and music, something called "The Best of Friends Must Part":

> What's that you say?
> No work today?
> Done lost your job?
> Where is your pay?[4]

It was a character song, ethnic around the edges, and though far from memorable, it was a big step up from "Marie from Sunny Italy," with its little birds and plinking mandolin. "The Best of Friends" may have lacked grace and lyricism (and humor, Berlin's hallmark, once he really became Berlin), but it had an appealingly unconventional social-realist grit.

"The only significance this song has," Berlin wrote almost seventy-five years later, "is that it was published [on February 6, 1908] in Tin Pan Alley on 28th Street by the Selig Publishing Company. I think Selig later became a silent movie producer." But he was being too hard on himself. The quality of the song aside, what it signified, both in content and execution, was the determination of a young man who had pulled himself up from nothing and meant, by hook or by crook, to go far higher.

He tried just one more song in 1908, and only a few weeks

after "The Best of Friends": an ethnic number—a "coon song," to put a fine point on it—called "Queenie." This time Berlin wrote just the lyrics (the music was by one Maurice Abrahams), which this time were barely serviceable—and so of their genre that there is no redeeming them:

> The moon above
> Am shining, love . . .[5]

Et cetera. The thing was published at the end of February, and he wrote nothing further that year. Perhaps, as he turned twenty, Izzy was rethinking his ambitions. But then, quite by chance, an itinerant song-and-dance man, his name lost to history, stopped by Jimmy Kelly's one night and inadvertently put I. Berlin on the path to becoming Irving Berlin.

In these more orotund days the dramatic recitation was a vaudeville commonplace: a rich-voiced ham could transfix an audience, move it to tears or laughter by intoning "Gunga Din" or "Casey at the Bat," or something in a funny Italian or Irish or African-American accent. And one night in early 1909, the song-and-dance man in question, booked to appear at Tony Pastor's and anxious for fresh material, went to the Folly for some liquid inspiration, heard Izzy the waiter perform one of his dirty parodies, and had an Idea.

The vaudevillian pulled the waiter aside. There was ten bucks in it for him if he could come up with a wop or a mick or a coon piece for the player to recite. Ten dollars was a lot of money. So, late one night, Izzy sat down with fountain pen and paper and scratched out "Dorando."

Dorando Pietri was an Italian runner who had been disqualified from the 1908 Olympic marathon after collapsing in the final stretch and being helped across the finish line. The incident drew the world's sympathy, and afterwards Dorando became a celebrity athlete, competing in several professional races in America, including one he lost to an Indian named Thomas

Longboat. Berlin's witty conceit—and this was the first time his native wit made an appearance in a formal lyric—was to imagine an Italian barber who sold his barbershop to finance a big bet on his compatriot and idol, and lost everything on the Longboat race.

The fledgling writer laid out his tale in marinara-thick dialect:

> Dorando! Dorando!
> He run-a, run-a, run-a like anything.
> One-a, two-a hundred times around da ring,
> I cry, "Please-a nunga [never] stop!"
> Just then, Dorando he's-a drop![6]

Three energetic stanzas tell the whole story: barber sells shop to bet on Dorando, Dorando collapses, Dorando explains his failure afterward. And the explanation makes a wacky kind of sense: it turns out that whoever fed the runner before the race gave him "Irish beef-a stew" instead of his favorite carbo load, spaghetti ("I know it make me run-a quick-a-quick").

Set aside your genteel modern distaste for ethnic humor, and what you find is an economic and effective piece of storytelling, charmingly based on current events—written by a sixth-grade dropout who served beer for a living.

And the song-and-dance man stiffed him on the ten bucks.

Ever resilient, Berlin took his lyric uptown to Ted Snyder, a music publisher on 38th Street, just west of the Sixth Avenue El. Snyder's office manager and gate guardian, Henry Waterson (aka Watterson), a big, bushy-browed, smiley-tough character, told Berlin he would listen to his recitation if he made it fast. Izzy went into high busking mode and gave him "Dorando."

"Well," said Waterson (according to Woollcott), "I suppose you've got a tune to this."

"Yes," lied the singing waiter from Jimmy Kelly's, thinking, if at all, that he would dig up a pianist and get a tune from him before noon next day.

"All right," said Watterson [*sic*], "I'll give you $25 for the thing, words and music. Just you trot into the next room to the arranger and he'll take your tune down for you."

In which moment of agony, Berlin could only clutch at his manuscript, and, as the yawning musician looked up with pencil poised, hum something that seemed to jog along somehow in step with the words there on the paper in his hand . . .[7]

Woollcott undersells the something that Berlin hummed. The melody, Furia writes, "was surprisingly intricate with shifting meters and tonalities. Following the usual practice of [Tin Pan] Alley composers of immigrant songs, Berlin casts his verse (introduction) in a minor 'ethnic' mode and his chorus in a more modern and 'American' major key. But at the point in the chorus where the barber cries, 'Please-a nunga stop!,' the music shifts back to the minor key to underscore the loss of the Italian runner."[8]

Berlin, in other words, had in an unguarded moment and under pressure revealed (probably to his own surprise) what was to be the engine of his genius: a gift for inventing melodies that were at once appropriate to the lyrics and something more: memorable.

Waterson's twenty-five-dollar offer was doubly significant: it was karmically equivalent to the sum that had gotten Izzy fired from the Pelham, and big-enough money that the neophyte couldn't pass it up. But in reality it was a sucker's deal, the kind that music publishers frequently made with hungry composers: the writer or writers got some flash cash; the song, and all subsequent profits therefrom, belonged to the purchaser. And profits could be substantial. Waterson, a horse player by avocation, had made a winning bet on "Dorando," which wound up making a decent-sized splash in vaudeville and earning the huge sum of twenty thousand dollars—not for Berlin but for the firm of Waterson and Snyder.

Yet the song earned something far bigger for Izzy: the name that appeared, alone, on the cover of "Dorando"'s sheet music—let the boys in the back room at Nigger Mike's or Jimmy Kelly's say what they would—was the name he felt entitled to take on at last: Irving Berlin.

* * *

Right out of the gate, Berlin, barely twenty-one, had demonstrated a prodigious ability to write witty, affecting, commercial lyrics: words that compelled and intrigued and lingered in the mind. With amazing suddenness he was able to speak in his own, uniquely charming, voice on the page. His public awaited. And Berlin kicked into gear.

Three weeks after "Dorando," he and a composer named Edgar Leslie published a comic song based on a serious topic: the scandal stirred up in New York the previous fall by Richard Strauss's opera *Salome*, with its severed head of John the Baptist and the title character's Dance of the Seven Veils. Instead of the stepdaughter of Herod, Berlin and Leslie's "Sadie Salome (Go Home)" gives us Sadie Cohen, a young singer who "left her happy home / To become an actress lady." And not just any actress lady, mind you, but a striptease artiste reenacting Salome's infamous dance. The rollicking chorus is in the voice of her sweetheart, Mose:

> Don't do that dance, I tell you, Sadie,
> That's not a business for a lady!
> Most ev'rybody knows
> That I'm your loving Mose,
> Oy, oy, oy, oy,
> Where is your clothes?[9]

This is truly a breakthrough song: light-years from "Marie from Sunny Italy"; miles, even, past "Dorando." Berlin could write effectively enough in the Italian dialect he remembered from the Lower East Side, but the Yiddish idiom was in his bones.

He would put ethnic songs aside as the fad waned in the nineteen-teens, its demise hastened by World War I's attendant xenophobia. For now, though, there was real gold to be mined from it. And all at once, employment: on the strength of the sheet-music sales of "Sadie Salome"—some quarter-million copies—Waterson and Snyder offered Berlin a job as a staff lyricist, at twenty-five dollars a week, plus royalties on any of his songs that the firm published.

He could quit Jimmy Kelly's and put his waiter's apron aside forever: he finally had his twenty-five dollars a week, his idea of heaven. Irving Berlin's heaven, however, turned out to be a place of unrelenting hard work.

* * *

The success of "Sadie Salome," combined with the confidence of a paycheck, liberated Berlin. A universe of possibilities opened up. At the barbershop one afternoon, he encountered a singer and occasional songwriter he was friendly with, one George Whiting. When Berlin asked Whiting if he was free to go to the theater that night, Whiting said that since his wife had gone to the country, he was on his own. Berlin, as he later recalled to a journalist, replied: "Gee, that's a good title for a song!"

> And we went back to the office, wrote it, and sang it that night at a café before an audience of thirty people. And it went—so much so that the orders were pouring in the next day, while in four days it was about the best known song in America.[10]

Even allowing for exaggeration, it's an amazing story, and it wasn't much of an exaggeration. The main hyperbole is the brevity of the phrase "wrote it." The two men slaved for hours, struggling to transcend the obvious and achieve the memorable —to fulfill, in short, the promise of the title line. Berlin again: "All night I sweated to find what I knew was there, and finally

I speared the lone word, just a single word, that *made* the song—
and a fortune."

The single word was "Hurrah!"—spelled thus in the title,
but pronounced *hurray*. "That lone word," Berlin said, "gave
the whole idea of the song in one quick wallop. It gave the
singer a chance to hoot with sheer joy. It *invited* the roomful to
join in the hilarious shout."[11]

It was probably well past midnight on a late-spring evening
when Berlin and Whiting repaired in triumph to Maxim's, next
door to the Waterson and Snyder offices on 38th Street. The
crowd had thinned in the wee hours; the nighthawks remaining
were hard-bitten show-business types, yet the effect of the song
on the men was electric:

> My wife's gone to the country,
> Hurrah! Hurrah!
> She thought it best,
> "I need a rest,"
> That's why she went away.
> She took the children with her,
> Hurrah! Hurrah!
> I love my wife but oh! you kid,
> My wife's gone away.[12]

With its racy implication of imminent debauches, the song
went, as Berlin said. The sheet music sold 300,000 copies, and
Berlin, under the terms of his new royalty deal with Waterson
and Snyder, made a penny a copy: three thousand dollars, the
equivalent of more than seventy thousand today. The just-
turned-twenty-one-year-old, who only a few months before had
been singing for tossed nickels and dimes at Jimmy Kelly's, suddenly had more money than he knew what to do with. Or rather,
amazingly enough for a twenty-one-year-old, Irving Berlin knew
exactly what to do with it. For one thing, he kept writing as
though the devil himself were prodding him with his pitchfork.

* * *

And he kept thinking, more and more, about writing music as well as words. He had taught himself to play the piano, after a fashion, back at the Pelham Café, where he'd tinkered in his off hours with Nick Nicholson's upright, at first (and then ever afterward) only in the key of F-sharp: the "nigger keys," in the coarse vernacular of the era; so called because F-sharp contained five black keys and only two white. And so used by many beginning pianists because, as Berlin later explained, "The black keys are right there under your fingers."[13]

At the Pelham he had also listened with astonishment to the visiting Harlem stride pianist Luckey Roberts—a tiny fellow with enormous hands (he could span a fourteenth) and prodigious rhythmic verve. Though Izzy could only gape at Roberts's (also self-taught) virtuosity, he was inspired rather than intimidated. The rhythm of ragtime was sexual and intoxicating, and he *felt* it, with the same high-wire certainty that guided all his early compositional efforts. "I know rhythm," he would solemnly inform a magazine writer in 1915, at the ripe old age of twenty-six.[14]

More and more, he also knew music. With his earnings, Berlin bought a secondhand upright piano—but not just any upright. His new instrument was a six-octave Weser Brothers transposing piano, with a control wheel mounted under the right side of the keyboard that allowed a melody played in one key to sound in another. Berlin could thus keep right on playing in F-sharp, but the music would come out in C, D, B-flat, or any other key, depending on the turn of the wheel.

In honor of that steering-wheel-like appendage (which in later models became a simple lever), he called the new instrument his Buick.

His new employers were nervous. They had hired him to write lyrics; and they wanted him to stick to his knitting. Ted

Snyder's disquiet certainly had to do with competitiveness. Seven years older than Berlin, "all full of tunes and knowing roughly twenty times as much about music as Berlin did," in Woollcott's words, Snyder was a lanky Midwesterner, a Ray Bolger type physically, all bones and Adam's apple and toothy smiles.[15] In 1909, though still in his late twenties, he was not only a successful music publisher but an estimable songwriter (he would go on to have a reasonably distinguished career: his two most famous compositions were 1921's "The Sheik of Araby" and, as cowriter, 1923's "Who's Sorry Now"); on the other hand, his ear was good enough that he may well have realized that this musically illiterate kid, this cheeky guttersnipe, had the potential to leave him in the dust.

Throughout the latter half of 1909, Berlin bided his time, dutifully penning the words to a string of Snyder tunes—such deathless compositions as "Do Your Duty, Doctor! (Oh, Oh, Oh, Oh, Doctor)," "Wild Cherries (Coony, Spoony Rag)," and "Some Little Something about You." In the meantime he was listening, playing, planning. The lyrics he wrote for his boss were strictly workaday, almost as though Izzy was holding something back for himself.

Out it popped at the end of November, with the third song for which he and he alone had composed both words and music: "Yiddle, on Your Fiddle, Play Some Ragtime." Like "Dorando," "Yiddle" had an unrestrained quality, an air of liberation. The verse begins in a solemn minor mode—in fact it's a direct musical quote of the Hebrew hymn "Hatikvah":

> Ev'ryone was singing, dancing, springing,
> At a wedding yesterday.
> Yiddle on his fiddle played some ragtime,
> And when Sadie heard him play . . .

That fourth line, though, shifts into major, signaling the upcoming effervescence of the chorus (it's Sadie who's talking):

> Yiddle in the middle of your fiddle, play some ragtime;
> Get busy, I'm dizzy, I'm feeling two years young . . .[16]

In fact it was Irving Berlin who was getting busy. The following month, he came out with another solo composition, also ragtime-y, also with a musical quote: "That Mesmerizing Mendelssohn Tune." The title's irreverent bounce is just the beginning of the tune's originality. The melody of the verse had an elegant lilt that any seasoned songwriter would envy. The first phrase of the chorus, "Love me to that ever-lovin' 'Spring Song' melody," was set to that selfsame Mendelssohn air—but then, as the syncopation kicked in, the love got a little lustier:

> Please me, honey, squeeze me to that Mendelssohn strain,
> Kiss me like you would your mother,
> One good kiss deserves another . . .[17]

Who had the gall to taint the sacred name and music of a classical composer with ragtime (and sex)? And who, by the way, put a word like "mesmerizing" in a song title? Who even knew what it meant?

Berlin, that was who.

Though he was barely old enough to vote, he was already learning to make his own rules. And the public was buying. In an age of schmaltzy, formulaic popular songs, no one had ever heard anything quite like "Mesmerizing" before. The song's tremendous swing and originality—not to mention its sweet-and-hot sex appeal—sold its sheet music through the roof, to the tune of (depending on which account you read) somewhere between a half-million and a million and a half copies. In any case, at two cents a copy—as both lyricist and composer Berlin earned double his initial rate, a factor that would have strongly encouraged him to continue writing words and music—his latest tune's sales put the modern equivalent of several hundred thousand dollars in the young songwriter's pocket.

And so this—seasoned performer, Bowery survivor, dazzlingly inventive songwriter, young man of wit and confidence and means—was the twenty-one-year-old who walked into a Manhattan studio soon after the New Year and recorded "Oh, How That German Could Love."

4

I Sweat Blood

It's a wonder that in the flush of his first success, in the expansiveness of youth and joy at his powers, Irving Berlin didn't treat himself to just a little excess. But the crucible of poverty seems to have both toughened him and wised him up. He also appears to have possessed some inner core of character, an innate moral compass: his lodestar seems to have been his family, and in particular, his mother. When he made his first songwriting money, the first thing he bought was not a new suit of clothes or a diamond pinkie ring or an automobile but a rocking chair for Leah.

And the minute he could afford it, he moved his mother and his sister Gussie from the chaotic and malodorous Lower East Side to the leafy streets of the Bronx. The 1910 U.S. Census shows the three-person core of what had once been the Baline family living—now under the surname of their semi-illustrious twenty-one-year-old breadwinner—at 854 Hewitt

Place: Irving, the twenty-four-year-old Augusta, and sixty-two-year-old Lena (as the census still listed her).[1]

Today the address is a vacant lot in a semi-industrial South Bronx neighborhood; in that prelapsarian past it was a fancy apartment building of recent vintage—ornate stonework; filigreed metal grillwork on the front doors—in a district of upward-striving middle-class families. Jewish, mostly. At least one family in the building had a live-in maid. The census lists the solid-sounding occupations of the building's family heads: merchant, petticoats; clerk, banking house; dealer, plumbing supplies. Cutter, ladies garments; salesman, cloaks and suits; attorney and counselor, law. The occupation of the family head in the Berlin apartment was listed as writer, music. Number of weeks out of work in 1909: zero.

Gussie—operator, petticoats—had been unemployed for a total of four weeks in the previous year, according to the census. Leah's occupation was listed as none—just as it had been back on Cherry Street in the 1900 census; only then, when she wasn't sweating over the household, she had midwifed to make a few extra coins. Now her youngest son had earned the old woman the freedom to rest.

Every morning he took the subway down to the offices of Waterson & Snyder to work at the business of writing popular songs. And it was a business, with bosses and rules and a merciless bottom line. Despite the huge success of "That Mesmerizing Mendelssohn Tune," 1910 was mostly an apprentice year for Berlin, spent cranking out routine lyrics to Ted Snyder's routine melodies.[2] He was solidifying his professional position, bringing home the bacon, doing his bit to keep Waterson & Snyder in the black. One exception to the humdrum was "Grizzly Bear," a catchy dance number with music by George Botsford, widely recorded and performed in vaudeville, and then, in a coup, interpolated into the *Ziegfeld Follies of 1910*. Actually, two

Berlin numbers made it into the *Follies* that year, the other being "Sadie Salome," which Florenz Ziegfeld had discovered when he heard Fanny Brice singing it on a vaudeville stage, a performance he liked so well that he grabbed both the song and the singer for his big show. This was the beginning of an important association between Berlin and Ziegfeld.

April's "Call Me Up Some Rainy Afternoon" was another song that demonstrated the magic Berlin could weave when he wrote words and music himself. On the surface, the tune is mere spun sugar, a kittenish come-on sung by one Nellie Green to her boyfriend, Harry Lee:

> Call me up some rainy afternoon,
> I'll arrange for a quiet little spoon.
> Think of all the joy and bliss,
> We can hug and we can—talk about the weather . . .

Sure enough, it rains, and Harry calls Nellie. When he goes over to her place, though, he finds his pretty Nell is not alone but, rather, "Singing to somebody in the hall: / 'Call me up some rainy afternoon . . . ' "[3]

And that's it. Love, sex, betrayal, all in one sweet package. The music-buying public ate it up: its sheet-music sales surpassed even those of "That Mesmerizing Mendelssohn Tune." The difference was that while "Mendelssohn" was a joyous romp, and Berlin's previous hits, "Dorando" and "Sadie Salome," were ethnic numbers, "Call Me Up" told a story that felt universal, with characters people could relate to. It had the ring of experience.

Personal experience, even. Outside of his two marriages, and an apparently unrequited crush he seems to have had on the actress Constance Talmadge in the late nineteen-teens, we know next to nothing about Irving Berlin's love life. He kept himself to himself, always. But his youthful expertise as an improviser of earthy lyrics shows a zesty and forthright interest in sex, as do the words to many of his early songs. And even given his powerful work ethic, Berlin, as a rich, handsome, natty young bachelor coming into his own as a songwriter/performer amid the lively show-business world of Manhattan in the years before World War I—a world filled with pretty and available young women—would almost certainly have gotten around.

*　*　*

Nineteen ten was also a schizoid year for Berlin, the last year of apprenticeship and subservience. His salary came from his employer, the man whose name was on the door, the tall, bony fellow who sat at the piano, smiling at the world and grinding out tune after mediocre tune. The big money in Izzy's bank account, though, was his and his alone. The question was whether he could make more of it, enough to light out on his own. He must have felt he could; on the other hand, there were his mother and occasionally unemployed sister in that nice apartment in the Bronx, and the monthly grocery bills and rent.

And so for the time being he played by Ted Snyder's rules, reporting to work each day in suit and tie, turning out the product with fountain pen and paper, though bubbling with words and music of his own—no, words-and-music; with him it was almost always a unified entity—and drawn irresistibly, treacherously, to that Weser Brothers transposing piano.

The Ted Snyder Company was, like every other successful publisher on Tin Pan Alley, a mill: a warren of small noisy chambers where not only the house talent but song pluggers and postulant composers pounded out would-be euphonies on battered uprights in cacophonous chorus. It would have taken a powerful imagination, not to mention an ironclad will, to conceive fresh musical ideas under such conditions: Berlin had both. One day in the summer or fall of 1910, a ragtime-flavored melody came to him, at work, "right out of the air," as he recalled a few years later. "I wrote the whole thing in eighteen minutes, surrounded on all sides by roaring pianos and roaring vaudeville actors."[4] The "thing"—the understatement is nothing short of colossal—was the tune (apparently lyricless at first) that would become "Alexander's Ragtime Band."

There is more than a touch of braggadocio to Berlin's account, and his word choice is interesting. *I wrote the whole thing in eighteen minutes.* Most songwriters did their writing in musical notation, on staff paper. Irving Berlin did not, because he could not. Instead, when a new tune occurred to him, he hummed it or played a rudimentary piano version of it in the presence of a musical secretary (soon the Snyder Company would hire a brilliant young pianist named Cliff Hess for this express purpose), who then wrote down the notes. That was the melody. Getting the harmonies right was a more complicated process. This time the secretary would sit at the keyboard and play chords while Berlin, who inwardly knew precisely what sounds he wanted, would either approve or disapprove. The secretary would note the correct chords, and by and by, a full song would emerge.

But despite his later boasting, Berlin was unimpressed enough at first by this new Thing he'd "written" that he didn't take the trouble to have it transcribed. Instead, he jotted a memo to himself about the melody, summing it up in a few words, then filed it away and forgot about it. It was only several months later, as he prepared to go on a winter vacation to Palm Beach—and here we must pause for a moment to consider the miracle of a twenty-two-year-old who in recent memory had sung for pennies in dives and slept in flophouses becoming a prosperous-enough businessman to vacation in Palm Beach— it was only as Irving Berlin puttered around the office before heading uptown to the newly built Pennsylvania Station to catch the Palmetto Limited, that he pulled from memory the melody that had popped out of the air months before. As a songwriter and journalist named Rennold Wolf wrote in a 1913 magazine article, "The Boy Who Revived Ragtime,"

> Just before train time he went to his offices to look over his manuscripts, in order to leave the best of them for publication during his absence. Among his papers he found a memorandum referring to "Alexander," and after considerable reflection he recalled its strains. Largely for the lack of anything better with which to kill time, he sat at the piano and completed the song.[5]

Wrote the words, in other words. Amazingly, not only could "Alexander's Ragtime Band" have easily been lost to oblivion but for a phenomenal act of musical memory on Irving Berlin's part; he also managed to throw the whole thing together while he waited for a train.

This was the exception that proved the rule: with the majority of his compositions, Berlin toiled for many hours, often through the deep watches of the night, sweating to come up with the right notes, the right words, the simplest essence of the song. Nothing, he discovered, was so complex as simplicity. "I sweat blood," he said. "Absolutely. I sweat blood between 3 and 6 many mornings, and when the drops that fall off my forehead hit the paper they're notes."[6]

The reality was less poetic. Woollcott said that Berlin suffered from "nervous indigestion"—a catchall that could have covered any number of disagreeable symptoms. "Most of his songs," he wrote, "always postponed to that last minute and then turned out in a kind of frenzy of application, had been written by a small composer twisted with pain. This was so well known that whenever his neighbors in Tin Pan Alley saw him looking especially wan and spent and frail, they would exclaim bitterly: 'Ah, hah, another hit I suppose!'"[7]

But from the beginning, "Alexander" was different. It's tempting to romanticize it as a thunderclap of sheer genius, but difficult to see it as anything else. As noted, 1910 was a journey-man year for Berlin, even if a profitable one: to look at a list of his titles for the period is to see a numbing succession of "Music by Ted Snyder"s, broken only occasionally by an all-Berlin composition, and only one of those times by a memorable one, "Call Me Up Some Rainy Afternoon." As also noted, "Alexander" songs had an ignominious lineage in American popular music. In May, Snyder and Berlin published one of their own, "Alexander and His Clarinet," a coon song in dialogue between a Colored Romeo (to quote another Berlin title from that year) and his Juliet, with a barely submerged Freudian subtext: " 'For lawdy sake [the female character sang], don't dare to go, / My pet, I love you yet, / And then besides, I love your clarinet.' "[8]

"Alexander's Ragtime Band" was light-years beyond this hackwork. For one thing, it was *about* something, unlike the bulk of the era's popular music (Snyder and Berlin's included), most of which merely lent humorous or sentimental animation to stock characters and situations. What's more, it was about something important. "Alexander" was a thrilling song, with a thrilling lyric, about the thrill of the new: a great new American art form, ragtime—which was, after all, jazz in embryo.[9] It didn't matter that the tune alluded to rather than embodied ragtime (it was really a march, with a mere hint of syncopation): it was a joyous tribute to African-American musical genius, the first great and lasting one in American popular song, from a Jewish-American musical genius. Even more: it was a celebration of America itself, a paean to—and very soon, a symbol of—emerging American cultural superpower.

"Alexander" also celebrated something else: its brilliant young composer. For in the end, who was Alexander but Irving Berlin himself?

And the song really did come straight out of the blue. "The gesture of the piece," writes musicologist Charles Hamm, "a first-person exhortation to anyone and everyone within earshot to come and listen to a band, has no precedent in earlier 'coon' songs or in any other songs of the Tin Pan Alley era, or even in the 'come-all-ye' command of British balladry to heed the words of the bard."[10] Berlin himself, sounding more like an academic than a tunesmith, reasoned that the exhortation was the song's secret.

> Its opening words, emphasized by immediate repetition— "Come on and hear! Come on and hear!"—were an *invitation* to "come," to join in, and "hear" the singer and his song. And that idea of *inviting* every receptive auditor within shouting distance . . .—an idea pounded in again and again throughout the song in various ways—was the secret of the song's tremendous success.[11]

"Alexander" caught on slowly in the first few months after publication (on March 18, 1911), then simply exploded, around the country and across the Atlantic in England (where Berlin would come to be regarded, reality notwithstanding, as the creator and sole genius of ragtime); even in France. Remember, radio wouldn't become a mass medium for a dozen years, and even phonograph records were a relatively new phenomenon. Record sales would help propel "Alexander's Ragtime Band," but it was sheet music—some two million copies sold by the end of 1912—that was the main measure of its success. By this gauge alone, "Alexander's Ragtime Band" was a megahit, earning Berlin forty thousand dollars in its first year and a half of publication, the equivalent of almost a million today.

But the money was only part of it. As early as September, *Variety* declared "Alexander" "the musical sensation of the decade"—and the decade had barely begun. The song turned Berlin into an international celebrity, and made him, at twenty-three, the king of Tin Pan Alley. To the dismay of many of the Alley's denizens.

Not the least of whom was Ted Snyder, who even as the song caught fire over the spring and summer of 1911, somehow failed to promote it or mention it in any of the company's advertising, finally capitulating only in August, when the tune's astonishing ubiquity finally rendered it and its composer undeniable. "'Alexander' was tinkled out on parlor pianos and belted out in cabarets and vaudeville theaters," Edward Jablonski writes. "In the latter, performers competed to use the song; the rule was that whoever got to the bandleader first got to do the number. Not only vocalists but acrobats, jugglers, and comedians seized on 'Alexander' to serve as their 'play-off,' or exit, music, a surefire stimulus to applause."[12]

"The Song Sensation of the Century," read the Snyder Company's full-page *Variety* ad (somewhat broadening the timeline) on August 19. "Managers, critics and the public want it. Any act can make good with it. . . . The instrumental lends class to any dumb or dancing act; in fact, it is the only song on the market to-day that makes 'making good' child's play." Another *Variety* ad in September went even further: "Acts are taking bows to the tune of it. I wonder why? Managers are asking acts to use it. I wonder why? **The whole world has fallen in love with it. THAT'S WHY.**"[13]

Snyder, of course, was tooting the firm's horn more than Berlin's; he couldn't be blamed for feathering his own nest. But even as he counted the receipts from the magic tune, he can't have been entirely happy to see the whole world falling in love with it and its youthful composer, who was after all his employee. Earlier in the year, the Friars Club had invited Berlin to join its august ranks, where he got to meet his idol, George M. Cohan, who recalled their first encounter thus: "You can imagine how surprised I was when I walked into the Friars Club one day and was introduced to this little boy."[14] In May, the organization further honored Berlin by asking him to sing "Alexander" at the opening performance of the *Friars Frolic of 1911* at the New Amsterdam Theatre. Did Ted Snyder sit in the audience, quietly seething? The *Frolic* then headed out on a twelve-city tour across the Northeast, with the composer reprising his star turn at every stop.

In September, Hammerstein's Victoria vaudeville theater, at 42nd and Broadway, booked the young songwriting sensation for a week, at one thousand dollars, to perform "Alexander," plus five more of his compositions, onstage, backed by the house orchestra. "It was," Woollcott wrote, "an honor accorded not because the management was struck by his gifts as a master of melody. It was struck by his qualities as a phenomenon." Hammerstein's, owned by Oscar Hammerstein I and managed by his resourceful son Willie (the father of Oscar II, the lyricist), was a kind of early precursor of reality television—a wildly successful venue with a lively subspecialty in novelty acts: performing dogs, famous pugilists, and the like. Everybody wanted to see the prodigy who'd written the most famous song in the land. Hammerstein's even had a life-size photo of Berlin in the lobby.

So stellar had the composer become that according to Woollcott, "word came up from Chinatown that some 200 of the old gang were planning to attend the first performance in a body. Their Izzy had made good in the big world and they were minded to celebrate."

The group, which attended the matinee, was "vociferous but refined," Woollcott continues.

> Berlin, hurrying to the theater just before the evening performance, was a little surprised to find two or three of his volunteer claque still loitering around the theater.
>
> "Gee, Izzy," one of them confided to him darkly, "We've been hanging around this bum joint for three hours trying to get a chance to pinch that swell picture of you in the lobby."[15]

But Izzy was more than a novelty act. On September 11, 1911, none other than *Variety*'s founder and editor Sime Silverman reviewed Berlin's opening:

> Next to last [the place of honor on a vaudeville bill] appeared Irving Berlin, who sang two of his newest songs, together with a neat medley of his own "hits," woven into a story. When you can do that you can write songs, and to see this slim little kid on the stage with a pianist [Cliff Hess] going through a list that sounded like all the song hits in the world is something to think about.
>
> Mr. Berlin looks so nice on the platform all the girls in the house fall for him immediately. . . . They were still applauding after Rayno's Bull Dogs came on to close the performance, but Irving wouldn't return.[16]

Yet even as the young colossus stood astride Tin Pan Alley, detractors were starting to saw away at his legs. As "Alexander" exploded, a weird rumor took hold among the popular-music community: that Berlin had paid a black man (or in some versions of the story, "a little colored boy") ten dollars for the song and published it under his own name. Risible as it sounds today, the rumor, fueled by dislike and envy for the composer, as well as his musical illiteracy, was given serious credence for years. Even Henry Waterson, to Berlin's annoyance, liked to joke about it.[17] Berlin contained his anger for a long time, but speaking to a reporter in 1916, finally let it out.

> When they told me about it, I asked them to tell me from whom I had bought my other successes—twenty-five or thirty of them. And I wanted to know, if a negro could write "Alexander," why couldn't I? Then I told them if they could produce the negro and he had another hit like "Alexander" in his system, I would choke it out of him and give him twenty thousand dollars in the bargain. If the other fellow deserves the credit, why doesn't he go get it?[18]

Some of the rumormongers mentioned a black pianist named Lukie Johnson as the possible composer; Johnson himself roundly denied the reports. "I wish to God I *had* written that song," he told Eubie Blake. "Irving Berlin don't buy no tunes from me. He writes them himself."[19]

5

At the Devil's Ball

IN JANUARY 1912 Irving Berlin's beleaguered boss bowed to the inevitable: "The Ted Snyder Co. goes out of business at once and will be succeeded by the Watterson-Berlin-Snyder company, a new $100,000 corporation," a notice in *Variety* read. "This means the taking into the firm of Irving Berlin, who has been the star writer for the Snyder Music Publishing Co."[1]

Between the dawn of 1911 and the March 18 publication of "Alexander," Berlin had written just two pallid little tunes, an ethnic number called "Dat's-a My Girl" and a collaboration with one Bernie Adler called "That Dying Rag." Between March 18 and the close of the year, on the other hand, he turned into a white-hot blaze, churning out no fewer than forty songs, sixteen of them in collaboration and twenty-four by himself. In his twenty-fourth year he had become a demon not just of productivity but of popular-music innovation, leaving George M. Cohan and Harry Von Tilzer in the dust.

Nothing Berlin did could touch "Alexander" as a breakout anthem of modernity, but amid the ethnic and novelty tunes that the commerce of the day demanded, he was writing more freely and freshly than ever—and than anyone else. Oddly, his first big splash after "Alexander" was a collaboration with Ted Snyder, "That Mysterious Rag." Berlin introduced the song during his September stand at Hammerstein's, it was a hit record for Columbia and Victor, and, like "Alexander," it made its way across the Atlantic. "'That Mysterious Rag' was one of many American songs about ragtime that captivated sophisticated European musicians," writes Robert Kimball in *The Complete Lyrics of Irving Berlin*. "When Erik Satie was composing his ballet score *Parade* (1917) for Serge Diaghilev's Ballets Russes, he used and parodied the rhythms and harmonies of 'Mysterious Rag' for the 'Little American Girl' section of his astonishing collaboration with Jean Cocteau, Pablo Picasso, and Léonide Massine."[2]

Astonishing would also apply to Berlin's growing presence on the world's stage.

In "Everybody's Doing It Now," a November composition, he once again demonstrated his ability to write a big hit all by himself. The song was bouncy, seemingly nonsensical fun:

> Ev'rybody's doin' it,
> Doin' it, doin' it;
> See that ragtime couple over there,
> Watch them throw their shoulders in the air,
> Snap their fingers—honey, I declare,
> It's a bear, it's a bear, it's a bear.
> There![3]

Though everyone knew what the song was *really* about. The bear reference was a wink at the latest spate of dance crazes, many with animal names, flourishing, as Laurence Bergreen writes, in the cafés and music halls—not the decorous waltzes favored by orchestras sawing away in hotel ballrooms—but a new breed of vigorous, highly sexual . . . black-inspired dances whose names alone had shock value: the rag, rock, turkey trot, monkey, maxixe, half-in-half, lame duck, gotham gobble, humpback rag, bunny hug, ostrich, and come-to-me tommy. To see them was even more shocking than pronouncing their names, for the dancers actually pressed their loins together on the dance floor, in full view of the public.[4]

As lively as Berlin's interest in sex may have been, commercial considerations always came first. While his show-business contemporaries were enjoying their wine, women, and song, he was slaving through the night to come up with his quota of three new songs a week. He was driven by more than the memory of his Pelham Café days. By his own early estimate, only one in ten of the songs he ground out was worth publishing. And while this assessment may have been overmodest—it wouldn't have accounted for the forty tunes he published in the *annus mirabilis* of "Alexander," unless he'd turned out something like eight per week—it does get at some essence of Berlin's huge lifetime output: if he was afraid of failure, that fear galvanized rather than paralyzed him.

* * *

In all too short a time, the titles of two songs Berlin published three days apart in September 1911, "There's a Girl in Havana" and "Don't Take Your Beau to the Seashore," would take on an eerily prescient ring. At the time, the tunes were mere trifles meant to be interpolated into other men's musicals; Berlin wrote them with a new collaborator, a cheerful, beefy young songwriter/lyricist from Buffalo named E. Ray Goetz.

Goetz had been accompanied on his move to the big city by his nineteen-year-old little sister Dorothy, a petite, vivacious brunette who seems to have aspired to become a singer, but about whom we know little except for the fact that sometime in late 1911 Irving Berlin fell for her, hard. The story of their court-ship has been lost, but since we know that Irving and Ray Goetz quickly became friends and that Berlin took the character of his friends quite seriously, we may easily infer the sister's appeal.

The suitor was young and impetuous and they married quickly, in February 1912, in a simple ceremony in Buffalo—simple, one suspects, because Irving was Jewish and Dorothy was not, and in those days, no temple or church would have been eager to have them. The fact that they married in her hometown, though, and not in a neutral location, indicates that her family, at least, was receptive to the union between their daughter and this great (and wealthy) young man.

The honeymooners headed to Havana. A shipboard pho-tograph of the pair in New York Harbor is molecular in its clar-ity: you can feel the icy cling in the air, a hint of incipient snow. And in its emotional clarity—they are as happy, as filled with life and hope, as any two young people can be. Irving, in his Homburg and tweed overcoat, is all wry alertness; Dorothy, in a full-length fur and glorious egret-feathered Edwardian hat, smiles with melting warmth at person or persons unknown. In the background, blurred fellow passengers watch the celebrated young couple having their picture taken. Try to imagine, if you will, any twenty-three-year-old and nineteen-year-old of the present or any recent era looking remotely as mature and assured.

Fate's hammer hit them soon after they returned to their love nest, a big apartment in the Chatsworth, a magnificent red-brick and limestone building (still standing) at 344 West 72nd Street, just off Riverside Drive. There had been an outbreak of typhoid in Havana: anything, a glass of water, a leaf of lettuce, could have spread it. Somehow, Irving didn't get sick; Dorothy did. Cough, a persistent headache, slowly rising fever; after a week, worsening fever and the onset of intestinal symptoms.

Delirium. Twenty years before antibiotics, the doctors could do little besides try to make her more comfortable.

Even Irving, with his steely ability to concentrate amid the banging pianos of Tin Pan Alley, would have been severely tested. According to Woollcott: "The doctors and the decorators were jostling each other in the hallway of this shiny new home, while the anxious bridegroom was locked up in the front room trying ludicrously to fulfill his contracts for jaunty songs long overdue."[5]

In the beginning of June, Dorothy developed pneumonia; when she breathed her last, on July 17, it was unclear to her doctors whether the typhoid or the pneumonia had killed her. The one thing certain was that Irving Berlin—precocious in many things, including sorrow—was a widower, at twenty-three.

* * *

Berlin, a consummate realist about his romantic-seeming craft, was always at pains to emphasize the tip-of-the-iceberg quality of his best work, and the genesis of the great song of mourning he published some five months later is no exception.

Two lyrics appearing to be earlier versions of "When I Lost You" reside in the Irving Berlin Collection of the Music Division of the Library of Congress. No music is known to survive for either, which makes a certain kind of sense: if Berlin was both grappling with his own grief and trying to figure out how to express it, words, rather than a tune, might have been what first came to mind.

And first drafts can be as painful to read as they are to write—especially if the emotions they spring from are as raw as Berlin's were. "They All Come with You," never copyrighted, begins,

> Sunshine and heavens of blue,
> Flowers and sweet morning dew,
> Innocent birds gaily sing
> Sweetest of all songs they knew . . .

and ends:

> Heavenly pleasures, a world full of treasures,
> My sweetheart, they all came with you.

And the chorus of "That's Just Why I Love You"—also unpublished—begins,

> I love the flowers that bloom in the spring,
> I love the birds in the treetops that sing . . .

and concludes, after touching on "church bells that solemnly ring," "the sweet morning dew," "angels who watch from above," and "the cooing of each little dove,"

> I love the things God wants me to love,
> That's just why I love you.[6]

Trying to make something good out of the awful thing that had happened, and paying tribute to his lost love, were laudable goals. Yet in pursuing them, Berlin was at first—for whatever reason, probably because of the overwhelming shock of what he'd just undergone—slipping all too easily into the maudlin key that turn-of-the-century songwriting deployed to express strong emotion. But Irving Berlin was a groundbreaker, not a follower. And now he broke ground by addressing grief straight on.

Just as the single word "hurrah" turned "My Wife's Gone to the Country" into a hit, two words—five letters—were the key to changing the dreadful (if sympathetic) hearts-and-flowers of "They All Come with You" and "That's Just Why I Love You" into lasting art. The words were "I lost."

> I lost the sunshine and roses,
> I lost the heavens of blue,
> I lost the beautiful rainbow,
> I lost the morning dew,
> I lost the angel who gave me

Summer the whole winter through,
I lost the gladness
That turned into sadness,
When I lost you.[7]

"Irving is a man of few words. But he keeps repeating them," his witty friend Wilson Mizner once said.[8] Though the crack poked mild fun at the simplicity of the songwriter's lyrics, it actually points to a great strength. In Berlin's hands, simplicity was power. He knew it; he sweated blood over it. The writer Anita Loos, a friend of his beginning in the 1920s, later recalled:

> I sometimes used to sit beside Irving at his tiny piano and listen while he composed. He would go over and over a lyric until it seemed perfect to my ears. Then he'd scrap the whole thing and begin over again. When I asked Irving what was wrong he invariably said, "It isn't *simple* enough."[9]

Repetition—as we have seen—was also an extraordinarily important component in Berlin's lyrics. "Repetition [is] the soul of a song," he wrote, in an outline for a projected but never completed book called *The Secret of Song Writing*. It is also, argue Amos Oz and Fania Oz-Salzberger, in *Jews and Words*, part of the soul of a people: "Reiterated lines sometimes beget music; and much of Jewish musicality grew from the resonance of repeated words."[10] Berlin may have stopped going to shul when his father died, may have worked hard on purging the greenhorn from himself and becoming a true American. "But his kind of assimilation was not denying his Jewishness," Mary Ellin Barrett says. "He was very much a Jew."[11] And his Jewishness permeated his songs.

In all likelihood, the words-and-music to "When I Lost You" came to him at once, as usual; and the music, too, was beautiful. The simple but haunting tune is in waltz time—an unusual signature in that ragtime-y era, and unusual for Berlin, too: it was the first (and most melancholy) of the great and melancholy waltzes that would mark his early middle period. The tempo implied a dance with the lost partner, underlining the song's sorrow.

"Publication, when he began writing it, was probably far from his intent," Jablonski writes.

> It has been intimated that this song constituted a commercial exploitation of Dorothy's death, but that is nonsense. Berlin wrote it because he felt it; it is guileless, lucid, and memorable, its sentiments simple, even obvious, but timeless. . . .
>
> When his partners heard the song, they voted for publication, even though ragtime was then still the main inspiration for Tin Pan Alley, and the waltz not especially salable.[12]

Published on November 8, 1912—in the same year that saw the world-shaking tragedy of the sinking of the *Titanic*—"When I Lost You" became an immediate smash hit: in sheet-music form, and then on piano rolls and phonograph records, it sold millions of copies, its popularity second only to "Alexander's Ragtime Band."[13]

Berlin's reaction to the song's success is unrecorded, though the sound of tenors like Henry Burr and Manuel Romain rendering his most heartfelt grieving with a theatrical throb might well have caused him some consternation. "It is probable," Woollcott wrote, "that he was acutely embarrassed when this, the first song of his heart, proved an immediate popular favorite. . . . It made a shining heap of dollars for the troubled youth who wrote it. There must have been times when he wished he had let no one hear it."[14]

It should also be pointed out that, as Alec Wilder reminds us, "none of the one hundred and thirty songs published up to this point in Berlin's career revealed this aspect of his talent, the ability to write with moving sentiment about personal trouble and pain."[15]

However mixed Irving's feelings, and however deep his grief

remained, something stirred in him that fall, perhaps unleashed by the not-so-simple act of expressing his bereavement. But even if writing "When I Lost You" brought a certain kind of release, what he did next seems nearly inexplicable: during that same November, he created two of the most joyous songs in his repertoire.

While "When the Midnight Choo-Choo Leaves for Alabam'" and "At the Devil's Ball" were never destined to join the ranks of Berlin's standards, they both hold up by the sheer force of their ebullience. "Midnight Choo-Choo" is very much of its period (though nobody else but Berlin could have written it): a romping paean to the thrill of train travel in the days when America still traveled by rail, and, not fifty years after the Civil War, a tribute to a mythical South, that sleepy, sunny (and thoroughly fictional) land of rural leisure and simple pleasures—a place, George S. Kaufman wrote in a *New Yorker* memoir about Berlin, "where the rhyming is easy."[16]

Even in 1912, the Arcadian South was already a songwriter's standby, if not a cliché. In his precociously prolific career, Berlin had already tried his hand at every musical platitude, from the coon song to the soppy ballad. At the same time, he was an original, working hard to bring his originality to bear. "Midnight Choo-Choo" shines, both in the syncopated vigor of the music and the startling vividness of the lyric:

> When the midnight choo-choo leaves for Alabam',
> I'll be right there,
> I've got my fare.
> When I see that rusty-haired conductor man,
> I'll grab him by the collar
> And I'll holler,
> "Alabam'! Alabam'!"[17]

"Rusty-haired" is a particular brilliancy: the gleam in the eye of a master portrait painter's subject. Berlin's best lyrics grab *listeners* by the collar by also making us *viewers*.

The same is true of "At the Devil's Ball," the first in a series of songs Berlin would write about hell and the devil between the pre–World War I years and the early twenties. Whether the subject(s) held a peculiar fascination for him or not, he had happened onto a rich new vein of songwriting material.

The tune is written in the first person, in the form of a dream (fifty years later, a no less brilliant Jewish songwriter, Bob Dylan, would employ the same conceit, to both comic and serious effect, in several of his early compositions[18]):

> At the Devil's Ball,
> At the Devil's Ball,
> I saw the cute Mrs. Devil, so pretty and fat,
> Dressed in a beautiful fireman's hat. . . .
> In the Devil's Hall,
> I saw the funniest devil that I ever saw
> Taking the tickets from the folks at the door;
> I caught a glimpse of my mother-in-law
> Dancing with the Devil,
> Oh! The little Devil,
> Dancing at the Devil's Ball.[19]

This passes beyond the comparatively gentle cartooning of "Midnight Choo-Choo," into sheer, surrealistic genius. However, unlike surrealism itself, which would be goaded into being only by the mechanized horrors of World War I (and which, in its attempts to mine the unconscious, often waxed pretentious or self-conscious), Berlin's early native Dada derived its great good humor from the brilliantly homely details: a coat check at the entrance to hell; the cute Mrs. Devil in her beautiful fireman's hat; and the masterstroke, the mother-in-law dancing with Old Nick himself.

* * *

In the year after his wife's death Berlin returned to his amazingly prolific ways, producing at exactly the same rate as he had in 1911, the year of "Alexander"—forty published songs (which means God knows how many others written and threw away), some of them even up to the Berlin standard. "I wrote more lousy songs than almost anyone else," he told Robert Kimball many years later. "Some of them may have seemed clever when they were written but they embarrass the hell out of me now. I would be happier if people did not perform them."[20]

"Berlin took such a dim view of his youthful offerings," Kimball wrote in *The Complete Lyrics*, "that when, late in his life, he assembled a special bound collection of 192 of his published songs to give to friends, he included only nine pre-1915 numbers. . . . That is an astonishingly low number considering how many wonderful songs he wrote during those early years."[21]

Maybe. But late in Berlin's life, as back in 1912 and 1913, business was business. Rather than being excessively hard on his younger self, the elderly Berlin was simply applying the same ruthless professional standard he had always lived by: every one of the pre-1915 numbers he chose to memorialize had been a major commercial hit. "The mob is always right," he was fond of saying.[22]

He was ambivalent about "That International Rag" in later years, including it in the bound collection but also dismissing it as "dated in the sense that it is about the effect of ragtime on people."[23] Berlin wrote the song for a show that the management of London's Hippodrome invited him to give in the summer of 1913—actually a show within a show: "Irving Berlin in selections from his repertoire." The primary entertainment, *Hullo, Ragtime!*, which had been running at the Hippodrome for six months and included "Alexander's Ragtime Band," had started a ragtime mania in England and engendered a great curiosity about the song's prodigious young composer, whom the theater's managers had lured across the Atlantic with a prodigious salary of twenty thousand pounds—the equivalent of more than two million dollars today.

Berlin sailed in June; he was a smash hit the moment he stepped out of his cab at the Savoy, to find that "the kid selling papers, who opened the door, was whistling 'Alexander.'" London music stores featured life-size photos of Berlin, surrounded by his sheet music, in their shop windows.

Yet certain snobbish elements in the country were laying for him and his tunes: the English press couldn't make up its mind whether the fact that he couldn't read or write music was remarkable or deplorable. He might well have felt defensive. He was a Jew, an upstart American, a mere kid. "It is almost impossible to believe," the *Daily Express* wrote, "that this boy— he looks nineteen—lathering his face to an unconscious tune one morning, four years ago [*sic*], hit on the jerky, spasmodic bars of 'Alexander's Ragtime Band.'"[24]

He disarmed them all. "That International Rag" was a hit, as was the Hippodrome show. Even the snooty *Times* softened its stance: "Once they have seen and heard him on the stage, only the most truculent could wish to have Mr Irving Berlin's blood," the paper wrote. A moment later, though, the tone shifted to highhandedness, as the writer opined, of Berlin's songs, "All their quaintness, their softness, their queer patheti-calness come out. They sound, indeed, quite new, and inno-cently, almost childishly pleasing, like a negro's smile."[25]

Two words in the statement are correct: "quite new." The rest reflected the reflexive condescension of empire—an empire that was, in early 1914, well along in the process of contraction. The twenty-five-year-old on the Hippodrome's stage repre-sented a new empire, one that was expanding by the day. And this small, curly-haired American Jew was not only this em-pire's representative but, at this point, one of its chief agents.

"Go where you will," the *Daily Express* wrote, "you cannot escape from the mazes of music he has spun. In every London restaurant, park and theatre you hear his strains; Paris dances to it; Berlin sips golden beer to his melodies; Vienna has forsaken the waltz, Madrid flung away her castanets, and Venice has forgotten her barcarolles. Ragtime has swept like a whirlwind over the earth and set civilization humming. Mr. Berlin started it."[26]

* * *

Three months after Berlin returned to New York, the Friars Club threw him a gala dinner at the grand Hotel Astor, in Times Square. In the spirit of the day, the after-meal speeches were richly sentimental; in the spirit of the Friars, the young songwriter who had rocketed to the top of his profession was brought down to earth.

George M. Cohan, who rose to a standing ovation, was pointed:

> I don't know whether to boost Irving or roast him. I feel the same toward Irving as a whole lot of other song writers feel. [Laughter] Of course you know I was a song writer. That is, I thought I was a song writer until this young man came along. . . . I heard all these Italian songs before I met him, and I thought he was a "Dago," but afterward I discovered he was a Jew boy, who named himself after an English actor and a German city [Laughter]. . . .
>
> Irvy writes a great song. He writes a song with a good lyric, a lyric that rhymes, good music, music you don't have to dress up to listen to, but it is good music. He is a wonderful little fellow, wonderful in lots of ways. He has become famous and wealthy, without wearing a lot of jewelry and falling for funny clothes. He is uptown, but he is there with the old downtown hardshell. And with all his success, you will find his watch and his handkerchief in his pockets where they belong.[27]

Cohan was a remarkable man, and he had given a remarkable speech: affectionate, condescending, candidly competitive, and piercingly accurate. And his self-deprecation, though humorous, had been right on the money: the twenty-five-year-old on the dais truly had surpassed his idol (whose photograph hung on the wall of Berlin's office, alongside a portrait of his other musical hero, Stephen Foster). All of thirty-five at the time, Cohan was the past; Berlin was the present and future.

6

Play a Simple Melody

ANOTHER PHOTOGRAPH: Irving Berlin, age twenty-six, sitting at his desk in the Waterson Berlin & Snyder offices at 112
West 38th Street. His back is to a window with the firm's name
printed on it; outside, a striped awning blocks bright sunlight:
it is spring or summer of 1914. Berlin is wearing a silk foulard
necktie and a beautifully tailored gray silk suit, and staring directly at the camera. He holds some folded papers in his hand
—probably business correspondence or contracts rather than
music—and his desk is also piled with papers. He is busy, in the
midst of business, and his gaze is intense and slightly forbidding. His dark hair is unruly, and a few locks fall on the side of
his forehead, emphasizing his youth—and then the fact of his
youth circles the viewer back to that splendid suit and tie, and
his name on the window, and the pile of papers in front of
him, and the fact that although he is four years from thirty, he

is already two years a widower, and immensely successful and powerful.

Nineteen fourteen was a banner year for Berlin: the year the songwriting dynamo joined the fledgling American Society of Composers, Authors and Publishers, ASCAP, as a charter member and member of the board of directors; the year he wrote his first score for a full-length musical; and the year he left Waterson Berlin & Snyder to found his own music-publishing firm, the Irving Berlin Music Company.

Yet Berlin's commanding gaze in the photograph also disguised a deep unease: "I was scared to death because I didn't know if I could continue to write hits," he recalled.[1] And he was fretting not just about his own inventiveness but about the shrinking profit margins of selling sheet music. Tin Pan Alley, the industry that had lifted him to fame, "was suffering from its own success," Philip Furia writes. The growth of the music industry had spawned too many publishing firms and generated "cutthroat competition," Berlin told *Theatre* magazine.[2]

The bold and seemingly counterintuitive move of hanging out his own shingle (along with his old friend and champion Max Winslow) in new offices at Broadway and 47th Street owed much to Charles Dillingham's plans for him. The veteran Broadway producer, famous for mounting the operettas of the Irish-born, German-trained Victor Herbert (*Babes in Toyland*, *Naughty Marietta*), had sat enthralled in the audience of Berlin's September 1911 stage performance at Hammerstein's Victoria. As Dillingham wrote in an unpublished memoir, "The first time I heard Alexander's Ragtime Band, I decided that the composer I.B. should write an entire score for me, and that was the start of 'Watch Your Step.'"[3]

Berlin had been yearning to evolve from a mere writer of songs into what he perceived as something more. "If I live long enough," he told the New York *Dramatic Mirror* soon after the triumph of "Alexander," "I shall write an opera completely in ragtime."[4] Old Europe still had its cultural hooks into America: opera equaled class. No doubt as a response to the hoopla that had arisen about his supposed primitivity, Berlin would keep mentioning his ragtime opera from time to time for years to come, without ever actually composing it.

Dillingham had nothing so staid in mind. Fresh winds were blowing through popular culture in 1914; youth was coming to the fore. The twenty-six-year-old Berlin and his songs seemed to be everywhere, as did the elegant young dance team of Vernon and Irene Castle, who had gained attention on both sides of the Atlantic with their genteel interpretations of dangerous dances like the maxixe and the tango—dances that had originated, in unapologetically sexual form, in the late nineteenth century in the portside slums of Rio de Janeiro, Buenos Aires, and Montevideo. By desexualizing these dances—they even invented a No-Hands Tango—the Castles made them safe for white audiences (and soon, participants) and became all the rage themselves. The slim and graceful couple modeled a panache that everyone wanted to imitate: Irene bobbed her hair and smoked cigarettes; many young women soon followed suit. And Charles Dillingham wanted to set the elegance of the Castles to the music of Irving Berlin.

In the years before World War I, the musical comedy as we have come to know it, with extensive scenes propelled by plot and dialogue and characters periodically breaking into songs that delineated their character, didn't quite exist. The legitimate musical theater (as opposed to vaudeville) was dominated by the operetta, as practiced by Victor Herbert and Franz Lehar. Operetta had originated in Europe, and the American variant still operated on a European model, with little in the way of book: the plot, such as it was, was carried along by the songs, which were sung by operatically trained singers.

And then there was George M. Cohan, who "had tried to wrest the American musical from the clutches of European operetta," Furia writes.

> Beginning in 1904, with *Little Johnny Jones*, he wrote shows that employed ragtime rhythms, colloquial speech, and contemporary American settings. . . . Songs such as "Give My Regards to Broadway" and "You're a Grand Old Flag" had a colloquial pugnacity that was a refreshing antidote to the Viennese schmaltz of Franz Lehar and Victor Herbert.[5]

But ten years on from *Little Johnny Jones*, Cohan was beginning to seem sentimental and slightly musty. Dillingham had something entirely new in mind: a freewheeling combination of legitimate theater and vaudeville, with known personalities—whether from vaudeville, the music hall, or elsewhere—performing a not too serious libretto and songs that more or less reflected the plot without advancing it too aggressively. Berlin responded enthusiastically, as both songwriter and businessman: writing the score to a musical that might propel a touring company around the country, he realized, could give his work a whole new platform.

His commercial fears notwithstanding, Berlin made an extraordinarily good deal for *Watch Your Step*. Though in 1914, "writers had little authority in a musical theater driven by producers and star power," as Jeffrey Magee reminds us, "Irving Berlin was different. From the start he exerted unusual control over his role as songwriter."[6] It was a pattern he would maintain for his whole working life: though filled with insecurities, he drove a very tough bargain when it came to protecting his music.

And with Dillingham he was in an excellent bargaining position. The producer had come to him, Berlin had a trunkful of hits, and when all was said and done, he was the man who had written "Alexander." The contract he negotiated placed a strict limit on the number of interpolations (songs by other composers) that would be allowed in the show, challenging a practice that had been rife throughout the history of American musical theater—and one from which Berlin himself had profited, and would continue to profit.

Yet as the deal was being finalized, he developed cold feet. "When he signed a contract with me to do a score, turning from song writer to composer," Dillingham recalled, "he became a little frightened and asked Harry B. Smith who was doing the libretto to write the lyrics."[7] Twice Berlin's age, Smith was the dean of his profession, with thirty years' experience writing the books for operettas, musicals, and revues (including five *Ziegfeld Follies*), as well as the lyrics to thousands of songs. But Smith was no Berlin. The librettist recalled the young songwriter in his own memoir:

> He is a genius in inventing unexpected rhymes. Most bards would think it hopeless to attempt to find a rhyme for "Wednesday"; but Mr. Berlin found one. In one of the songs in this piece [*Watch Your Step*], a matinee idol describes his persecution by women and alludes to the elderly worshippers who attend the afternoon performances:
>
> > There's a matinee on Wednesday,
> > I call it my old hens' day.[8]

Smith told the youngster: "Irving Berlin, don't let anybody ever help you with your lyrics."[9]

Berlin took heed. And once he got going, he barreled ahead with a fiery energy over the summer and into the fall, turning out almost thirty new songs in various styles: rags, ballads, a polka, a waltz. An orchestrator named Frank Sadler arranged the pieces for a twenty-piece orchestra, a breathtaking leap for a songwriter who'd previously been used to hearing his tunes played by, at most, a piano and ten, as a vaudeville orchestra was called.

The show was essentially a revue, a mishmash—Berlin's score was really just a disparate collection of charming songs, and as for the libretto, the program read: "Plot (if any) by Harry B. Smith." What counted was the spectacle of the thing. Who cared if the action shifted, with little to no explanation, from a law office to a stage door to a rural town to the Metropolitan Opera, where the angry ghost of Giuseppe Verdi appeared, berating the chorus for singing his work in syncopation?

But the show's real gem, more or less buried amid the gaudy foolishness, began as a girl singer crooned plaintively,

> Won't you play a simple melody
> Like my mother sang to me . . .

and then the boy singer went into the syncopated counter-chorus:

> Oh you musical demon,
> Set your honey a-dreamin,'
> Won't you play me some rag?[10]

"Simple Melody" was the first of Berlin's great double songs—songs consisting of two separate melodies written to be sung by two voices, successively at first, then together in counterpoint. It was an astonishing feat for a songwriter who couldn't read or write music, and therefore had no certifiable knowledge of harmony. But for Berlin, the astonishing was commonplace: as always, the harmonies were right there in his head when he needed them. "The musical part didn't give me any trouble," he recalled many years later. "The difficulty was getting two lyrics so that they wouldn't bump into each other."[11]

"Simple Melody," like *Watch Your Step* itself, represented a clash between the old-fashioned and the newfangled that turns into sweet, contrapuntal harmony. The show opened at the lavish New Amsterdam Theatre, at 214 West 42nd Street, on December 8, 1914. The plot's implausibilities mattered little to the first-nighters (among whom sat Leah Berlin, next to her son and two of his sisters). What did matter was that the spectacle was fresh and new, a perfect showcase for the talents of the Castles and Berlin, but especially Berlin. When the house lights came up, someone called, "Composer! Composer!" "He walked up the aisle, mounted the stage, and acknowledged the applause," Bergreen writes.

> When the composer appeared before them, the audience drew its collective breath. He looked tiny, and although he was now a twenty-six-year-old widower, he scarcely seemed out of his teens. He made a brief speech of thanks, but his words were drowned out by the roar of approval.[12]

Just as astonishing to *Variety*'s reporter was Berlin's behavior after the premiere. "Seldom has a successful first night occurred in New York when the one most responsible for it could not be found after the performance at the most famous Broadway restaurant, the center of a large and admiring crowd," he wrote.[13] But instead of basking in the admiration, Berlin got in his hired car with his mother and sisters and saw them home. And then returned to his apartment with Cliff Hess to await the reviews.

They were worth waiting for. Berlin "stands out like the Times building does in the Square," *Variety* wrote. "That youthful marvel of syncopated melody is proving things in 'Watch Your Step,' firstly that he is not alone a rag composer, and that he is one of the greatest lyric writers America has ever produced."[14]

As far as the *Times* was concerned, Berlin was the story:

'WATCH YOUR STEP'

IS HILARIOUS FUN

Irving Berlin's Revue at the
New Amsterdam is Fes-
tivity Syncopated.

But, the piece went on to insist, a revue was what it was. "So many things have been called musical comedies that 'Watch Your Step' might as well be called one," the anonymous reviewer wrote.

> It is really vaudeville done handsomely. . . . More than to any one else, "Watch Your Step" belongs to Irving Berlin. He is the young master of syncopation, the gifted and industrious writer of words and music for songs that have made him rich and envied. This is the first time that the author of "Alexander's Ragtime Band" and the like has turned his attention to providing the music for an entire evening's entertainment. For it, he has written a score of his mad melodies, nearly all of them of the tickling sort, born to be caught up and whistled at every street corner, and warranted to set any roomful a-dancing.[15]

The message was mixed, but in essence it was the same as George M. Cohan's: Berlin may have moved uptown, but he was still there with the old downtown hardshell. So what if he hadn't reinvented musical comedy? He was a vaudevillian at heart, a writer of madly hummable hits, and what was wrong with that?

* * *

Charles Dillingham was eager to repeat the success of *Watch Your Step*, but by 1915, World War I had broken out, the English-born Vernon Castle had enlisted in the Royal Flying Corps, and the dance team was no more.[16] Dillingham's solution was to build his new musical, *Stop! Look! Listen!*, around Irving Berlin and the French dancehall sensation Gaby Deslys.

With less than three months to write twenty-five numbers, Berlin produced a ragtag score that seemed like an assemblage of reworked castoffs from *Watch Your Step*—and then there was "I Love a Piano." The comedian and dancer Harry Fox (who gave his name to the Fox Trot) introduced the number, accompanied by no fewer than six pianists (playing either six different instruments or a spectacular prop keyboard that spanned almost the entire stage; accounts vary). But no special effect was needed to assure the immortality of the song, whose tune is sheer, ringing joy and whose lyrics are among Berlin's wittiest:

> I know a fine way
> To treat a Steinway. . . .
> So you can keep your fiddle and your bow,
> Give me a P-I-A-N-O, oh, oh—
> I love to stop right
> Beside an upright
> Or a high-toned baby grand.[17]

This is simplicity at its simplest—and of course its most complex: one shudders to think of the blood Berlin sweated to get it right. And the lyric, if one reads between the lines (as if the lines themselves weren't perfect enough), is as autobiographical in its own way as "When I Lost You": here we have intertwined the composer's insecurity and awe in the face of the many more talented keyboard artists he has encountered with his sensuous, highly metaphoric connection to the instrument that is the source of his wealth and fame. This is a song that's every bit as erotic about the piano (right down to that *O, oh, oh!*) as the many sexy tunes that would be written about cars from the 1930s through the 1960s. And a song that gives us the complete transition of the whip-smart boy who sang dirty parodies at Nigger Mike's to full-fledged artist.

* * *

Hamstrung by Gaby Deslys's diva behavior, *Stop! Look! Listen!* ran for just over two months. Yet even as the Dillingham production was closing, a musical that had opened almost simultaneously with it was settling into a long run, and its composer was helping to create a new American art form.

Very Good Eddie opened on December 23, 1915, at the Princess Theatre, a tiny bandbox of a house (299 seats) at 104–106 West 39th Street; the librettist was an English-born American named Guy Bolton, and the composer was the Manhattan-born Jerome David Kern. At thirty-one, Jerry Kern was three years older than Irving Berlin, and unlike Berlin, a refined genius rather than a primitive one, having studied piano and composition in New York and Heidelberg and having begun contributing songs to Broadway shows, and musicals in London's West End, while still in his teens.

From a strict musical standpoint, Kern could write rings around Berlin, bringing refinement to a thirty-two-bar popular song that the younger songwriter could only dream of. As proof, there was his watershed 1914 hit "They Didn't Believe Me," a song that sounds timeless today because it was modern then.

"Critics tried to group them together: Kern and Berlin, the next generation of Broadway composers," Bergreen writes. "But Berlin resisted the notion of seeing his name bracketed with anyone else's; he wrote his own music and lyrics, published his own songs, and on occasion, performed them himself. He displayed scant interest in developing the collaborative skills required by a musical."[18]

Meanwhile, down on West 39th Street, Jerry Kern was making collaborative magic. *Very Good Eddie* was the second of the so-called Princess Theatre plays: musicals with American settings, few scenery changes (a simplicity born of necessity in the tiny theater), farcical action by Bolton, and beautiful songs by Kern. Soon P. G. Wodehouse would add his romance-spoofing lyrics to the equation, and the trio would proceed to revolutionize the American musical theater with a series of shows that were matchlessly funny, sophisticated, and character-driven.

In the meantime, Irving Berlin—who would not write a truly successful, truly integrated song-and-story musical until 1946's *Annie Get Your Gun*—would go his own way. Also in the meantime, he fell in love.

* * *

To all appearances, Berlin's chief romance since Dorothy's death had been with his Weser Brothers transposing piano. He had moved from the Chatsworth, with its doleful associations, to an apartment on West 70th, where he lived, as well-to-do young bachelors of the era often did, with a couple in service, a Swedish cook and valet. Every night, the pair left at midnight and Irving repaired to the piano, tapping at the black keys and scratching out lyrics with his fountain pen until the sky began to lighten. Now as in the early years—the early years were all of a decade ago now—his overnight hours were dedicated to work, not play.

But were they really? He'd been a widower for four years; he worked in show business, where the temptations were many; he was young and magnetic and beautifully dressed and quite well off. And both the words and the music of his songs seem to reveal, at the very least, a healthy libido. Is it reading too much into tunes like 1914's "If You Don't Want My Peaches (You'd Better Stop Shaking My Tree)" and 1915's "Take Off a Little Bit" ("A man must see/An inch or three/To keep him interested/An ankle now and then/Will catch the best of men/So take off a little bit.")—not to mention those syncopated rhythms!—is it over-imaginative to imagine that this songwriter was writing from a standpoint that wasn't merely academic?[19]

But in 1916, his output suffered markedly, both in quality and quantity: between the March closing of *Stop! Look! Listen!* and November, he published a mere seven songs, none of much interest to posterity except as curios—though that fall the eighteen-year-old George Gershwin made a piano roll of one, "I'm Down in Honolulu (Looking Them Over)."

Berlin might have been sidetracked in May by the Friars Frolic, a charity gala in which he performed, and for which he wrote both a long, rhyming speech, and a song, "The Friars'

Parade." He was almost certainly distracted by his collaboration with Victor Herbert on the score for an upcoming Flo Ziegfeld extravaganza, *The Century Girl.*

And then there was eighteen-year-old Constance Talmadge.

"Dutch" Talmadge—she'd been so nicknamed as a little girl, because of her round face and blond hair—was the youngest of three daughters of a feckless, alcoholic father and a legendary stage mother. When her husband's desertion left her destitute, Peg Talmadge got her three good-looking girls to Hollywood as fast as she could. The oldest, Norma, the tragedian of the family, was the first to go to work in the movies; Natalie, the middle sister, turned out to have little interest in acting but would later marry Buster Keaton. Dutch, a natural comedian, quickly outshone them both, snagging a role in a very serious project: D. W. Griffith's epic *Intolerance.*

After Constance's contract with Griffith ran out, her mother brought her daughters back east—the movie business was bicoastal in those days. And one night, at a party at the Ritz Hotel, Norma Talmadge met Berlin's old Bowery pal Joe Schenck, who fell hard for her.

Schenck and his younger brother Nicholas had recently joined Marcus Loew in the movie-theater business, and Joe aspired to run a studio. And here, in one beauteous twenty-two-year-old package, was his ticket. In Norma Talmadge Joe Schenck saw both a future wife and a Galatea, a girl he could mold into a star. He set to work on his project, deputizing his best friend Irving to sound out Norma's feelings for him. Irving discovered that Norma liked Schenck well enough (the two would marry that October), and somewhere along the way, in the turbulent year of 1916, Irving discovered Dutch.

Long-chinned and tomboyish, Dutch Talmadge wasn't as conventionally beautiful as her older sisters, but she compensated with a teasing vivacity that made her formidably sexy. Yet she was also still a girl, and a certain hard-hearted flightiness was part of her charm.

In 1917, Berlin would publish a song called "Whose Little Heart Are You Breaking Now?," with the line "I wonder whose feelings you're hurting/When he catches you flirting."[20] A couple of years later, his friend Anita Loos asked him to think of a title for a screenplay she'd written for Constance. Irving had it: *A Virtuous Vamp*. Maybe the virtue applied only where he was concerned.

7

I Wasn't Much of a Soldier

THE FIFTY-SEVEN-YEAR-OLD Victor Herbert was the anti-Berlin: large, bibulous, gregarious, lecherous. He was also a brilliant musician, not only as a composer but also as a cellist, conductor, and master orchestrator. "Berlin, the untutored, was embarrassed by the disparity in their musical learning," Jablonski writes. "In Herbert's presence he felt, as he would tell Herbert's biographer, Edward N. Waters, 'like a man who could talk, but could neither read [nor] write.' "[1]

One day during rehearsals for *The Century Girl*, the story goes, the two men lunched together at the Lambs Club. After making some nervous small talk, Berlin finally popped the big question. "Victor," he asked, "people say that if I studied music, it would overwhelm me. Do you agree with them?"

Herbert replied, "Irving, you have a natural talent for putting music and words together. Mind you, a little science wouldn't hurt."[2]

And so (the story goes) Berlin decided to take piano lessons. Long story short: it didn't take. "I was never a good student," he told Michael Freedland, many years later. "I was much too impatient. I studied and practiced for two days and then gave it up. I realized I could have written two songs and made myself some money in that time."[3]

The stories of Berlin's musical incompetence are legion—and in many cases, highly exaggerated. (Draw your own conclusions from the fact that the storytellers were sometimes fellow songwriters.) In fact, he eventually learned to both read and write music—Mary Ellin Barrett has guessed it was sometime in the 1920s.[4] As for his keyboard technique, "at some point, the piano playing cleaned itself up," Barrett, who was born in 1926, recalled. "When I was thirteen," she said, "he would sit down at the piano and play for me and my friends—not his songs, but other people's. If somebody called for 'Night and Day,' he didn't embarrass me. Now, he wasn't Gershwin, or, for that matter, Harold Arlen, who was a wonderful jazz pianist. But he was wonderful at the piano."[5]

With Victor Herbert conducting the orchestra, *The Century Girl* opened on November 6, 1916, on the eve of what was to be an extraordinarily close presidential election between the incumbent Woodrow Wilson and Charles Evans Hughes. Both men had campaigned on promises to keep the United States out of the war in Europe, and the revue reflected the isolationist/patriotic schizophrenia of the moment. Herbert and his lyricist Henry Blossom contributed a pair of flag-wavers, "When Uncle Sam Is Ruler of the Sea" and "Uncle Sam's Children," but Berlin, who'd written an antiwar song ("Stay Down Here Where You Belong") soon after the commencement of hostilities in 1914, and had come to regret it, stuck to show business.

And it was a hell of a show. Critics and audiences had derided the revue's eponymous theater the Century, a great white elephant on Central Park West and 62nd Street, for its poor acoustics and distance from Broadway, and Flo Ziegfeld was out to prove them all wrong—or go broke trying. He (and Charles Dillingham, who coproduced) pulled out all the stops, spending lavishly on scenery, costumes, and talent to create a gargantuan spectacle, a full four hours long, whose chief point, in the Ziegfeld tradition, was a celebration of American womanhood. Hazel Dawn, Elsie Janis, May Leslie, and Lilyan Tashman, among others, provided the pulchritude; there was also a full complement of vaudeville stars, including Marie Dressler, the comedians Sam Bernard and Leon Errol, and the comic singing team of Van and Schenck.

Alexander Woollcott, then the *New York Times* drama critic, called the show both "spectacle and vaudeville, glorified beyond anything we have had in the music hall world and multiplied by ten."[6] *Variety*'s notice was somewhat less glowing: "As there are only about 90 to 100 minutes to be taken out, it doesn't require much of a knife, just a hydraulic dredger."[7] The public, perhaps in the mood for escapist excess with a war raging in Europe, ate it up anyway: *The Century Girl* ran for two hundred performances.

But the show's music was hardly the point, and songs like "It Takes an Irishman to Make Love" and "The Chicken Walk" were no ornament to Berlin's reputation. A new kind of popular music was bubbling to the surface at the hinge of 1916–17. Only a year before, Berlin's "Everything in America Is Ragtime" could triumphantly climax a show; suddenly, everything in America wasn't ragtime anymore, and the man who had been dubbed (however inaccurately) the King of Ragtime was in danger of becoming irrelevant. Jerome Kern, the songwriter with whom Irving Berlin had so often been bracketed, was entering an astounding period of creativity, preparing the scores for no fewer than three musicals, while Berlin found himself at what looked very much like a creative impasse. Then history stepped in to help him out.

* * *

From the evidence of the songs, he remained a pacifist, though not an outspoken isolationist, well into the Great War, perhaps maintaining an immigrant's wariness about sticking his neck out. "Stay Down Here Where You Belong," published in October of 1914, was his first musical reference to the hostilities, and his second hell-based tune. In it, the Devil was conversing with his son, who wanted to go up on Earth, "Where I can have a little fun."

The Devil replied in the chorus:

> Stay down here where you belong;
> The folks who live above you don't know right from wrong. . . .
> Kings up there are bigger devils than your dad:
> They're breaking the hearts of mothers,
> Making butchers out of brothers—
> You'll find more hell up there than there is down below."[8]

A devil's advocate might almost hazard the opinion, in light of World War I's unprecedented mass carnage, that this lyric was as acute as any Berlin ever wrote.[9] The Battle of the Somme— better labeled by the Germans *Der Schlacht an der Somme*, the Slaughter on the Somme: more than a million killed or wounded —was just winding down as that gauzy entertainment *The Century Girl* opened in November of 1916.

But by then, Berlin's pacifism had begun to transform into something else. He may have had a genuine change of heart; he may also have been affected by the rise of Teutonophobia in America, which would result in, on the lighter side, the renaming of hamburgers to liberty sandwiches, sauerkraut to liberty cabbage, and dachshunds to liberty pups, and, on the not so light side, the banning and burning of German books and the conflation of things German with things Jewish. Suddenly, Berlin didn't look like the greatest name choice.

In 1915, the songwriter—still technically a resident alien—

started an application to become a naturalized citizen, a three-step, two-year process beginning with a formal renunciation of "allegiance to Nicholas II, Emperor of all the Russias." By the beginning of 1917, Germany initiated unrestricted submarine warfare on U.S. ships crossing the Atlantic, and on April 6, President Wilson declared war on Germany. On May 18, Wilson signed into law the Selective Draft Act, requiring all American men between twenty-one and thirty to register for possible service in the armed services. Irving Berlin, still not a U.S. citizen, was exempt.

Not long afterward, George M. Cohan introduced his immortal war anthem "Over There"—and in May, just before his twenty-ninth birthday, Berlin published his first war song, the less than immortal "For Your Country and My Country":

> It's your country, it's my country,
> With millions of real fighting men;
> It's your duty and my duty,
> To speak with the sword, not the pen.[10]

Ponderous lyrics aside, though, the tune was sprightly, and the 1917 Duo-Art piano roll (recorded by the increasingly ubiquitous George Gershwin) listed it as a "jazz one-step."[11] Just like that, ragtime was passé. With a single song, Berlin had entered two new territories at once.

* * *

In October, Berlin filed his petition for naturalization; and on February 6, 1918, in the county clerk's office at City Hall, he raised his right hand and once again renounced any loyalty to Russia (which was now under the control of a Bolshevik regime rather than a czar), solemnly promising, "I will support and defend the Constitution and laws of the United States of America against all enemies, foreign and domestic; and that I will bear true faith and allegiance to the same."

How thrilled he must have felt to say these words! And,

with the war still raging, and doughboys now fighting and dying in Europe, how glad Berlin would have been to heed the call of his friend Elsie Janis, late of the cast of *The Century Girl*, to come over to France and help her entertain the troops . . .

Until the draft notice arrived, just days after his thirtieth birthday.

The army wanted him while it could still get him: in a year he'd no longer be eligible. Despite his wholehearted patriotism, "the board's bland acceptance of him had come as a disagreeable surprise," Woollcott wrote, citing Irving's chronic stomach trouble: "For all his own doctors had insisted that no army would take him as a gift. Indeed, for years he had writhed with a nervous indigestion which had led him from doctor to doctor and made him the profitable plaything of each new specialist arriving in New York."[12]

And so the rich and coddled bachelor, so used to the pleasant and largely nocturnal rhythms of his life on West 70th Street, with a cook and valet in service and a chauffeured car at his beck and call, found himself transported to Camp Upton, in Yaphank, N.Y., the home of the 77th Infantry Division, a huge grid of hastily built barracks and dusty parade grounds set among the desolate potato fields of central Long Island.

"There Pvt. Berlin was issued an ill-fitting khaki uniform (his tailor would remedy that on his first weekend pass), wraparound leggings, a campaign hat (similar to those worn by Boy Scouts), cumbersome shoes, and a steel helmet," Jablonski writes. "In addition, he received two olive-drab blankets and a gun with a bayonet. This last did not make much sense to Pvt. Berlin."[13]

"I found out quickly I wasn't much of a soldier," Berlin recalled. "There were a lot of things about army life I didn't like, and the thing I didn't like most of all was reveille. I hated it. I hated it so much that I used to lie awake nights thinking about how much I hated it."[14]

The first night was especially hard. "Ten o'clock found me lying on an army cot in the dark," he remembered, years later.

> The large wooden barracks was filled with dozens of men who would soon be asleep. As a civilian I never went to bed before two in the morning. The thought of having to lie there awake for hours depressed me. . . . Suddenly, I got very hungry. I knew it was one o'clock because I always get hungry at that hour of the morning. I thought of my apartment in New York. The night before some friends had been there for a farewell dinner. What was left of a turkey was still in the ice-box when I started for camp. Nothing could have brought home the seriousness of my position more than the fact that I couldn't be in my kitchen at one o'clock in the morning. I have no idea what time I fell asleep but I awoke with a start and heard for the first time the bugler who was to become my pet aversion and be the inspiration for "Oh How I Hate to Get Up in the Morning."[15]

* * *

The song was, appropriately enough, a march—a madly infectious march. The tune, and the lyric, rose up out of the chest with gusto:

> Oh! How I hate to get up in the morning,
> Oh! How I'd love to remain in bed . . .

The whole thing appeared utterly straightforward, yet dizzily clever: Berlin's trademark, of course. The words' rebelliousness lay somewhere between naïvely wholehearted and carefully calibrated: a corollary of the Berlin trademark. The kicker was in the song's final verse:

> Someday I'm going to murder the bugler,
> Someday they're going to find him dead.
> I'll amputate his reveille and stamp upon it heavily,
> And spend the rest of my life in bed.[16]

More elegant, hard-won simplicity: the repetition of "someday"; the giddy, bloodless malevolence of "amputate"; the brilliance of rhyming "reveille" and "heavily"; the fond dreaminess of the last line: all pure Berlin.

And the genius of Berlin was that he could give you bloodlessness without saccharine. Though the song was not the plaint of a front-line soldier, who would have had far more to gripe about than having to get up early, its universality cleared it of pettiness, and its sheer catchiness and good humor turned it into an instant anthem.

And turned Private Berlin into a Camp Upton celebrity—upon whom great privilege quickly descended. As the song caught on, and his fellow soldiers were shipped off to France humming it, Berlin—now promoted to sergeant—stayed stateside. Clearly he was a special commodity. In short order, he was summoned to meet with the camp commandant, Major General J. Franklin Bell.

In one version of the story, General Bell tells his celebrity charge, "We want a new community house—a place where friends and relatives of you men can be made a little more comfortable when they come to visit. It could cost a lot of money—perhaps $35,000—and we thought perhaps you could put on a little show to make money."[17]

In the other version, it's Berlin who wants to Put on a Show, in order to capitalize on the talents of the other show-business draftees in the camp—and with a certain other agenda in mind. As soon as General Bell agreed to the production (so the story goes), Berlin said, "Here's the thing, General. I write at night. Sometimes I work all night when I get an idea. And I couldn't do that if I had to get up in the morning at five, you understand."

Suddenly, the general was all generosity. "Why, you don't have to get up at five," he told Berlin. "You just forget about all that. *You write this show.*"[18]

If the army brass had visualized a winsome little talent show out at Camp Upton, they were in for a surprise. Irving Berlin wasn't thinking small—he was thinking colossal. That spring, the U.S. Navy had staged a revue (distinguished mainly for its chorus line of uncomfortably convincing female impersonators) at no less a venue than Manhattan's Century Theatre. Berlin proposed to outdo the navy, returning to the site of *The Century Girl* with a limited-run staging of his own singing, dancing army revue, with an all-Berlin score and a complement of more than three hundred soldiers. To sell the thing, he gave it an attention-getting title: *Yip! Yip! Yaphank*. And Major General Bell was sold. He even assigned Sergeant Berlin a supervisory board consisting of a major, a captain, and a lieutenant. The clever sergeant would have allowed these important officers to feel they were supervising while he, of course, saw to every detail of the show himself.

* * *

From Tin Pan Alley he enlisted a (civilian) musical secretary, the twenty-two-year-old songwriter Harry Ruby, the future author of "Who's Sorry Now?," "I Wanna Be Loved by You," and "Three Little Words," as well as several Marx Brothers film scores. As Ruby sat by with pen and staff paper, Berlin began to generate songs for his revue: lightly satirical, military-themed tunes with titles like "Kitchen Police (Poor Little Me)" ("Against my wishes/I wash the dishes,/To make this wide world/Safe for democracy"), "Ever Since I Put on a Uniform," and "Bevo"—the name of a nonalcoholic wartime beer brewed by Anheuser-Busch and particularly loathed by soldiers everywhere ("You may taste like beer but you're only a bluff,/You may be near it but you ain't near enough").[19] He also wrote a romantic number, with the clunky and referential title "The Sterling Silver Moon." (Edward Madden and Gus Edwards's mega-hit "By the Light of the Silvery Moon" had been published nine years earlier.) Revised and much improved, Berlin's song would reappear in the *Ziegfeld Follies of 1919* as "Mandy" ("there's a minister handy").

Yip! Yip! Yaphank! premiered on Monday, August 19, 1918, and the New York theater world had never seen anything quite like it. *Variety's* Sime Silverman, now a Berlin follower of seven years' standing, turned in an effusive review. "As a show, it's a wonder," he wrote. "Here were 350 men, all from Camp Upton, giving a show that moved with the precision of a clock. In the opening scene . . . 277 were on the stage at the finale—and not a miss!"[20]

Of course in a climate of patriotic fervor, service comedies had an automatic leg up. And while the *New York Times's* unbylined reviewer applauded the genre in general, he went on to say that *Yaphank* was markedly better. The reviewer felt the piece was at its best when the music was playing: "Most of [the songs] will probably soon be more than familiar, for they are certain to find their way into vaudeville or musical comedy when 'Yip! Yip! Yaphank' is permitted to pass.[21]

This would have been music to Berlin's ears. Not only had he not lost professional momentum during his army stint; he had, through sheer pluck (not to mention overwhelming talent), raised his professional profile even higher. And—as the *Times* neglected to say—the man who put over the revue's showstopper was the songwriter himself.

It was late in the evening, close to 11 P.M., after the big chorus numbers had made their impact, when the lights dimmed and a military tent materialized onstage. "Sergeant Berlin!" someone called, but the sergeant failed to appear. Finally, two soldiers entered the tent and dragged out the show's author and star, in uniform and to all appearances, asleep on his feet. "Of course there was a welcome that rocked the theater," *Theatre* magazine's critic wrote, "but to his credit as a good actor, there he stood . . . staring dreamily ahead, and buttoning up his coat. Then he introduced, in his peculiar, plaintive little voice, the chorus that began: 'Oh! How I hate to get up in the morning.'"[22]

It was, in its shy, sly way, a knockout performance—a fact that Berlin, with his thorough understanding of theatricality, would have understood perfectly. That peculiar, plaintive little voice, with its pronounced Lower East Side accent (in which "murder the bugler" came out as "moider" him) commanded more attention than a back-row-reaching tenor with rolled R's and perfect enunciation would have: his charisma was concentrated, absolute. And he was the star of the evening, lest anyone think otherwise.

It was a power even his commanding officer had to acknowledge. At the end of the show—a blockbuster finale in which the entire company, in full battle gear and with rifles on their shoulders, streamed up the aisles singing "We're on Our Way to France" ("Bye-bye, mothers and all the others / Who'll come to shed a little tear")—Major General J. Franklin Bell stood in his box and addressed the audience: "I have heard that Berlin is among the foremost song writers of the world, and now I believe it," he said. And then: "Berlin is as good a soldier as he is a songwriter, and as popular in Camp Upton as he is on Broadway."[23] He then called on the diminutive sergeant to speak.

The applause rose to a crescendo and continued for a full ten minutes as, amid shouts of approbation, Berlin stood smiling, bowing, and speechless. His reticence, he knew well, spoke far louder than any oration would have. And his show, limited as its run might have been, kept his light burning brightly on the Great White Way. Jerry Kern may have conquered musical theater, but Irving Berlin had found his own way to rule alongside him.

* * *

Berlin had written another song at Upton, an unashamedly patriotic number intended to be the finale of *Yip! Yip! Yaphank!*

"As you may remember," the composer recalled in a 1954 letter to Abel Green, the editor of *Variety*,

> The finale—the boys were alerted in the scene before that they were going overseas, and in overseas outfits, including helmets, they marched through the Theater . . . boarded a transport, and as the lights lowered, the transport, on wheel[s], slowly moved off stage. It was a very touching and emotional scene. . . .
>
> Having that finale in mind, it seemed painting the lily to have soldiers sing "God Bless America" in that situation, so I didn't use it.[24]

In fact, Berlin had misgivings about the song almost from the moment he wrote it. "There were so many patriotic songs coming out everywhere at the time," Harry Ruby remembered. "Every songwriter was pouring them out. He'd already written several patriotic numbers for the show, and then, when he brought in 'God Bless America,' I took it down for him, and I said, 'Geez, *another* one?' "[25]

"Just a little sticky" was Berlin's own verdict on the number, which he relegated to his song trunk.[26] It would stay there for twenty years.

8

Work for Yourself!

REENTERING CIVILIAN LIFE was easy; bringing all his businesses back up to speed was not. For a couple of months in
early 1919, Berlin even considered signing with another publisher instead of reopening his old shop. With a brand-new
song in hand, he paid a visit to Max Dreyfus, the head of T. B.
Harms, the highly successful publisher of Jerome Kern. The
number, based on the tumultuous recent events in Russia, was
called "That Revolutionary Rag":

> That Revolutionary Rag—
> 'Twas made across the sea
> By a tricky, slicky Bolsheviki . . .[1]

But though he had the lyric on paper and the tune in his
head when he walked into the Harms offices, he didn't yet have
a *song* written down on a lead sheet: Cliff Hess had remained at
Waterson Berlin & Snyder, the publishing firm that still con-

tained Berlin's name but no longer contained Berlin. Accordingly, Berlin asked Dreyfus whether the publisher had somebody on the premises who could take down the music for him.

"I have a kid here who can do it," Dreyfus said.

He walked Berlin to a room where a long-jawed, dark-haired youngster sat at a distressed upright. The kid was none other than George Gershwin, twenty and a house pianist and song plugger for Harms. Since Berlin claimed, then and later, not to have remembered their 1915 meeting (the then-seventeen-year-old had brought him some songs for possible publication; Berlin had been more impressed by the boy's piano playing), Gershwin reintroduced himself. His face may have been only vaguely familiar, but those fingers! After Berlin had hummed the tune and Gershwin obediently written down the notes, the kid played a bouncing, iridescently chorded version, arranged in his head on the spot: the song "was so good I didn't recognize it," Berlin would later joke.[2]

He recalled the meeting to Robert Kimball in 1973. "Gershwin had heard that Berlin was looking for a musical secretary and he said he would like the job," Kimball and Alfred Simon wrote in *The Gershwins*.

> Berlin replied that his plans were unsettled and asked him what he really wanted to do. Gershwin said he wanted to write songs. Berlin listened to some Gershwin songs . . . and said, "What the hell do you want to work for anybody else for? Work for yourself!"[3]

By June, Berlin had decided to take his own advice and go back into the music-publishing business, setting up a new firm, Irving Berlin, Inc., at 1607 Broadway, between 48th and 49th. Once again he brought in Max Winslow to help him, giving his trusted old friend the title of professional manager; he also hired as business manager a character to whom all accounts refer (for reasons that will become clear) as "one Saul Bornstein." Berlin's new musical secretary was a gifted twenty-one-year-old composer, conductor, pianist, and arranger named Arthur Johnston, who would go on to become a successful Hollywood songwriter himself ("Pennies from Heaven," "Cocktails for Two").

The new shop opened two days after the premiere of the *Ziegfeld Follies of 1919*, which featured no fewer than fourteen Irving Berlin numbers. Suddenly Berlin was back in a big way. Those fourteen songs—especially the showstopper, "A Pretty Girl Is Like a Melody," which came to symbolize Flo Ziegfeld and his dazzling product, and a whole early-twentieth-century style of musical theater—were central to the success of the 1919 *Follies*, which ran for 171 performances, more than any of its predecessors.

The show would have run even longer had it not been for the mid-August interruption of an Actors Equity strike, an event that divided Broadway management and talent and proved fateful for Berlin. At the Friars Club earlier in the summer he had run into an old friend, the producer Sam H. Harris. Excited by his big role in the revue's success, Berlin—not ordinarily given to impetuousness in speech or action—had blurted, "If you ever want to build a theater just for musical comedy, I've got a great name for it—the Music Box."

Good name, Harris said; then he changed the subject.[4] At forty-seven, the producer was a wise old head of the Great White Way, best known for his long association with George M. Cohan, which had begun in 1904 with *Little Johnny Jones*, sometimes credited as being the first American musical, and best known for introducing the numbers "Yankee Doodle Dandy" and "Give My Regards to Broadway."

But after fifteen years and eighteen shows with Harris, Cohan was giving his regards to Broadway for real, so upset by the strike and his partner's perversely—so it seemed to him—pro-labor stance that he'd decided to retire from the stage (temporarily, as it turned out) at age forty-one. And the theater world was shocked at his departure: Harris without Cohan made no sense. *Broadway* without Cohan made no sense—a general feeling that was borne out in the spring of 1920, when Harris's first show without his former partner, *Honey Girl*, with a score by Albert Von Tilzer, Harry's younger brother, flopped badly.

Sam Harris phoned Irving Berlin. "Irving," he said, "you remember that Music Box idea of yours?"

"Will I ever forget it?" said Berlin, who, having been awakened by Harris's call at the crack of noon, had no idea what the producer was talking about.

Harris told Berlin that he'd just bought a piece of land three brownstones wide on West 45th Street, across the street from the Hotel Astor. "You can have your Music Box whenever you want it," the producer said. "You're my partner."[5]

Sam Harris was a grand old Manhattan character, a fearlessly venturesome gambler who'd worked his way up to Broadway producer by selling cough drops, running a hotel laundry business, and managing a prizefighter named Terry McGovern. Now he was proposing to share the biggest gamble of his career with Irving Berlin. To pay off the loan on the 45th Street property, raze the brownstones, and erect the new theater would take an estimated $947,000—very serious money in 1919, the equivalent of some $14 million today. Berlin was quite well-heeled, but he didn't happen to have $473,500 lying around.

He went to Joe Schenck. His best friend had now achieved his dream of movie moguldom, having transformed his young wife Norma Talmadge (she called him Daddy) into one of filmdom's brightest stars. In the years after World War I, when New York was still America's motion-picture cocapital, Schenck was running an honest-to-God movie empire out of a three-story brick building on East 48th Street, presiding over the offices and studios of the Norma Talmadge Film Corporation, occupying the first floor, the Constance Talmadge Film Corporation, on the second floor, and the Comique unit, whose stars included Fatty Arbuckle and Buster Keaton, on the third. The former pharmacist, who was not only making pictures but also exhibiting them in the chain of theaters he co-owned with his brother Nicholas and Marcus Loew, had become a very wealthy man.

And Irving Berlin was a very nervous one when he sat down in Joe Schenck's office. "Joe, I want to let you in on something," he began, tentatively.

Schenck, who was almost a decade Berlin's senior and had been around the block a few times, fixed his old friend with a poker player's stare. Irving changed tack.

"Joe, I'm in trouble," he said.

"Who's the girl?" Schenck asked.

"Not a girl, a theater," Berlin said.

"Why do you want me?"

Irving remembered Sam Harris's line. "You're my partner," he said.[6]

It was the Open Sesame. Schenck put up half of Berlin's half, and construction proceeded on West 45th Street.

"The Music Box would be the first and only Broadway theater ever built to accommodate the songs and scores of a single composer," Bergreen writes.[7] But Jablonski asserts that this was not Berlin's original intention—that he always wanted to stage the works of other composers besides himself. When Harris proposed naming the theater Irving Berlin's Music Box, Irving objected. "Too much Berlin," he said.[8]

Nevertheless, there was never any other plan for the theater's premiere production than an all-Berlin revue. All he had to do was write it.

*　*　*

He spent the summer of 1921 shut in his suite at Atlantic City's grand Traymore Hotel, with Arthur Johnston in attendance, following his own nine rules for writing popular songs, including injecting "heart interest" into each number, sprinkling the lyrics with "open vowels" for euphony, and most important of all, rule #9: "The song writer must look upon his work as a business, that is, to make a success of it, he must work and *work*, and then WORK."[9]

"The only breath of salt air I got for weeks at a time," Berlin reminisced years later, "was when I leaned out of a window and flew a kite."[10]

"Berlin will have been fiddling at his piano for weeks," Woollcott wrote,

> until he has verse, chorus and melody pretty much as he likes it. Now he plays it for Johnston, who, sitting with pencil poised in the manner of a bored stenographer, makes strange, negligent flytracks across a scrap of paper. At the end [Johnston] takes over the piano stool and plays what he has written, while Berlin, with beach robe trailing, paces the far corner of the room. . . .
>
> Then, once the melody is there on paper, there is the lyric to be completed and the second chorus to be written.[11]

In the meantime, 120 miles to the north, his beautiful new theater rose.

Berlin's Music Box was a jewel box: small (a cozy 1,010 seats, compared with the Shubert's 1,400, the Winter Garden's 1,570, and the New Amsterdam's 1,702) and beautiful, inside and out. The architect was Detroit's C. Howard Crane, whose greatest fame would come later, from his designs for huge concert halls and movie palaces. But Crane was also a master of acoustics, and in the days before onstage amplification, acoustics were crucial. The theater's interior—ornately neoclassical yet warm and inviting, giving the feeling of an elegant English country house into which one had been specially admitted—was a place where every note and every word would be heard and savored.[12]

And the building's flat-stone-finished Georgian exterior made it look like a place into which one wanted to be admitted.

With its second-story portico, pilasters, and dual Palladian windows, its four-dormered slate roof above, it too conveyed the look of a luxurious house, at once stately and intimate. The Music Box signaled both what Irving Berlin wanted to signal about himself—elegance and success—and what he couldn't help signaling: warmth mixed with coolness, fun and emotion dispensed with a certain professional distance.

But even before the building was finished, it was considered a folly. "It stinks from class," said the comedian Sam Bernard.[13]

"As the plasterers and painters were putting the final touches on the Music Box," Woollcott wrote,

> all Broadway was shaking with laughter. . . . Rival managers, standing in knots on nearby street corners, could be seen figuring happily on the backs of envelopes and announcing: "If they sell out every seat for the next five years, they'll lose money."[14]

All indications seemed to bear out the dire assessment. For one thing—and it was a big thing—that $947,000 would only get the place built. Mounting the theater's first show would cost extra—plenty extra. As plans for *The Music Box Revue of 1921* began to gel, the production budget rose. And rose. To almost $188,000: a huge sum, more than triple the average cost of mounting a Broadway musical at the time.[15] To direct the revue, Berlin and Harris had hired the brilliant Englishman Hassard Short, a former actor with an exquisite sense of lighting and stagecraft—and a fine disregard for the cost of realizing his designs. He had a particular love for big hydraulic elevators that rose up from beneath the stage bearing actors and choruses, an effect that never failed to elicit gasps of pleasure and surprise from audiences. He had designed such a mechanism, magnificent and supremely costly and temperamental, for the Music Box. It became known as Hassard Short's Elevator.

And the revue itself became known, among the cast, as *The Harris and Berlin Worries of 1921*. No one had to look any farther than the composer's face to see how accurate the joke was. Irving had returned from Atlantic City not suntanned but pale and drawn. Working through the nights on the many songs required to fill a three-and-a-half-hour show, and still fine-tuning the material, he was barely sleeping at all; his characteristic nervous indigestion—"songwriter's stomach"—made eating more a duty than a pleasure. His already birdlike frame had turned stick-thin.

"From the beginning," John Lahr writes, "Berlin kept his eye on both the music and the money."[16] And it wasn't just the Music Box's costs that were eating at him: it was also the competition. "Revues . . . were becoming increasingly commonplace on Broadway," Furia writes.

> The *Music Box Revue* would have to compete not only against Ziegfeld's annual *Follies* but against its many imitations, such as George White's *Scandals*. . . . New York audiences had already begun to weary of the formulaic glamour of these shows, so producers relied on profits from extensive tours in other cities; but the fledgling owners Berlin and Harris lacked the road companies to mount such tours.[17]

Berlin's half-partner paid an inspection visit to the theater during dress rehearsal. While a nervous Irving showed Joe Schenck around, Hassard Short's beautiful elevator, intended, in one breathtaking piece of stagecraft, to carry sixteen lovely chorines from a well in the basement to the top of the proscenium, had stalled midway between stage and ceiling. Stranded in midair, the young women made their distress known, vocally.

"What's that?" Schenck asked.

"Oh," Berlin said, "that's just one of our little effects."

His partner roared with laughter and slapped Berlin on the

back. "Never mind, Irving," Schenck said. "After all, it's no more than you or I would lose in a good stud game and never think of it again."[18]

Spoken like a movie mogul. But as Berlin and Sam Harris knew all too well, Broadway was a different game altogether. On opening night writer and producer, wearing tuxedos, sat in a suite in the Astor overlooking the theater and picked nervously at a room-service dinner. They were, Berlin would later recall, "two very frightened men."[19]

But soon, a crowd of celebrity watchers had gathered. "By eight-thirty," Woollcott wrote, "the mob had made the sidewalks impassable and the police were clearing paths for the nobility of Broadway"—the likes of Douglas Fairbanks, Metropolitan Opera star Geraldine Farrar, society beauty Mrs. Lydig Hoyt.[20] It was a fair omen that the big gamble of Berlin and Harris—and Schenck—might not be in vain. The composer and the producer shook hands.

"Go to it, Irving," Sam Harris said.

"Go to it, Sam," said Berlin.

* * *

As the tuxedoed pair stood watching in the wings, the actors hit their cues and performed flawlessly, Short's complex stagecraft functioned smoothly, and, most important of all, the swell audience ate up every moment, laughing and applauding effusively and at just the right spots. Twenties theater audiences demanded little more than fun and excitement, but Berlin was giving them more. His froth had bite to it. The show's opening numbers, a series of linked segments, toyed with the fourth wall and addressed the composer's insecurities about the entire enterprise, both the expensive theater and the expensive show. The first number, "What's in the Queer-looking Bundle?," was set on the roof of the Music Box itself. A stork flies over and drops a bundle; four stagehands examine it as they go into a song:

What is it?
It's a revue!
A revue?
Good God, another revue!²¹

This was how Berlin laid the competition low, evoking knowing laughter by letting the audience in on the joke. The patrons were delighted with the show, and with themselves. And now that the chief convention of the revue, its strength and its weakness—the fact that one thing leads to another only in the most loosely associative way—had been both mocked and embraced, Berlin could go on being Berlin to his heart's content, giving the crowd tune after catchy tune.

Sensibly, he saved his strongest material for the end of act one: two songs—the first deep and heartfelt, the second fast and jazzy—that the businessman in him knew would send that sophisticated crowd out to intermission shaking their heads in wonder and delight.

"Say It with Music" was the first, and Irving had put into it not only time and effort but high hopes, for he intended it to be the theme song of the Music Box itself. The number was rich and romantic, its tune a first cousin to that of "A Pretty Girl Is Like a Melody" and its lyrics as unashamedly romantic as the tune:

> Say it with music,
> Beautiful music;
> Somehow they'd rather be kissed
> To the strains of Chopin or Liszt.²²

But the audience applauded with heart-sinking politeness—the simple staging, just a boy and a girl and an earnest song, was simply less than they wanted to see. Standing in the wings, Irving sweated bullets: one more chance to win them over.

Dignity and earnestness were thoroughly beside the point with the act's closer, "Everybody Step," sung in close harmony by the Brox Sisters, a talented and comely young trio from Tennessee.[23] The tune leaped headlong from the foursquare meter of conventional stage music straight into the Jazz Age:

Ev'rybody step
To the syncopated rhythm;
Let's be goin' with 'em
When they begin

The song was breathless, it was thrilling, it was irresistible, and it would quickly become considered as important a leap forward in American popular music as "Alexander's Ragtime Band" had been a decade earlier—important enough that the distinguished American composer John Alden Carpenter would cite it "as one of the greatest works of music, the only American composition on a list that also included works by Bach, Beethoven, Chopin, Debussy, Mussorgsky, Stravinsky, and Wagner."[24]

This was very nice, but it was also very hyperbolic, and in any case it was beside the point. "Everybody Step" was popular music—superb popular music, without any need to be put on a classical pedestal. More relevant was the question: was it jazz?

Critics and audiences would answer in the affirmative, immediately and emphatically. "Everybody Step" instantly established Berlin—the man who in 1915 had boldly asserted, "I know rhythm"—"as a 'jazz composer' and even 'king of jazz,'" Jeffrey Magee writes.[25] The latter honorific would also be laid, more lastingly, though not more truthfully, on the white bandleader Paul Whiteman.

Ignorance and fear were behind the era's purposeful whitening of jazz, whose origins and governing genius were African American. Like its cousin the blues (and as ragtime had been, to a politer extent), real jazz was hot and unapologetically sexual, and it was quickly targeted from pulpits and editorial pages as the theme music for all the excesses of the twenties.

In the spring of 1921, four months before the premiere of

the *Music Box Revue,* another show opened at the Cort 63rd Street Theatre, a mile uptown and just to the west of Central Park: an all-black, musical comedy called *Shuffle Along,* with a jazz-rich score by the great African-American songwriting team of Noble Sissle and Eubie Blake.

Shuffle Along, a sensation from the get-go, created traffic jams on 63rd Street and ran an amazing 484 performances: 44 more than the *Music Box Revue's* amazing run of 440. And Irving Berlin would have been keenly aware of the show—might even have taken it in before heading to Atlantic City and writing "Everybody Step." Yet musically speaking, he always went his own way.

Magee makes much of the contrast between black jazz and Berlin's jazz as presented by the Broxes, who "sang as one in tight, lockstep harmony—never once venturing even a short phrase of solo or duet." Their high voices had "a coy nasality," their phrasing "a deliberate rhythmic rigidity," their stage style an "innocent naughtiness." Their entire presentation "formed a stark contrast to the hefty, dark-skinned, matriarchal, and lower-voiced African American vaudeville blues singers such as Mamie Smith and Ma Rainey."[26]

Berlin's jazz, in other words, was white jazz. But that loaded phrase embodies a musical spectrum ranging from striped-vest-and-straw-boater Dixieland to white giants like Bix Beiderbecke and Benny Goodman, Gerry Mulligan and Bill Evans. And Irving Berlin, as lyricist and composer, belongs in the empyrean range of that scale. He knew rhythm, and he knew his audience.

* * *

As a public figure and inveterate ham, Berlin put himself in the show that night: in the prime slot, the second-to-last scene. Just after the hugely expensive production number "The Legend of the Pearls," he bustled onstage with The Eight Little Notes, who were playing reporters sent to ask him, as he recalled to the *New York Times*'s Mel Gussow fifty years later, "how you write a song."

"I write my songs very easily," he warbled, self-deprecatingly. "When I need a melody, / If I hear a tune that appeals to me, / I go right home and write it."

Berlin then sang them an example: a slightly wistful but oddly jaunty number, a song whose spirit he would transform into another, far more powerful, composition three years later:

> All by myself in the morning,
> All by myself in the night . . .[27]

It was, or at least felt like, Irving at his most confessional: how could his solitary habits not have worn on him? (Constance Talmadge had married a wealthy Greek-American tobacco merchant at the end of 1920.) But now that he was nearing his midthirties, he would diligently set about finding company. Of all sorts.

9

What Shall I Do?

A TIME TRAVELER transported back to the Manhattan of the 1920s would find it filled with a familiar push and hustle and crackling energy, of which Irving Berlin—songwriter, music publisher, theater co-owner, and producer—was an important part. His two centers of operation, at 1607 Broadway and 239 West 45th, were in the thick of it: in the middle of Midtown, just a couple of blocks apart. And so, not long after the opening of the first *Music Box Revue*, and flush with the show's success, Berlin moved to the neighborhood—the easier to commute to work and the better to keep his eye on business. Twenty-nine West 46th Street was a six-story brownstone just a five- to ten-minute walk from both the Music Box and Irving Berlin, Inc. The building had a family-run grocery store on the main floor and five tenant apartments above; at the top, reached by a tiny elevator, was a duplex penthouse, with a view across rooftops under what was in those days a far bigger sky.

Irving pulled out all the stops in decorating his plush bachelor pad. P. G. Wodehouse, who with his writing partner Guy Bolton visited Berlin there with an outline for a musical called *Sitting Pretty*—Berlin would eventually withdraw from the project—remembered the place with awe:

> There was a broad corridor that descended in a series of steps, each step an eight foot square platform, to the big living room that faced the street. Molded glass panels by Lalique lighted this handsome passage. These were fringed with big potted plants, and standing in front of two of them were tall wooden stands on which stood a pair of brilliant-hued toucans. They added the final touch of magnificence.[1]

Lalique! Toucans! At last, it seems, Irving was allowing himself a bit of indulgence, a few of the fruits of his mighty labors. And yet—speaking of time travel—there's a haunting, Ozymandias-esque passage in Mary Ellin Barrett's memoir in which, in the fall of 1989, just a month after her father's death at age 101, she visits the penthouse at 29 West 46th for the first time since she left it, as an infant, in the late 1920s. Berlin lived there for just a half dozen years, she writes, but held onto it for six more decades "for sentimental reasons." Disused, the place became a storage facility for the vast detritus of a huge career; underneath all the junk, though, was a time capsule of her father's life in the early to midtwenties.

> I felt like an intruder as I picked my way through the clutter, the framed, discolored posters of hit shows of long ago, the rusted filing cabinets, the trunks and cartons and iron boxes filled with papers and manuscripts; opening this door and that . . . imagining ghostly voices, laughter, the sound of a cocktail shaker—a silence—then the piano, the sweet, wispy voice.[2]

It could be a scene from a movie: the dusty light, the crumbling artifacts, the spectral party voices and music. And what would the sweet, wispy voice have been singing, to his own sparse piano accompaniment, but one of the sweetly sad waltzes with which he ornamented that frantic decade?

* * *

One night in late November 1923, Dorothy Parker and the artist Neysa McMein gave a birthday party at McMein's studio for their fellow Algonquin Round Table member, the humorist Donald Ogden Stewart. Irving Berlin showed up with a couple of bottles of champagne hidden under his overcoat, in deference to Prohibition—and, no doubt, with a puckish grin on his face.

"While we all sat around," Stewart recalled, "celebrating and drinking the champagne, Irving went to the piano and kept on playing the first part of a song he had written. It was called 'What'll I Do?' But he hadn't been able to finish it. He played the part he had over and over, and we all liked it—but the best part of the evening was that after Irving had had enough of his champagne, he was finally able to finish the song that night."[3]

Neysa McMein's big skylit studio, on the top floor of a nondescript three-story brick building at the northeast corner of Sixth Avenue and 57th Street, was the second home to the Algonquin Round Table and "the nearest thing to a salon this country has ever seen," one visitor commented.[4] "On a typical day," writes the Dorothy Parker biographer Marion Meade, one "might find Charlie Chaplin, Paul Robeson, Ethel Barrymore, Jascha Heifetz, and playing duets on Neysa's piano, Irving Berlin and George Gershwin."[5]

McMein was tall and beautiful, an ardent and well-publicized suffragist and feminist, as well as an energetic advocate of sexual liberation: "All New York knew," Anita Loos wrote, "she was the heroine of a succession of romances with extremely prominent men"—including Chaplin, Harpo Marx, the playwright and producer George Abbott, and Robert Benchley—but not Irving Berlin.[6]

Although all of New York's bright young men seemed to fall in love with McMein, and her personal style—smart, free-spirited, a little lofty—was right up Berlin's street, he doesn't seem to have been drawn to her erotically. He had female friends: Loos, Parker, the novelist Alice Duer Miller. If there was an occasional fling with one of the *Ziegfeld Follies* beauties or a *Music Box Revue* chorine, he hid it well.

He was, we know, a prodigious worker; by all evidence he was also a prodigious sublimator. With money, fame, charm, and good looks, he could quite easily have cut a romantic swath through early-twenties Manhattan; instead, driven by vaulting ambition, genius, and extreme anxiety—the first *Music Box Revue* was a big success, but then, quickly, there was another to write, and another, and another—he appears to have preferred the late-night companionship of his most faithful mistress, WORK.

"What'll I Do?," on the other hand—if we are to believe Stewart's testimony—was composed not only amid merry company but under the influence. At any rate, the song was a breakthrough, pure and simple. Nobody else had ever done anything like it—more important, Berlin had never done anything like it. He had written waltzes before, yet "What'll I Do?," which seemed so simple, was utterly different. The Stewart story is a nice one, but it stands to reason that if Berlin did in fact finish the song that pixilated night in McMein's studio, what he finished was the music only. Kimball claims that the number was written "in Palm Beach, Florida, where Berlin was vacationing with E. Ray Goetz"—and, thanks to a dated photograph, we know that Berlin was in Florida in January 1924, a month or so after the party at Neysa's.[7] (We also know—make of it what you will, including nothing—that McMein and Parker were in that Florida photograph with Berlin and Goetz.)[8] Berlin himself said, "Sometimes music comes first like 'What'll I Do?' That began as a musical phrase and I had to work hard to find the words to fit the melody."[9]

Some vacation. The words did indeed fit the melody, but some of the rhymes fell in unexpected places:

When I'm alone
With only dreams of you

Genius that he was, Berlin was simply writing his own rules. Earlier in his career, he had told a reporter, with a bracing absence of false humility, "I established the syncopated ballad and I have shown that the metre can be 'chopped up' to fit the words."[10] He had been doing it for years, but never before so simply, elegantly, and emotionally. And strangely.

But—

What'll I do
When I am wond'ring who
Is kissing you

—who was "What'll I Do?" *for?*[11]

He privileged perspiration over inspiration, and he was at great pains to keep his private life private and to assure the public that (with the single exception of "When I Lost You") his own life had nothing to do with his compositions: "It has always been assumed that whenever I've written a ballad I've been through some heartbreaking experience. But the real reason is that the public would rather buy tears than smiles—and right now they happen to want sob ballads."[12]

But he was not a machine, and the better ballads feel a lot like emotion recollected—or at the very least, emotion repurposed—in tranquility. He was a man of powerful feelings, and the fact that he was deeply private didn't mean that he didn't use those feelings in his work. In 1920 Berlin had written a great torch song, a strange hybrid of ballad and march called "After You Get What You Want, You Don't Want It," whose lyric is hard not to read as a direct apostrophe to the inconstant Dutch Talmadge:

If I gave you the moon,
You'd grow tired of it soon . . .[13]

In 1922, the year before he composed "What'll I Do?," he had suffered two major losses. The first was most grievous. To a great degree, in the unapologetically pre-Freudian way of the early twentieth century, Berlin's mother was still the central female figure in his life. And in the summer of that year, Leah, now an elderly seventy-four, grew ill and then gravely ill, her chronic nephritis complicated by pneumonia. Beginning July 18, a Dr. H. Schumer attended her daily at the Bronx apartment, but she declined rapidly and died on the morning of the twenty-first.[14] It was ten years, almost to the day, after Dorothy's death.

And in December, four days before Christmas, Mike Salter died. Berlin's emotional bond to his old employer was nowhere near as deep as the connection with his mother, but the link to his past was profound. Would Irving have ever dipped his toe into the unknown waters of songwriting, much less persisted with what turned out to be the backbreaking task of composing "Marie from Sunny Italy," without Salter's goading? And if he hadn't, where might Izzy Baline have ended up? "Treat him as kind as you can," Berlin asked a *New York Herald* reporter at the funeral. "He was no angel, maybe, but there are a lot of guys on the street today who would have been in jail if it hadn't been for Nigger Mike."[15]

* * *

Saul Bellow once wrote of the solitary writer's need for "rejoining mankind, taking a humanity bath."[16] Irving Berlin, as fiercely dedicated to his solitary art as Bellow, seems to have felt a similar need, and for a couple of years in the early twenties the Algonquin set, both in situ and at Neysa McMein's, seems to have filled it.

The cast of characters revolved to some extent but centered around Woollcott, Parker, F. P. Adams, Benchley, the playwrights Robert Sherwood and Marc Connelly, the editor Harold Ross and his soon-to-be wife (and with him, cofounder of the

New Yorker) the writer Jane Grant, and the columnist Heywood Broun. Others, like George S. Kaufman, Edna Ferber, McMein, Alice Duer Miller, Harpo Marx, Herman J. Mankiewicz, Tallulah Bankhead, and Alfred Lunt and Lynne Fontanne, popped by from time to time, but Aleck Woollcott was the group's linchpin, and the setter of the comic tone, which was quick and frequently nasty.

He was an odd duck, and to most everyone, a thoroughly disagreeable one. Short, fat, and piercingly intelligent, he was acutely self-loathing, with plenty of bile to spare for others: his specialty was the bitchy put-down. He appears not to have had an active sex life of any kind. "As a substitute for sex," Marion Meade writes, "he indulged himself by wearing scarlet-lined opera capes, insulting friends with greetings like 'Hello, repulsive,' and eating enormously and exquisitely until his weight swung up to a blimpish 255 pounds."[17]

The Algonquinites were, or at least thought of themselves as, the crème de la crème: the most sophisticated wits in America's most sophisticated city. Several of them wrote newspaper columns, especially Adams, whose "The Conning Tower" occupied some of the most influential newspaper space in America, so the group was in a prime position to chronicle its own aphorisms, wisecracks, and opinions. There was an innate quality of insularity and self-congratulation, and, ultimately, there was backlash. "The Round Table was just a lot of people telling jokes and telling each other how good they were," Dorothy Parker later said. "Just a bunch of loudmouths showing off, saving their gags for days, waiting for a chance to spring them. . . . There was no truth in anything they said. It was the terrible day of the wisecrack, so there didn't have to be any truth."[18]

It was into this nest of vipers that, one day in 1922, one of the group—perhaps McMein, perhaps Benchley—introduced Irving Berlin.

Berlin was too innately reserved and work-minded to want

to spend long, lubricated lunches engaged in, or more likely feeling pressured to bear admiring witness to, volleys of witty repartee. Nevertheless, Aleck Woollcott fell head over heels for him.

Of course carnal love had nothing to do (consciously) with the critic's crush. Rather, it was all that Irving had done—the sheer magnitude, beauty, and wit of his achievement—and the way he carried himself: a magnetic amalgam of self-effacement, quiet confidence, nervousness, and shy humor, with an under-lay of toughness. *This* was a giant—at age thirty-four—and everyone around that round table would have known it, especially Woollcott, whose *Times* beat exposed him to a great deal of mediocrity. (Some two hundred Broadway shows opened every year in the early twenties, the vast majority of them not great or even very good.) And critics by definition possess the capacity for self-criticism, and what they feel about themselves isn't always pretty. Aleck Woollcott would have understood, deep down, the engine and irritant of his caustic humor: his own artistic sterility. "I never had anything to say," he admitted near the end of his short life: he would die at fifty-six, in 1943.[19]

And thus it was that Irving Berlin gained an idolator and, in the strangest of admixtures, a close friend. As well as, in due course, a biographer.

* * *

Our lives hinge, more than we are willing to admit, on mere chance. Who knows how differently Berlin's life might have turned out had he not received a last-minute invitation to replace an extra man, a last-minute dropout, at an uptown dinner party on the night of Friday, May 23, 1924?

The party-giver was one Mrs. Allen Gouverneur Wellman, a society lady, Berlin's eldest daughter writes, "with ties to the Long Island crowd . . . and a taste for the newer, livelier company of theater people. . . . It was a time in New York for smart, intimate dinners that crossed lines."[20]

And it was a perfect spring evening in New York—bell-clear, cool but not cold. Here at age thirty-six was one of Manhattan's most eligible bachelors, happily girding himself for a social evening in swell company—not unlike the singer of a song he would write a decade later, "Top Hat, White Tie and Tails": putting on his dinner jacket and tying his bowtie, brushing his unruly hair, and striding out into a city that seemed to move to the rhythms of the songs he had written . . .

And yet.

The fourth *Music Box Revue* was in the offing, and he was worried about it. Though the third had run eight months and turned the unknown Grace Moore into a star, the reviews had been mixed: the first two in the series had had such verve; were Berlin's *Revue*s, so smart, so sharp and au courant, losing their edge?

He always took criticism more personally than he let on, and in this case the criticism was all bound up with his passionate, almost bodily feelings about his gorgeous new theater, his prized showplace.

And as one whose eye on the popular-music business was just as keen as his ear for a tune or a lyric, Berlin might still have been mulling over the February concert at Aeolian Hall mounted by Paul Whiteman and billed as "An Experiment in Modern Music." The program included works by Victor Herbert, George Gershwin, and Berlin, who was said beforehand to have been preparing a "syncopated tone poem."[21] But on the day of the concert there was no tone poem, only a Ferde Grofé–orchestrated "Semisymphonic Arrangement of Popular Melodies"—a fancy name for a medley—of "Alexander's Ragtime Band," "A Pretty Girl Is Like a Melody," and, from that year's *Music Box Revue*, "An Orange Grove in California."

Gershwin's piece was the world premiere of "Rhapsody in Blue."

The public response to "Rhapsody" was justifiably rhapsodic: it was an age-defining work, an instant classic. The "Semi-symphonic Arrangement," on the other hand, was quickly forgotten, even if two of the three songs it contained were destined for immortality. And that was the way Berlin's career seemed to be going: the long, important works, the ragtime and jazz operas he had promised himself and the public (not to mention the symphonic tone poem), were mere chimeras; what was solid and substantial were the songs. Young Gershwin—"the kid," Irving called him; "the only songwriter who became a composer"[22]—could not only write "Rhapsody in Blue"; he was also in the midst of preparing, along with his lyricist brother Ira and Guy Bolton, a new Broadway musical to premiere that December, *Lady Be Good*. The show, with a fully integrated book and score, would be a breakout hit, running 330 performances and introducing not only the title song and "Fascinating Rhythm" but also Fred and Adele Astaire.

The most significant song to emerge from the third *Music Box Revue*—which, that night in May 1924, had just closed—was Berlin's first great waltz of the twenties. Dance bands everywhere were playing it, and sheet music of it and the Paul Whiteman Orchestra's recording of it had already sold into the hundreds of thousands. The record would soon be omnipresent on the radio.

And so what could Irving Berlin be but bemused and amused, when, in the Park Avenue citadel of Mr. and Mrs. Allen G. Wellman, the fresh young thing with pale intelligent wide-set eyes, pert nose, and cleft chin stared at him admiringly "and said in the soft, clear fluting, slightly affected accents of old New York, 'Oh, Mr. Berlin, I do so like your song "What Shall I Do?"' "[23]

* * *

He set the record straight but pretended her version was more correct. "Where grammar is concerned, I can always use a little help," he told Ellin Mackay.

"She was embarrassed but not too," their daughter writes. "He was amused. A spark was struck. She was a great heiress, a spoiled, stuck-up darling; he was a world-famous composer with the pride and assurance of a self-made man. But both had lifesaving senses of humor, and their humors matched—fast, playful, sometimes a little rough on others."[24]

She was also twenty-one to his thirty-six. And this was only the beginning of their differences. On both sides there was, in the modern parlance, baggage. He was a widower. Did he imagine ever marrying again, having children? Perhaps he did. Single men go to parties for several reasons, but one above all: you never know who you might meet.

Yet even if twenty-one was older in those days, she was still a girl. On the face of it, just another in the welter of socialites afoot in twenties Manhattan. And she was certainly very rich. Her father, Clarence Mackay (the surname was pronounced Mackie, accent on the first syllable), was an heir to the Comstock Lode, the richest vein of silver in Nevada history, and the chairman of Western Union's chief competitor, the Postal Telegraph Cable Corporation. The family seat was Harbor Hill, an enormous Stanford White mansion on 688 acres (with 134 servants in attendance) in Roslyn, N.Y., at the highest point on Long Island's Gold Coast. In the normal order of things, she would have—much like Mrs. Allen G. Wellman—married an appropriate young man, a Harvard, Yale, or Princeton man in finance, and ideally in the Social Register too.

But those young men were bloodless and boring, and she was sharp-witted and restless and headstrong. She'd dropped out of Barnard because her classmates, and even a favorite teacher, had ostracized her for being wealthy. She seemed to have a talent for writing: maybe she would become a novelist like her mother's cousin Alice Duer Miller.

And there were other reasons Ellin Mackay didn't quite fit in. Money smoothed many rough edges, but her father's money was new, only one generation removed, and the Mackays were Irish Catholic—not Social Register material. There was more. Her mother, the suffragist and socialite Katherine Duer Mackay, also smart and restless and headstrong, had bolted, leaving her husband and three children in 1914 (Ellin was ten at the time) to marry Clarence Mackay's personal physician, Dr. Joseph Blake. Ellin had been brought up by servants and her anxious, hovering father, a peppery little man with glittering blue eyes and a bushy mustache. But for a child whose parent has left, there is always a dark uncertainty at the center of things, and Ellin Mackay, at twenty-one, seemed on the verge of imitating her mother and slipping her tether.

This was the girl who looked Irving Berlin in the eye and told him she did so like his song "What Shall I Do?"

10

Always

CLARENCE MACKAY collected Renaissance art and suits of armor; he also kept an expensive mistress, the concert and opera singer Anna Case. He devoted a similar possessive zeal to the three children of whom he had gained complete custody after his wife's unthinkable desertion. His nickname for his younger daughter, and hers for herself when she wrote to him, was Angel Child. This was more than mere banter for an observant Catholic. Mackay doted on his golden-haired daughter, and expected angelic behavior in return, suffering the predictable consequences. Ellin, her mother's daughter in many ways, grew up confident and willful, with undertones of doubt and defiance. When her father ordered her to give her solemn oath that she would stop seeing this utterly unsuitable man—fifteen years older, a show person, and (worst of all) a Jew—she looked him in the eye and said, "No. I won't promise."[1]

A kind of steeplechase ensued. Clarence exacted a promise

from Ellin to go abroad, far away from this Irving Berlin, for six months. If at the end of that time she hadn't got him out of her system, father and daughter would talk. A draconian bargain, but being a dutiful daughter as well as a rebellious one, she accepted. At the end of September 1924, father and daughter, along with Clarence's valet and Ellin's French maid and Irish chaperone, sailed for England on the S.S. *Aquitania*.

She was playing for time. Ellin had fallen deeply in love with Irving; she wrote and cabled him (unbeknownst to her father) almost every day from Europe. Irving responded more sparsely. He loved this girl deeply but worried about all the things there were to worry about, including the loss of his independence.

And then there was the problem of the fourth *Music Box Revue*. "I really am delighted with a good deal of my stuff," he wrote Ellin, "but I have lived with it so long and gone over the numbers so often that they have become stale. Then again, as I told you so many times, the thrill of the Music Box has gone and now it has become a job that I love most when it's finished."[2] In the meantime, Clarence Mackay had hired private detectives to dig up whatever dirt they could about Irving Berlin.

After a few weeks Mackay returned from Europe to attend to his affairs, leaving his daughter well chaperoned as she saw the sights in the south of France, in Rome, in Egypt and the Holy Land. All the while, Ellin continued to write to the person she called her "young man": three or four letters to every one he wrote her.[3] And Berlin continued to write the 1924 *Revue*. It premiered in early December, to mostly good notices and strong ticket sales, though business would soon flag, and—due mainly to theatergoers' waning interest in the form (and growing interest in book musicals)—the show would run for only 184 performances, the least of the four *Revue*s.

The last show Berlin wrote for his theater contained virtually no songs that would stand the test of time, although a pair of slight but ravishing curios from the show made it onto *Irving Berlin, 1909–1939*, the double LP that I so eagerly bought in 1975. The exquisite Grace Moore (who soon after the *Revue* would make her Metropolitan Opera debut, as Mimi in *La Bohème*) sang both. "Rockabye Baby" was a shamelessly schmaltzy lullaby ("Rockabye baby, / Hushabye, dear, / Slumber, my sweetheart, / Mother is near . . ."). And the waltz "Listening" was an equally sentimental hymn of yearning to an absent lover:

> Listening,
> Listening for you,
> All alone,
> Feeling kind o' blue . . .[4]

A cannibalized bit of this minor number (dropped from the show after the first week) formed the basis of a major one. Over the summer, while Berlin ground out the score in his suite in Atlantic City's Ritz-Carlton Hotel, he wrote one song that he apparently felt was too good to sit around till December: instead he had it interpolated, at once, into the post-Broadway tour of the third *Music Box Revue*.

The new number was also a waltz, also wistful, and as lyrically terse as "Listening," but, by the scarcely analyzable alchemy that makes some tunes memorable and others forgettable, a classic instead of a trifle. The nakedly revealing verse went:

> Just like the melody that lingers on,
> You seem to haunt me night and day.
> I never realized till you had gone
> How much I cared about you—
> I can't live without you.

The song was the great "All Alone." The bare-bones sparseness of the chorus made the verse look positively florid:

> All alone
> By the telephone,

Waiting for a ring,
A ting-a-ling . . .

And the windup, with its almost brutally effective repetition, is nothing short of majestic.

Wond'ring where you are
And how you are
And if you are
All alone too.[5]

If Irving's letters to Ellin tended to be over-newsy and slightly withheld emotionally, a song like this more than made up for it. And if the gimlet-eyed girl who had fallen so hard for him could fall any harder, this song would have seen to it.

Three recordings of "All Alone" were made quickly; remarkably, all three—by Al Jolson, by Paul Whiteman and His Orchestra, and by the great Irish tenor John McCormack—became best sellers. The song has been recorded dozens of times since 1924. Thirty-eight years later, the Frank Sinatra album *All Alone*, containing the title number as well as four other Berlin waltzes ("When I Lost You," "What'll I Do," "Remember," and "The Song Is Ended"), was also a commercial success.

* * *

"Remember" is a story in itself. Berlin wrote the song in December 1924, when Ellin had been away almost three months, and while at first its tone of intense longing seems nothing if not autobiographical, the lyric then takes a left turn:

Remember we found a lonely spot
And after I learned to care a lot
You promised that you'd forget me not
But you forgot to remember.[6]

Philip Furia accuses Berlin of protesting too much by insisting there is no connection between his sob ballads and his own experience, and I tend to agree. At the same time it's important to keep in mind the ability of any gifted and thoroughly professional composer of popular songs to write in character—see also: Stephen Sondheim.

But it's *also* important to keep in mind that there is such a thing as the unconscious, that we all have one, and that it's a faculty with which artists tend to be on good, even speaking, terms. Irving Berlin, having been separated by death from one wife and both his parents, would have had every reason (including some very practical reasons) to fear that for all his young woman's ardor, she too might leave him.

On Christmas afternoon of 1924—his work ethic knew no bounds—the sensitive creator invited his two business partners, Winslow and Bornstein, to his studio at the Music Box to hear his latest number. "I sang it, certain that I had a hit," Berlin recalled, about a year later. "When I finished, Bornstein said that it was not so good. Winslow said it was terrible. . . . They tried to persuade [*sic*] me from publishing it and suggested that I throw it into the wastebasket and forget about it."[7]

What caused Winslow and Bornstein to react so violently against this sweet and winsome tune? Perhaps Berlin, with his limited piano skills and small, reedy voice, simply failed to put the song across to his partners. We will see again and again that he wasn't always the best salesman of his own work. Whatever the case, the incident was traumatic. "It seemed that a song was going to be my downfall," Irving said. "That Christmas Day was the worst one I ever spent in my life. . . . I never want another day like that. It was one of mental torture."

He went on:

> During the spring and the summer I remembered "Remember" and worried about it. I thought I had lost my skill, my talent. I was afraid to write anything for fear Winslow would say it was terrible. I was developing an inferiority complex, which is the greatest hindrance a writer can have. . . . I worried so much that I was becoming a bundle of nerves.[8]

This went beyond songwriter's stomach and approached emotional disorder. Berlin was speaking in December 1925, recalling his crisis to a reporter from the *New York Telegraph*—was he exaggerating to make a good story? It seems he was not, for his period of misery coincided with the second half of Ellin's exile, and the most tumultuous period in the courtship.

It was a time when the New York tabloids picked up on the secret engagement and began publishing imaginative stories about the glamorously mismatched couple. In June the *New York Daily Mirror* printed an entirely fictitious account of a meeting between Berlin and Clarence Mackay, in which Mackay supposedly threatened to cut off his daughter without a penny, and Berlin allegedly countered that in that case he'd give her $2 million himself. It was a time when Berlin formally asked Ellin's mother for her daughter's hand in marriage, and Katherine, now married to Dr. Blake (and as her life story demonstrated, a believer in romance), gave her blessing. And during the same period Berlin's lawyer, Dennis O'Brien, met with Mackay and Mackay's lawyer, Max Steuer, who informed O'Brien that private detectives had discovered that Berlin was a drug addict, that he suffered from a venereal disease, and that he had relatives who were mobsters.

O'Brien coolly informed Steuer and Mackay that all three allegations were incorrect. The drug rumors, probably a result of Berlin's early days around Olliffe's Pharmacy and the opium den–rich neighborhood around the Bloody Angle and the Pelham Café, had been around for a while (and weirdly, would cling to Berlin for the rest of his life and after his death). Nor did he have V.D. Nor was he connected to organized crime through any close or distant relatives.

Persuaded, Mackay then did an astonishing thing: he apologized. And presented Berlin's lawyer a reasonable argument for further postponement. His daughter and Berlin "were both delicate, high-strung people," the tycoon contended. While he respected Berlin's considerable achievements, he worried—quite accurately—that "creating music put a strain on his health." He also fretted, again sensibly, that his own well-publicized objections to the relationship and the accompanying newspaper hoopla "might have fanned the flames of romance artificially."[9]

Mackay's change of tone wasn't a change of heart: it was the iron hand in a velvet glove. His "suggestion" was to send his conflicted daughter—who upon returning from Europe in April had faced reporters with her arm linked with Clarence Mackay's and said, "The truth of the matter is that if I were to marry I would surrender the companionship I have with my father . . . and I cannot bear to think of parting with him"[10]— on *another* trip, this time to western Canada and California. Berlin had no choice but to comply. Over the two months she was gone, in the summer of 1925, there was, in marked contrast to her European trip, scant if any communication between Ellin and her young man. It isn't clear why this was so. At any rate, Mackay nearly achieved his aim: while Ellin traveled out west, there came a point when the romance seemed hopeless, and the two decided to part forever. In the meantime, Berlin had fallen into the hands of the Marx Brothers.

* * *

Chico (Leonard), Harpo (Arthur), Groucho (Julius), and Zeppo (Herbert) Marx, successful vaudevillians since before World War I, had recently made a successful transition to Broadway with a nominally scripted but largely ad-libbed revue called *I'll Say She Is.*[11] Even if that format was tired, the anarchic humor of the brothers Marx was fresh and new to legitimate-theater audiences, and the New York critics—notably Alexander Woollcott—fell hard for them and made the show a runaway hit. Big producers, Ziegfeld and Dillingham and the Shuberts, began approaching the brothers to do another show, but, as

Harpo Marx later recalled, "The one guy who didn't go after us was the one guy we wanted to work for—Sam Harris."[12]

Harris, the old Broadway hand, liked to have control over the product. Sensibly, he feared mounting a show in which, on any given night, the script might be thrown out the window. But Harpo, whom Woollcott had taken up as a kind of Round Table mascot, now had access to important theater people, one of whom was Irving Berlin, who had seen *I'll Say She Is* and loved it. And so, on one of Irving's rare visits to the Algonquin, Harpo prevailed upon him to go to bat for him and his brothers with Harris. Who agreed to produce a Marx Brothers show— if George S. Kaufman wrote the book and Irving Berlin wrote the score.

And so, in the summer of 1925, Berlin and Kaufman went to Atlantic City to work on the show that was to become *The Cocoanuts*, a musical about the land boom in Florida. The only problem was the music. Only one Marx Brother actually sang— Zeppo, the least interesting one. And for his part, Kaufman would have been happy if nobody sang at all: the playwright tended to see characters breaking out in song as pointless intrusions into his superbly witty dialogue. "Funny thing about Kaufman," Ira Gershwin said, years later. "It's very funny, considering he did so many musicals—he hated music, you know."[13]

Moreover, while Berlin and Kaufman were writing a light comedy with songs, there had to be a love story, and Kaufman, the ultimate cynic, didn't believe in love. The show's composer, of course, not only believed in it but happened to be in it— painfully—during the writing of the show. In a wry 1960 *New Yorker* memoir, Kaufman recalled working with Berlin:

> We had adjoining rooms at the hotel, and along about the second week Irving woke me up at five o'clock one morning to sing me a song he had just finished. . . . The song was the little number called "Always," and its easygoing rhythms

were just up my street. I learned it quickly, and as dawn broke we leaned out of the window and sang it to the Atlantic Ocean—its first performance in any hotel. It was destined to be sung millions of times after that, and invariably better.[14]

Yet while Kaufman implies—and some accounts assert—that Berlin composed "Always" for *The Cocoanuts*, Berlin himself shot down the notion, in a 1959 letter to Groucho Marx. "I didn't write it to be part of the score of this show," he said, "but I did write it during that period. I remember singing it for George Kaufman and he didn't seem too enthusiastic."[15]

Maybe, to be fair to all concerned, Irving *floated* the idea of putting the song in the show. In any case, Kaufman had a bucket of cold water ready: " 'Always,' I pointed out, was a long time for romance. . . . I suggested, therefore, that the opening line be just a little more in accord with reality—something like 'I'll be loving you Thursday.' "[16]

"Thinking back," Berlin wrote to Groucho in another letter, "if I had put it in the show, I wonder who could have sung it outside of yourself."[17]

* * *

The tune to "Always" came to him quickly, Berlin recalled, but the problem of creating a lyric that was both simple and memorable bedeviled him. "Off and on, I spent a year on it," he said two decades later. "If I'd hurried, the melody would have been the same, but the words wouldn't have been so plain and simple."

Writing a lyric that would hold up alongside the powerful closing words of his other great waltzes of the period, "What'll I Do," "All Alone," and "Remember," was especially problematic. "I just couldn't get the last three lines," he said, "so I ad-libbed—'Not for just an hour, not for just a day, not for just a year—but always.' And there it was—exactly what I wanted to say."[18]

* * *

Berlin turned out the requisite number of songs for the actual *Cocoanuts* score: twenty-odd tunes, including the three ("Florida by the Sea," "When My Dreams Come True," and "The Monkey Doodle Doo") that so charmed me when I first happened upon them, plus an almost equally winsome triad of others ("A Little Bungalow," "Lucky Boy," and "Tango Melody") that can be heard on early recordings. One unrecorded number, "Family Reputation," contains some arresting lines:

> In a restaurant, should a debutante
> Depart from the dull convention?
> Scandal papers review her capers
> With a curt little hurtful mention . . .[19]

But despite its fleeting—and today, nostalgic—charms, the score was generally undistinguished: "he never talked about *The Cocoanuts*," Barrett writes, "except to say it wasn't the best score he ever wrote."[20] How could it have been? He was massively distracted—by Kaufman, by the Marxes, and most of all by his roller-coaster romance. When Ellin returned in September, she ended the engagement in despair. Yet somehow the broken relationship sputtered along while Irving traveled to out-of-town tryouts of *The Cocoanuts* attempting to keep the faltering musical alive. "They occasionally see each other in New York," Ellin's mother wrote a friend in November, "and I think she is still in love with him and very unhappy."[21]

As was Irving, for all kinds of reasons. Audiences in Boston and Philadelphia were underwhelmed with the show. Berlin and Kaufman were barely speaking. The Marxes were doing just what Sam Harris had feared they would do: mangling or omitting lyrics, ad-libbing profusely. (During one run-through, Kaufman famously said, "You know, I think I just heard one of my own lines.")[22]

In the meantime, Ellin channeled her unhappiness into a

new pastime. Encouraged by her literary cousin Alice Duer Miller, she penned a short, semifacetious essay about Manhattan social life among the young upper orders; Miller, who was on the board of Harold Ross's new (and struggling) *New Yorker,* commended the piece to him, and the magazine ran "Why We Go to Cabarets: A post-debutante explains" in its November 28, 1925, issue.

The piece was a little arch and a little starchy, though it pointedly called out her class's much starchier older generation —read: Clarence Mackay—for its hypocrisy, and lambasted the unbearable socialites she was burdened with ("all the numberless, colorless young men . . . with whom, if they so choose, she must continue to dance at every party").[23]

The cheeky squib caused a stir among the *New Yorker's* rarefied readership (and to Ross's delight, raised the magazine's circulation). But flippancy aside, it was a remarkably graceful piece of writing for a twenty-two-year-old—and, beneath the mannered prose, a remarkably passionate one: a real cri de coeur, implicitly protesting her hidebound father's intransigence and pining for the young man of genuine substance with whom she was in love.

*   *   *

The Cocoanuts opened at the Lyric ten days afterward, on December 8, and—all out-of-town indications to the contrary —was a smash on Broadway, where it counted. The Marxes were New Yorkers to the core, and the city had fallen for them once again. And they were the show's true stars; Berlin's score was background music, counterpoint to their anarchy.

But Irving and Ellin were the cynosures of opening night. For a year the story of the impossible romance of the Society Girl and the Jazz Composer had been a bonanza to the New York papers—even the *Times* had put Mackay's return from Europe and her denial of the engagement on the front page in April—so the fact that she gave Berlin a "box party" at the

Lyric on premiere night, and the fact that they were clearly together later, at a dinner at the home of *New York World* editor Herbert Bayard Swope, set tongues wagging.

The next weeks were fraught. Berlin showed his young lady off to his circle; by and large, his circle disapproved. "Those clever friends of Irving's . . . were so mean to newcomers," Helen Hayes recalled. "They only wanted to pounce on this society belle whose overbearing father disapproved of their Irving, their God. She seemed very fragile. Both of them seemed fragile, two fragile beings."[24]

On New Year's Eve, Bergreen says, the couple danced together at the Mayfair Hotel and Berlin told Mackay he was sailing for Europe in two days, with her or without her.[25] Barrett says only that her parents had once again "parted forever," that her father planned to sail on January 2, and that her mother thought he'd left.[26]

In fact, on Saturday night the second, Berlin was still in Manhattan, playing poker with some of the Algonquin crew and—understandably distracted—losing steadily. On Sunday he stewed. Then on Monday morning he phoned his grieving fiancée—to her complete surprise and delight[27]—and said, "Ellin, I want you to decide one way or another."[28] And so she decided.

They were married, at City Hall, at noon on Monday, January 4, 1926. Mr. and Mrs. Max Winslow attended as witnesses, along with Irving Berlin Inc. publicity manager Ben Bloom. In hopes of throwing off the press, the wedding party had taken the subway downtown: it was the bride-to-be's first trip on the proletarian conveyance. Clarence Mackay found out about the wedding two hours after the fact, and was furious. The *Times* declared him "stunned," and continued: "He issued a brief statement saying that the wedding had been performed without his 'knowledge or approval,' and added that he would have nothing further to say on the matter."[29]

The bride and groom made their way to Atlantic City and declared themselves ecstatic to the clamoring press. Ellin expressed the hope that Mackay would come around: "We are very anxious that father should give his consent and blessing," she said. "I hope he is not too angry."

"We are hoping that it will be granted," Irving added, curtly.[30]

It was not granted. Both the tabloids and the respectable papers had made Mackay, the Disapproving Tycoon, an essential part of the narrative, so the disapproved wedding was the most public possible humiliation for him. In retaliation he cut his wayward daughter out of her third of his $30 million estate (roughly half a billion today)—though he was powerless to revoke the substantial trust fund he had set up for her. Clarence and Ellin wouldn't set eyes on each other again for almost three years, and only tragedy would bring them together.

* * *

Irving Berlin, for all his protestations about the chasm between his compositions and his personal life, admitted, quite simply, " 'Always' was a love song I wrote because I had fallen in love."[31]

It made perfect sense, then, that he presented this perfect song to Ellin—music, words, copyright, and royalties—as a wedding gift. It also made psychological sense as a demonstration to his bride that his own power was nothing to be sniffed at.

* * *

They went to Europe on an extended honeymoon, finally leaving behind the surging, hovering, pestering press, which had made their first week of marriage a nightmare. The crowd that greeted the couple at London's Waterloo Station by bursting into "The Drinking Song" from *The Student Prince* turned out to have mistaken Berlin for the theater producer J. J. Shubert, who had also crossed on the *Leviathan*.[32] At the Crillon in Paris, the throng of reporters and newsreel cameramen the couple steeled themselves to face were in fact awaiting a visiting maharajah.[33]

They would be gone for seven months in all, in London, Paris, and Madeira. In March, Ellin began to feel overpowering nausea; a doctor confirmed the reason. A joyous Irving immediately went to Cartier's and bought her an inch-wide bracelet of pavé diamonds. They were happy; he was happier than he had ever been in his life, he wrote his sister.[34]

11

---◆◖◆◗◆---

Never Saw the Sun Shining So Bright

AND SO THE STORIED COURTSHIP, with all its thrill and drama, became Married Life, bearing its own set of joys and challenges. The press, smelling unexploited controversy, continued to hound the couple. But having been both wounded and toughened early on by her parents' divorce, the postdebutante had learned well how to protect herself—and how to strike back when necessary. Early in the honeymoon, when a *Herald Tribune* reporter reached Mrs. Berlin at the Crillon in Paris and asked if it was true that she was expecting a baby in June, she said coolly, "I was married in January."

"Do you wish to deny it, then?" he asked.

"I have no comment," she told him. "But if you print the rumor, I will sue you and the paper for everything you have."[1]

The rumor was not printed. When the newlyweds tried to return from Europe in secret, sailing to Quebec City instead of New York—it was August 1926—the New York papers somehow found out, and a crowd of importunate reporters met the couple dockside. Mrs. Berlin, now six months pregnant, proceeded to quite lose her patrician composure, cursing out the newspapermen in language that would have impressed a sailor —and remembering nothing of the incident afterward.

Conscious or unconscious, it achieved the desired effect: the newshounds backed off.

The baby, Mary Ellin, was born in New York City on Thanksgiving Day. On Christmas—the morning was cold and rainy, but the West 46th Street bachelor pad, now refitted for a young family, was cozy and filled with fresh flowers—she turned one month old. A double celebration. Later, Irving would commemorate it with an inscription on the sheet music of a composition he completed during that eventful month:

> For Mary Ellin, her song. Christmas 1926
>
> > Blue days all of them gone
> > Nothing but blue skies from now on.[2]

The immortal song was born under strange circumstances. Some say that Flo Ziegfeld, whose new musical *Betsy* was floundering in its Washington, D.C., tryout, had importuned his old friend Berlin to write him a hit that might perk up the show's prospects. This was a delicate matter. The production's composers, the twenty-four-year-old Richard Rodgers and thirty-one-year-old Lorenz Hart, whose *Garrick Gaieties* hits "Manhattan" and "Mountain Greenery" heralded, according to *Variety*, a "lyrical renaissance,"[3] had a noninterpolation clause in their contract.

But Broadway producers are not delicate creatures, and *Betsy* was in trouble. In another version of the story, it was Belle Baker, the show's star, who reached out to Berlin the night before the December 28 Broadway opening. Baker, a Yiddishe-mama belter in the style of Sophie Tucker, was a longtime friend of the songwriter's and an important interpreter of his tunes

("Cohen Owes Me Ninety-Seven Dollars"; "Always"). According to her son Herbie, she phoned Berlin in desperation, saying, "Irving, I'm opening in a show tomorrow night, and there isn't a 'Belle Baker song' in the score. . . . What can I do?"[4]

Herbert Baker, just six years old at the time, claimed to remember Berlin showing up at his parents' place with an uncompleted song from his trunk: the first eight bars of "Blue Skies." According to him, Irving labored all night over the song's middle section, keeping the little boy awake, and finally coming up with the great bridge, one of the very greatest bridges in popular music ("Never saw the sun / Shining so bright . . ."), at, appropriately, dawn of the morning of the twenty-eighth.

It's a terrific story. The only problem with it is the fact that Berlin had written the song, according to one of the scrupulously accurate copyright cards he kept in his office, on or about December 16, 1926.[5]

What all parties agree on is that "Blue Skies" was the smash hit of the show's premiere, thoroughly upstaging an unpleasantly surprised Rodgers and Hart. Like the audience, the two young songwriters were hearing Berlin's tune for the first time when Belle Baker belted it out at the beginning of act two. And the audience was wowed, demanding encore after encore—twenty-four encores in all. So overwhelmed was Baker by this rapturous reception that on the twenty-third reprise, she blanked on the lyrics. "Berlin stood up—he was sitting down in the front row," Herbert Baker recalled, "and he threw her the words—and they finished the next chorus singing together!"[6]

"It really didn't take a trained ear to appreciate that . . . 'Blue Skies' was a great piece of songwriting, easily superior to anything Larry and I had written for the production, but at the time I was crushed by having someone else's work interpolated in our score," Rodgers recalled.[7]

Ziegfeld's scheming was to no avail: *Betsy* closed after thirty-nine performances. But "Blue Skies" simply caught fire: five different orchestras recorded it in just the first month of 1927, and Ben Selvin and the Knickerbockers' version outsold them all. Later that year, Al Jolson sang the song in *The Jazz Singer*, billed as the first talking picture (but actually a silent movie with songs dubbed in and a little dialogue).[8] Fifty-one years later, Willie Nelson's version was a number one country music single. Fifty years from the moment you read this, the tune may well chart once again. "Blue Skies" will continue to be recorded as long as there is recorded music: its simplicity and emotional wallop, driven by the alternation of major and minor in the melody (a device that future songwriters John Lennon and Paul McCartney would also employ to great effect), and by the repetition of the word "blue" in alternately light and dark senses, are that powerful.

Who else but Berlin would have put the arrestingly strange word "noticing" in the lyric of a popular song? And used it in a line that conveys both the joy of life and life's transience?

> Noticing the days
> Hurrying by—
> When you're in love,
> My, how they fly![9]

Who else but Berlin, whose sense of loss and the frailty of human happiness ran so deep, could have written such a hauntingly sad song about happiness?

* * *

He was approaching forty, and he had lost precious work time in the precious business of living: the year of courting Ellin; the weeks and months now blissfully bonding with his young family—*noticing the days hurrying by* . . .—all the while trying to, somehow, remain Irving Berlin. But something had changed; his old, fierce drive had altered. And in the meantime, Broadway was passing him by. Wounded as Rodgers and Hart were by the fiasco of *Betsy*, they almost simultaneously opened another show, *Peggy-Ann*, which ran for 333 performances. And toward the end of 1927 the team would score another big success with *A Connecticut Yankee*, which introduced "Thou Swell" and "My Heart Stood Still."

Nineteen twenty-seven was a dazzling year in general for musical theater written by composers other than Irving Berlin. *Good News*, with songs by the ace team of Ray Henderson, Buddy DeSylva, and Lew Brown ("The Best Things in Life Are Free"), would run for 557 performances. George and Ira Gershwin had two hit musicals that year, the Wodehouse-Bolton confection *Oh, Kay!* ("Do, Do, Do"; "Someone to Watch Over Me") and *Funny Face* ("'S Wonderful"; "He Loves and She Loves"), which brought Fred and Adele Astaire back to Broadway. And then there was Jerome Kern and Oscar Hammerstein II's epochal *Show Boat*, after which musical theater would never be the same.

That year, Berlin's old friend and onetime brother-in-law Ray Goetz, now a producer and married to the winsome and very French musical star Irène Bordoni, asked Irving to write a show around her, to be called *Paris*. Feeling less than qualified to tackle a Gallic theme, Irving referred Goetz to his young old friend Cole Porter, who was living a glamorous expatriate life on the Continent. "You can find him in Venice," Berlin said.[10]

The theater producer Elisabeth Marbury had first introduced Berlin to Porter in the mid-1910s, when Cole, fresh out of Yale, was dazzling New York's upper crust at parties with his witty songs. The young Broadway aspirant, three years Berlin's junior, also dazzled Irving with his wide knowledge of his work, and a lifelong friendship, based on affection and profound mutual respect, was born.[11] *Paris* would open in October 1928—at the Music Box—and its showstopper, "(Let's Do It) Let's Fall in Love," would put Porter on the map for good.

Through the spring and summer of '27 Berlin commuted to the city from Dobbs Ferry (where he was renting a house so that Ellin and the baby could breathe some country air) to write a dozen songs for that year's edition of the *Ziegfeld Follies* —though only one, "Shaking the Blues Away," possessed anything like his old verve.[12] Still, he continued to prove he could turn out stand-alone hits, publishing both "Russian Lullaby" and the great "The Song Is Ended (But the Melody Lingers On)" that year.

Watching *The Jazz Singer* that fall, Irving became intrigued by the possibilities of writing songs for the newly audible medium. At the end of the year he took his young family to Palm Springs, for Ellin's health (she was underweight and anemic), and, while he was there, to talk about potential projects with Joe Schenck, now president of United Artists, and Columbia Pictures head (and former Waterson-Berlin-Snyder song plugger) Harry Cohn.

But musical theater was his preoccupation. He had conceived of an upstairs-downstairs show about the wealthy and their servants, with a book to be written by Anita Loos: he wrote a first draft of a new tune, "Puttin' on the Ritz," for the prospective production. He'd also started work on an ambitious (and serious) musical about a minstrel man, called *Mr. Bones;* and he still dreamed of writing an opera, perhaps for the young acting and singing sensation Paul Robeson.

Yet there was also a new, personal difficulty. In the summer of 1928, the newly pregnant Ellin and the baby removed to the Adirondacks while Irving stayed in a rented house in Port Washington, working on songs and an extensive plot treatment for *Mr. Bones.* "I realize very clearly that with me and my friends and the baby and my constant demands . . . it is impossible for you to do good work in the house," his young wife wrote him from Loon Lake.[13]

The missive is solicitous and self-deprecating, but it also contains a germ of reproach and even despair. Husband and wife are nearly different generations: she has recently turned twenty-five, and in May, Berlin turned forty. And though he was a youthful and vigorous forty, twoscore was a relatively advanced age in 1928. He also had intimations of mortality. "I hope I live long enough to see [Mary Ellin] in her first long evening dress," he wrote his wife, worrying and annoying her.[14]

That her father still refused to acknowledge the marriage—and now his granddaughter—was a continual source of tension. As were the husband and wife's complex personalities. She could be irritable; he could be uncommunicative. At bottom was the fact that both were subject to bouts of depression, a malady that dared not speak its name in those times. Both had suffered profound early loss: it was one of the unsaid things that drew them to each other.

And then the unspeakable.

The baby, a boy—Ellin and Irving named him Irving Berlin, Jr.—was born on December 1 and brought back to the family's new home, a townhouse with a garden, overlooking the East River at 9 Sutton Place. And early on Christmas morning, the nurse found the infant dead in his bassinet.

It was crib death, now called sudden infant death syndrome, or SIDS: even now, little is known about its causes. Then, there was nothing to explain it, no way to describe it except as an excruciating, unendurable hammer of fate.

Strangely, the death brought Irving Berlin and his father-in-law together for the first time, Clarence Mackay coming to Sutton Place to offer his condolences. Barrett declares the confrontation between the two "unimaginable," then proceeds to imagine it deftly: "What words could have been exchanged between the heartbroken husband and the grieving, still disapproving father? Condolences gravely offered and accepted; the formality desperate, under cover of a shared, overwhelming concern for Ellin."[15]

Always afterward, Christmas would bring the sharpest kind of pain.

* * *

Escape was the only balm. And so, soon after New Year's, leaving Mary Ellin in the care of her nurse, the two of them fled to Miami and then, over the summer, to Europe: Paris, Munich, Baden-Baden, the Black Forest, Venice. The complex business of healing the unhealable zigzagged forward—now and then they were able to forget, until they were seized by deep guilt over having forgotten.

Berlin went to Hollywood twice that year, the year of the Crash: alone, in the spring, to write the songs for King Vidor's *Hallelujah!*, the first all-black, all-sound musical; then in September, with his wife and daughter, setting to work on two projects for Joe Schenck and Sam Goldwyn at United Artists: *Puttin' On the Ritz*, starring the Al Jolson wannabe Harry Richman and Joan Bennett, and a story Berlin had come up with himself, a tale of a shipboard romance turned on its head by the stock-market crash, first called *Love in a Cottage*, later *Reaching for the Moon*. The picture was to star Douglas Fairbanks, Bebe Daniels, and a young Bing Crosby.

The film adaptation of *The Cocoanuts* was released in May, and—despite the initial displeasure of the Marx Brothers, who were so appalled by it that they tried to buy back the negative and prevent the picture's release—it was a big box-office hit.[16] Most of moviegoing America, of course, had never witnessed the Marxes' wild comedy, which, despite the film's primitive production values, came as a revelation. Berlin's score—including a new number, "When My Dreams Come True"—was another story. "It is as a funny picture and not as a musical comedy, not for its songs, pretty girls, or spectacular scenes, that *The Cocoanuts* succeeds," John Mosher wrote in the *New Yorker*. "To the Marxes belongs the success of the show."[17]

Berlin himself would later admit that after marrying he had coasted a bit. By his standards, maybe more than a bit. In one 1929 letter to Hollywood—they continued to correspond frequently when apart—Ellin wrote, "I'm not belittling what you have done. But while talent and facility withers with years, genius matures. And I don't think you've ever stopped long enough to listen to that maturing genius."[18]

It was both loving and devastating. Was it true?

On December 2, 1929, the same day as he published one of his (admittedly) worst songs, "To My Mammy," Berlin published "Puttin' on the Ritz," one of his best. With its breathlessly syncopated beat and intricate rhyme scheme—

> If you're blue and you
> Don't know where to go to

—the number was no less thrilling than 1921's "Everybody Step," yet it also incorporated a quantity that had been present in Berlin's lyrics since the beginning, one that was now ripening and deepening: social observation. Its sharp-eyed portrait of poor but flashy Jazz Age Harlemites—

> Spangled gowns upon a bevy
> Of high browns from down the levee,
> All misfits

—was loving, if also, in tune with the times, patronizing.[19] But it was photographically keen, and wildly catchy.

It was also a rare gem amid the general dross of Berlin's output at the turn of the decade. In another letter to Hollywood that past spring, Ellin had told her husband how anxious she was that he have "a big success." She had a "horrible feeling" that he hadn't "done so well" since their marriage; now that she was strong again—three months after the death of the baby—she wanted to help him. "It's simply grand about *Mr. Bones*," she wrote, with desperate cheer. "I feel you are going to do wonderful work for it. . . . You sound ambitious again for the first time in months and I'm so happy I could cry."[20]

But what happened next was decidedly less than grand: Berlin's big idea for a show about a minstrel man went into the Hollywood meat grinder and emerged as a mediocre Al Jolson vehicle called *Mammy*. Only one tune from the movie, "Let Me Sing and I'm Happy," is remembered today, less as a standard than as a classic Jolson barn burner.

Irving Berlin was neither the first great artist nor the last to be lured by Hollywood's gold, only to discover to his sorrow what the gold could cost. What made him different was that unlike most of those other writers and composers, he wasn't in dire need of the money: he simply liked being well paid for his work. The former was about to change.

In the last week of October, 1929, Wall Street laid an egg, as the famous *Variety* headline put it. And just like that, Irving Berlin's nest egg vanished, like the savings of so many others. Five million dollars, the equivalent of some seventy million today: just like that. His daughter writes that he made a joke of it—he was lucky to have a rich wife, Irving said. Ellin's trust, invested outside the stock market, was unaffected. (Her father was less fortunate: all but cleaned out by the Crash, Clarence Mackay had to move from his mansion to the original manor house of the property, fire most of the staff, and sell off his art collection.)[21] But Irving wasn't happy about accepting her help, Ellin said.

All of a sudden he wasn't happy about much of anything, especially writing songs.

* * *

Ellin and Mary Ellin returned east the following February —Ellin's mother was dying—but Berlin stayed on in Hollywood alone. Though he felt a powerful pull to go with his family, and his professional instinct told him to bring his shipboard-romance story back to New York and make a Broadway musical of it, he felt he owed it to his friend Joe Schenck to do *Reaching for the Moon* as a movie. His professional pride also longed for a silver-screen success, a solid score to redeem the mediocrity of *Mammy* and Harry Richman's *Puttin' on the Ritz.*

In the meantime, Irving had a visitor.

Sam H. Harris wanted badly to talk his old friend and business partner into coming back to Broadway, and he had the perfect lure: a new farce on the timeliest of topics, the recent advent of sound in the movies. The play was called *Once in a Lifetime*, and its writer was a twenty-five-year-old prodigy named Moss Hart. Harris loved it, and decided that Irving Berlin should team with Hart to turn *Once in a Lifetime* into a musical.

On the face of it, it was a great match: Irving had learned quite a bit in a short time about the talkies' impact on Hollywood. And Berlin and Hart had something important in common: Moss Hart, too, was the son of dirt-poor Jewish immigrants and had grown up in tenements, in his case in the Bronx and Brooklyn. The future playwright's dreams of Manhattan glamour had been fired by Franklin P. Adams's "Conning Tower" columns in the *New York World*, with their tales of glittering opening nights and dazzling raillery at the Algonquin Round Table.

Berlin was interested in working with the young man. Was the young man interested in collaborating with Berlin? Of course it was barely a question at all. How could any young playwright pass up the chance to work with the great Berlin? Yet Hart claimed in his memoir, *Act One*, that with all the effrontery of youth and talent, he dismissed the idea out of hand. "I do not write musical comedies," he huffed to Sam Harris's general manager, Max Siegel. "I'm a playwright. I write plays— *only* plays."[22]

Amazingly, Hart hadn't talked himself out of a production. Music or no music, Harris liked the youngster's play well enough to want to produce it at the Music Box—if Hart would agree to collaborate with George S. Kaufman on a rewrite. Thus was born a great partnership: *Once in a Lifetime*, opening at Harris and Berlin's theater in September of 1930 (Kaufman also directed, and acted in, the show), would run for more than four hundred performances.

*   *   *

Missing his wife and daughter keenly, Berlin hunkered down to write the score for *Reaching for the Moon*—fourteen tunes in all, this despite the formula he had revealed to *Photoplay* in June: "In my opinion, no picture except an operetta should have more than four songs, but these four should be sung often."[23]

At that point, Berlin had no more idea of the ideal recipe for a Hollywood musical than anyone else in Hollywood. In the three years following the release of *The Jazz Singer,* moviemakers, thrilled by the possibilities of sound, had begun turning out musicals in vast profusion. But by the middle of 1930, Depression audiences, worried about their pocketbooks and tired of the genre, stopped buying tickets to movie musicals, and the studios slammed on the brakes.

Reaching for the Moon's production costs had risen to more than a million dollars, a huge amount at the time, and the film's music would have accounted for a large portion of the budget. United Artists decided to cut its losses and turn *Reaching for the Moon* into a straight comedy. Berlin's score was jettisoned just like that, except for the title song, played only as an instrumental under the credits and behind a love scene, and a throwaway called "When the Folks High Up Do the Mean Low Down," sung by that smooth-faced newcomer Crosby.

Devastated, Berlin repaired that November to a mineral-spring health spa in French Lick, Indiana, to, in the parlance of the day, take the cure. This was a euphemism: he had fallen into a serious depression. His wife and daughter came to his side. Someone—probably Ellin—took an adorable snapshot there of father and daughter, holding hands on an autumnal lawn. The day looks wet and gray. Mary Ellin, about to turn four, wears a cloche hat and a caped wool coat; Berlin is dressed for golf, thirties-style, in broad newsboy cap, jacket and tie, and plus fours. He looks elegant but painfully thin, and his smile, while warm, also contains a certain irony. Where has the sleek and self-assured artist of just a few years earlier gone?

Always an acute reader of public moods and trends, Irving Berlin is suffering, like America, from a shattering loss of confidence. It will take a brisk wind to blow the black clouds away.

12

Good God, Another Revue!

It was a depressed Berlin who was returning to New York in the winter of 1930–31, and a depressed New York he was coming back to.[1] America's economic collapse was now a year old: the worst was yet to come, but the breadlines had already begun; unemployed men, some in business suits, were selling apples on the streets of Manhattan. The same cold winds buffeted Broadway. Theater audiences were declining as cheaper entertainments beckoned—movie tickets cost cents instead of dollars; the radio was free. Theater stars were heading west, where the money was. The Great White Way's 1929–30 season had seen 233 productions; in 1930–31 there were 187.[2]

Broadway wasn't dying in the early thirties, but it was growing smaller and denser. Ziegfeldian extravaganzas, overblown revues with high ticket prices and long-legged chorines, were no longer economically feasible or artistically desirable. Operettas retained their popularity; and the new Young Turks—the

Gershwins; Cole Porter; Rodgers and Hart; DeSylva, Brown, and Henderson; Harbach and Kern—continued to turn out musicals that the people continued to come to see. A genre that had seemed outmoded began to come back.

Between mid-1929 and early 1930, a revue called *The Little Show*, starring Fred Allen, Libby Holman, and Clifton Webb, ran for 321 performances at the Music Box. A brilliant new team, the thirty-two-year-old Howard Dietz and twenty-eight-year-old Arthur Schwartz, had written most of the score, including a song that was to become one of their signatures, "I Guess I'll Have to Change My Plan." *The Little Show* was a new brand of revue, one whose hallmarks were wit and intimacy with hints of satire rather than escapist grandeur.

Satire, a rich vein of humor in fearful times, was in the air. Prohibition was still in force and responsible for much national misbehavior; the country was grappling with terrible financial demons that an ineffectual Republican administration was doing little to overcome. (In tribute to the president, the shantytowns that were springing up around the country would soon be dubbed Hoovervilles.) And in New York City, Mayor James J. Walker, Irving Berlin's songwriting friend Jimmy, was facing a gathering storm of corruption charges that would soon force him out of office.

Satirical themes, stirred up by the excesses of the twenties, had begun to find their way into Broadway entertainments even before the Crash. In 1927 George S. Kaufman wrote the book for the Gershwin brothers' musical *Strike Up the Band*, whose story revolved around a nonsensical war between the United States and Switzerland. The show shut down quickly after its Philadelphia tryout, prompting Kaufman's famous definition of satire as "what closes on Saturday night." But as revised by Morrie Ryskind, *Strike Up the Band* had a moderately successful run in 1930. And in 1931, the Gershwins, along with Kaufman and Ryskind, wrote *Of Thee I Sing*, a still darker satire about the fatuous presidential campaign of one John P. Wintergreen, who runs on a "love" platform. Opening at the Music Box the day after Christmas, the show would win the 1932 Pulitzer Prize for drama, a first for a musical.

All this was in the air while Berlin lay fallow.

But Sam Harris had no intention of letting his old friend and business partner stay on the sidelines. Unlike other Broadway producers, Harris was riding high, largely because of his acumen about this brilliant boy Hart, whom he had wisely placed under a five-year contract.[3] *Once in a Lifetime* was minting money for the Music Box, putting Berlin in the peculiar position of feeling successful and unsuccessful at the same time. And Harris felt certain the boy had more hits in him, and that Berlin did, too.

In the spring of 1931, Moss Hart was riding a cross-country train home from California, where a Los Angeles production of *Once in a Lifetime* was playing to packed houses, when he started sketching out ideas for a new show—a new *Music Box Revue*, of all things, to be written in collaboration with the man he'd previously declined to collaborate with, Irving Berlin. In fact Hart revered Berlin, whose songs he had fallen in love with while working in a Bronx music store as a boy; as a teenager during the first *Revue*, the future playwright had waited at the Music Box's stage door for a glimpse of his idol.[4]

Hart broached the revue idea to Harris over dinner after returning to New York. The producer became so excited that he had a telephone brought to the table and immediately called Berlin, saying, "Come right down here, Irving. Moss Hart has an idea for a new *Music Box Revue* and I like it."[5]

Unable to get right down there (or more likely, saving face), Irving joined Harris and Hart for lunch at Sardi's the next day. Berlin liked the young playwright's revue idea, except for the revue part—what he really wanted to do next, he said, was a book musical. "He did, however, see a distinct possibility [that my] idea could be translated into the kind of musical story he wanted," Hart would recall, a few years later,

> and suggested that I immediately pack a bag and move down to Long Island for two weeks. . . . I stayed for four months and then moved back to New York and lived with him for eight months more. . . . You not only write a show with Irving Berlin, you live it, breathe it, eat it and were it not for the fact that he allows you to sleep not at all, I should also say sleep it.[6]

Hart, an inveterate embroiderer of his own legend, was exaggerating how long it took him and his forty-three-year-old collaborator to write the musical satire that resulted from their labors: they began work in June and opened *Face the Music* the following February. He was also omitting a crucial part of the picture—Berlin's ruined self-confidence, his utter terror at getting down to serious work once more. Each major project he'd completed over the past five years had eroded his certainty rather than building it up. At first, he found, he was just going through the motions.

"For two months I went along as I always have, picking out tunes and fitting in the words," he would later recall.

> Then my troubles started. I realized I had used tunes and lyrics that had been loafing around in my head; realized I had written them down because they were easy, not because they were good. If I could have revived any self-assurance it wouldn't have been so tough, but a song writer is only as good as his last show, and I was constantly afraid.[7]

His young collaborator couldn't help but be affected by the older man's unease, which was exacerbated by Berlin's customary nervous energy: Irving was a pacer, a gum-chewer, a fast talker. Hart himself was "a nervous type," he confessed; but "compared to Irving Berlin," he wrote, "I am Buddha incarnate."[8] Hart agreed to hew to Berlin's schedule: hard labor from midnight to nine A.M. and sleep during the day. The problem was that Hart, like Berlin, was an insomniac. The frazzled atmosphere seemed to have defeated them—then something clicked. Between July and early September, the songwriter produced a stream of fresh, lilting songs, by turns sprightly, witty, and romantic: "Let's Have Another Cup of Coffee," "Soft Lights and Sweet Music," "You Must Be Born with It," "On a Roof in Manhattan," "I Say It's Spinach."

The dry spell was over.

* * *

The Music Box being quite busy (*Of Thee I Sing* was in the midst of a 441-performance run), *Face the Music* opened at the New Amsterdam in mid-February 1932, and was a hit—for a while: the show would close after 165 performances, a victim of Depression-flattened ticket sales and the departure of its widely adored female lead, Mary Boland, for Hollywood. But it burned bright at first. Gorgeously staged by Hassard Short and expertly directed by the multitentacled Kaufman, who gave the revue a relentless, breakneck pace, it was in a way an even more ambitious satire than *Of Thee I Sing*. *Face the Music* took on not just one big target but three: politics, show business, and the Depression. The show featured broke millionaires and millionaire cops, and named New York politicians without mercy: Governor Al Smith, Mayor Jimmy Walker, and also Judge Samuel Seabury, who even as *Face the Music* opened, was leading the corruption-hunting committee that would soon bring about Walker's downfall.

The opening number, depicting Manhattan's upper crust reduced to dining at Horn & Hardart's Automat, set the gaily stinging tone. Much as he had in "At the Devil's Ball," Berlin deployed his cartoonist's sensibility masterfully, depicting

> Missus Belmont passing by,
> Putting mustard on a Swiss-on-rye

and

> Missus Astor with a grin
> And a dab of ketchup on her chin.[9]

Except that now, in addition to being snapshot-crisp and sweetly funny, the musical portraits had a topical barb. Also sweet, and also barbed, was the infectious and sprightly "Let's Have Another Cup of Coffee." One of the Depression's great anthems, it predated the classic "Brother, Can You Spare a Dime?" by a half-year, and worked more subtly than Jay Gorney and E. Y. Harburg's powerful lament. Berlin's verse was a subtle dig at songwriters who "see the world through rose-colored glasses"; the chorus then proceeded to do just that:

> Just around the corner
> There's a rainbow in the sky,
> So let's have another cup o' coffee,
> And let's have another piece o' pie![10]

Tellingly, the irresistible recording by Fred Waring's Pennsylvanians omitted the verse, giving the Depression-blasted public what Waring apparently felt it wanted: sheer uplift, without shades of gray.

Around this time, Berlin moved his family from the dark halls of the Warwick Hotel to a sunny penthouse triplex atop East End Avenue. But while the reviews for *Face the Music* were glowing ("As brilliant a Broadway lampoon as ever laughed at trouble . . . the score is out of Irving Berlin's top shelf," wrote the *Herald Tribune*'s Percy Hammond),[11] Berlin's inner critic gnawed at him. Rather than feeling triumph at being "back in town with a hit," his daughter writes, Irving was "subdued, exhausted, after too many disappointments and uncertainties." Ellin, who had just given birth to the couple's second child, Linda, was in the grips of a severe postpartum depression. Then, in July, Boland left for Hollywood and Sam Harris closed *Face the Music.* According to Barrett, the show "barely broke even"; other sources claim it wound up deep in the red.[12]

Vacationing with his family in the Adirondacks in the summer of 1932, Berlin was cheerful on the surface, but in a precarious state underneath. Composing the musical's bright, natural score had been such wrenching labor that he feared the dry spell might return. He was still second-guessing himself: "I had written 'How Deep Is the Ocean?' but didn't like it and convinced everyone in the office it wasn't good enough," he recalled. "Soon after, I wrote 'Say It Isn't So,' which I also discarded."[13]

But while Berlin was away, Max Winslow slipped "Say It Isn't So" to Rudy Vallee. Vallee introduced the song on his coast-to-coast broadcast, Thursday night, September 1, singing it with the deepest possible feeling: his wife, the actress Fay Webb, was in the midst of divorcing him, and Vallee was hoping against hope that Berlin's plaintive words and music might change her mind.[14] America knew the story; the song took off. (The divorce went through anyway.)

Heartened by the success, Berlin published "How Deep Is the Ocean?" in late September. As he explained many years later, the germ of the song had sprung from the humblest possible source:

> In the early days of sound films I wrote a very awful movie for Al Jolson. One of the songs was a true horror called "To My Mammy." But in the middle of it I had a couple of nice lines. . . . Years later I took out those nice lines and wrote a new song around them called "How Deep Is the Ocean." . . . I think it's one of my best songs—taken from one of my worst.[15]

Paul Whiteman and His Orchestra, with Jack Fulton on the vocal, introduced the tune on an October broadcast, and it too caught on fast—and has stuck around ever since. Unlike "Say It

Isn't So," which, while lovely, seems permanently scented with the wistful, cigarette-smoke and muted-trumpets perfume of a Depression-era fox trot, "How Deep Is the Ocean?" is, quite simply, a towering song, and a timeless standard.

* * *

Shortly before *Face the Music* closed, Berlin told Moss Hart that he wanted to work with him again. "We both agreed that we had no desire to do a conventional sort of revue with the usual blackout sketches, songs and dances," Hart recalled. "So we hit upon the idea of writing a topical revue right off the front pages of the newspapers."[16] The idea would become *As Thousands Cheer.*

It was a brilliant notion. "The idea unifying *As Thousands Cheer* was so obvious," the Hart biographer Steven Bach writes, "one wonders why no one had hit on it before: a musical revue pretending to be a daily paper, with weather reports, political bulletins, human interest stories, society gossip, a Sunday roto-gravure (picture) section, even comics."[17]

The use of actual celebrities rather than thinly disguised characters would markedly sharpen the satire. The writers could range as freely as the news would allow them, covering comedy and tragedy and all the stops between. And, having learned that critics and audiences liked what they created together, the two could have fun creating it. "Mr. Hart was a very funny man," Barrett recalled. "He and my father laughed a lot when they were together. From the way they laughed you would have thought writing a show was a lark."[18]

Of course no job was ever a lark for Irving Berlin—he still sweated blood to achieve simplicity, and always would—but creating *As Thousands Cheer* gave him nothing like the torment *Face the Music* had. He knew, once again, that he could write hits.

That spring Berlin lent Hart five thousand dollars to take a leave of absence from MGM, where he was doing hackwork for Irving Thalberg, and accompany him to Bermuda to write

As Thousands Cheer. The work there and back in Manhattan over the spring and summer went smoothly. The newspapers provided endless inspiration. Hart churned out barbed sketches about the boldfaced names of the day: FDR, Mahatma Gandhi, the celebrity evangelist Aimee Semple Mcpherson, the Rockefellers, Noël Coward, the divorcing Joan Crawford and Douglas Fairbanks, Jr. Berlin wrote songs around personalities—"Mr. and Mrs. Hoover," about the outgoing president (later dropped from the show); "How's Chances?," about the Woolworth heiress Barbara Hutton—and newspaper sections: the advice-to-the-lovelorn column ("Lonely Heart"), the comics page ("The Funnies"), and the weather forecast ("Heat Wave"). But one section stumped him at first. "I was stuck for a song for the Rotogravure Section," he later recalled.

> I'd written a couple of old-fashioned-type songs but they were lousy. So I reached back to something I had written in 1917. It went, "Smile and show your dimple, you'll find it very simple. . . ." Except that now, of course, I made the words apply to an Easter Parade.[19]

Of course. The song that would become one of Irving Berlin's most enduring standards became the act I closer of *As Thousands Cheer.*

The second number in act II struck a decidedly different note. After "Metropolitan Opening," a lighthearted sketch about the Depression's decimation of the formerly swell firstnight crowd at the Metropolitan Opera, a curtain fell, bearing the headline UNKNOWN NEGRO LYNCHED BY FRENZIED MOB. The curtain then rose to reveal a black woman standing by the dinner table in a southern shack and singing a Berlin song in an entirely new key:

> Supper time—
> I should set the table,

'Cause it's supper time;
Somehow I'm not able,
'Cause that man o' mine
Ain't comin' home no more.[20]

Berlin had written the number with full knowledge that the
tune wouldn't go down easily with an audience out for an evening's light entertainment. "People told me I was crazy to write
a dirge like that," he said, years later. But he was equally convinced that a musical dealing with headline news needed at least
one serious piece.[21]

And in the spring of 1933 he found the woman he wanted to
sing "Supper Time." Ethel Waters was a national star, and the
headliner that spring at Harlem's Cotton Club, where her closing number was Harold Arlen and Ted Koehler's new masterpiece, "Stormy Weather." The thirty-six-year-old singer led a
turbulent professional and personal life, and the song "was the
perfect expression of my mood," she wrote in her memoir. "And
one night Irving Berlin, the frail little Jewish man who has written the great love songs for two generations of Americans, came
up to hear me sing that song."[22]

Berlin declared that he had to have Waters in *As Thousands
Cheer*, and not just to sing "Supper Time" but for three other
numbers as well, including a Josephine Baker takeoff called
"Harlem on My Mind" and the great "Heat Wave."

The show had a successful tryout at Philadelphia's Forrest
Theatre in early September, although opening night was marred
by an ugly incident all too in tune with the times: the stars Clifton Webb, Marilyn Miller, and Helen Broderick refused to
take a bow with Ethel Waters. To his everlasting credit, Berlin
told the three that of course he would respect their feelings—
only in that case there needn't be any bows at all.

They took their bows with Waters at the next show.

According to Waters, Miller and Webb also openly expressed their discomfort about "Supper Time" early in the try-out, ostensibly because they had to follow the song with "a flip-pant bedroom dance": "Society Wedding," a number that begins with a chorus of bridesmaids and ushers singing the praises of the upper-crust bride and groom—and ends on the ribald note of bride and groom waking together on their wedding morning.[23]

To *his* everlasting credit, "Sam Harris, having witnessed the audience's fervid reaction to ['Supper Time'] in Philadelphia, simply said, 'It stays in,'" Jeffrey Magee writes. "Harris was not chiefly trying to make a social statement; he was recognizing good theater when he saw it."[24]

Berlin, of course, was doing both.

As Thousands Cheer opened at the Music Box on Saturday night, September 30, 1933, and was an immediate smash. "[The show's] satire is as daring as it is convulsing," wrote John Mason Brown of the *New York Evening Post*.[25] At the end of his review, however, he added a "P.S.": "I do wish Miss Waters could find another number to take the place of 'Supper Time,' which neither fits her gifts nor fits into the general scheme of things at the Music Box."[26] And after praising the show, the *New Yorker*'s Wolcott Gibbs sniffed, "I was only mildly distressed by one item—Miss Ethel Waters is supposed to be a Negress whose husband has been lynched, and she sings a song about it, which definitely seemed to belong somewhere else. In Mr. Harris's safe, possibly."[27]

That he was supposed to be distressed by the song seems not to have crossed Wolcott Gibbs's mind.

The *Times*'s Atkinson lauded all the stars, but saved his highest praise for Waters: "[She] takes full control of the audience and the show whenever she appears. Her abandon to the ruddy tune of 'Heat Wave Hits New York' . . . and her pathos in a deep-toned song about a lynching give some notion of the broad range she can encompass in musical shows."[28]

That final plural is interesting: perhaps the *Times*'s critic was writing prescriptively, for *As Thousands Cheer* marked the first time a black woman had ever starred in a Broadway musical.

"Heat Wave," the third number in act I, was Waters's introduction to the audience. One can only imagine the effect she created. Statuesque (five-foot-nine) and sinuous in her bandanna headdress and Caribbean wrap skirt, she shimmied as she belted, purred, and growled her way through Berlin's superbly witty paean to hot weather, hot dancing, and hot sex ("She started the heat wave / By letting her seat wave").[29]

Berlin was back in full force, musically and lyrically. His longtime fascination with syncopation had advanced; his sweat-tested brilliance at writing simple yet piercingly clever lyrics was sharper than ever. The song's bridge, with its jaggedy beat and peekaboo rhymes, was as elegant as a Swiss chronometer:

> It's so hot,
> The weatherman will
> Tell you a record's been made.
> It's so hot,
> A coat of tan will
> Cover your face in the shade . . .[30]

Overwhelmed by the avalanche of critical praise in the Monday papers, Berlin wired Max Winslow in Hollywood: "Dear Max, the notices for show this morning are better than they were for the first Music Box Revue. It is bigger hit than I ever hoped for. Stop. Best to everybody. Irving."[31]

13

Before They Ask Us to Pay the Bill

As Thousands Cheer would play for four hundred standing-room-only performances at the Music Box, then take to the provinces on an extended road tour. The show's success would change Berlin's life once again.

Not just financially—although the multiple streams of income generated by the hit allowed him to forget, at last, about the money he'd lost in the Crash.[1] Though he would turn forty-six in May of 1934, he was invigorated, bubbling with ideas. Against received wisdom, Berlin and Hart began writing a sequel to *As Thousands Cheer*—titled, not very imaginatively, *More Cheers*.

The received wisdom seemed borne out when *Let 'Em Eat Cake*, the follow-up to the Gershwins' Pulitzer-winning *Of Thee I Sing*, closed in the first week of January, after a miserable ninety performances. It wasn't just that the show's plot was even darker than *Of Thee I Sing's*—in a season of rising fascism overseas, *Let 'Em Eat Cake* depicted a fascist takeover of the United States—but that the depths of the Depression were a miserable time commercially for Broadway musicals, *As Thousands Cheer* being one of the very few exceptions.

Berlin and Hart went ahead with their sequel anyway.

And Irving continued to enjoy the fruits of his comeback, including the bittersweet—and in his household, ecumenical—pleasures of the Christmas season. "The menorah was set up on a living room windowsill," Barrett writes. "Settled into the white damask sofa, my mother read the story of Judas Maccabaeus. . . . A few nights later, there she was again, on the same white sofa, reading the Gospel according to Luke."[2]

Soon after Mary Ellin's birth Ellin's suggestion that the child be raised as a Catholic led to the first bad fight in her marriage.[3] Afterward she and Irving reached a compromise, albeit one tilted in his favor. "I believe the children should be brought up in their father's faith," she later told Berlin's secretary Mynna Granat. "My children are going to be brought up as Jews, and when they are fourteen or fifteen I'll teach them about Catholicism, and then they can decide for themselves."[4]

Barrett remembered that year's Christmas dinner as a lively mixed-family affair with a boisterous Mackay contingent including the once-wealthy Clarence and his former mistress, now wife, the voluptuous and resplendent opera singer Anna Case, "plus the somewhat more dignified Balines," led by Irving's brother Ben, a successful furrier in New London, Connecticut.[5] She enjoyed watching her father talking with his older, grayer brother, and felt similarly warmed by the sight of Irving and Clarence in conversation,

> both smartly dressed in dark blue suits, men of the world being hearty with each other, talking about Europe, Long Island, mutual friends like Otto Kahn and Herbert Swope, my grandfather . . . calling my father Irvin or Irwin, my fa-

ther calling my grandfather Mr. Mackay. Not by a flicker was
anything betrayed. Long afterward my mother once said,
"Your father probably never forgave your grandfather."[6]

* * *

Spring of 1934 was a season of triumph. "Easter Parade"
was ubiquitous, a national hit. On Sunday nights from early May
through the beginning of June, NBC aired a five-part celebration of Berlin's music on Gulf Oil's *Good Gulf Program*, featuring Irving himself with commentary and special material and
a hundred Berlin songs rendered by various artists.[7] On May
28 he achieved the popular-culture coronation of the day, the
cover of *Time*, which featured a brooding portrait of the composer seated at the piano, over the odd caption "Jerome Kern
was reminded of Wagner."

In a quote for Woollcott's biography of Berlin, Kern had
said that like the German composer, Berlin "molds and blends
and ornaments his words and music at one and the same time,
each being the outgrowth of the other."[8] The observation worked
well enough in 1924, but it was a curiously tone-deaf comment
to adduce in 1934, as Hitler and the Nazis consolidated their
power in Germany and the Führer expressed his open admiration for the notoriously Jew-hating Wagner. Yet *Time* went even
farther: "Wagner, too, was a shrewd businessman. And his inspiration never seemed to run dry."[9]

A more than superficial assessment of Irving Berlin would
have noted that his inspiration had run dry, terrifyingly so, just
four years earlier. But the shrewd businessman part, as much
as it fed into antisemitic stereotypes, was true enough. Art and
commerce had been tightly interwoven in Berlin's mind since
the sheet music for "Marie from Sunny Italy" had hit music
stores a quarter-century earlier. He still frequented the stores,
monitoring the movement of his product by running his finger
over his sheet music (and that of the other composers pub-

lished by Irving Berlin Inc.) to check for dust—and if there was dust, promptly returning to his Broadway offices to learn the reason why.

He reported to 799 Seventh Avenue every weekday, as diligently as any garmento—though, in keeping with his insomniac schedule, rarely before noon. The office was a noisy, messy, cheerful warren, stacked with show-business newspapers and sheet music, alive with the sound of pianos being played and songs being auditioned and people shouting on the telephone. It was a place of busyness and of business, its lord and master a great artist with a keen eye on the bottom line.

Though Berlin and Hart continued to hammer away at the sequel to *As Thousands Cheer*—in the summer of 1934 they even sailed to Naples together aboard the S.S. *Rex*, on a "working holiday"[10]—Berlin the businessman was increasingly impressed by the commercial possibilities of movie musicals in general, and by the musicals of RKO Pictures in particular.

The Gay Divorcee premiered on Columbus Day, 1934. The picture was sheer, high-toned fluff about romantic mix-ups, set in England, but the brilliance of the players and of the studio's musical unit, set against the escapist elegance of the mise en scène, made the film catnip for Depression audiences. And central to the movie's charm was the first official teaming of Fred Astaire and Ginger Rogers.[11] Mark Sandrich directed, and Pandro S. Berman produced. Working closely with Astaire, the twenty-four-year-old Hermes Pan choreographed, and together they forged a new epoch in dance on film. Cole Porter's great "Night and Day"—and Astaire and Rogers's magnificent courtship dance to it—stood, and still stands, at the core of the movie's artistic splendor.

"Night and Day" was a groundbreaking song, with unusual, Middle Eastern–tinged harmonies and a forty-eight-bar structure, in the form ABABCB—with C representing the song's release or bridge—instead of the standard thirty-two-bar, AABA form. And it had inspired Irving Berlin, who knew greatness when he heard it, to write a fan letter to Porter in Paris in January 1933:

> Dear Cole,
>   I am mad about "Night and Day" and I think it is your high spot. You probably know it is being played all over, and all the orchestra leaders think it is the best tune of the year—and I agree with them. . . .
>   As ever.
>   Irving[12]

It wasn't only the bands of the day that were playing the song all over—Fred Astaire's recording of "Night and Day" with the Leo Reisman Orchestra was one of the best-selling records in the nation in 1932. This was well before Astaire had sung the tune on film, where his acting and dancing helped put it across. The world learned early on that while his voice was anything but rich and powerful, Fred Astaire was, as Irving Berlin would say many years later, "not just a great dancer [but] a great singer of songs. He's as good as any of them—as good as Jolson or Crosby or Sinatra. He's just as good a singer as he is a dancer—not necessarily because of his voice, but by his conception of projecting a song."[13]

As a boy vaudevillian in the nineteen teens, Astaire (born in 1899) had frequented music publishers' offices in Tin Pan Alley, looking for material: at Jerome H. Remick's he had struck up an enduring friendship with the teenaged song plugger George Gershwin. Yet though Astaire often visited Waterson-Snyder-Berlin, and while by the fall of 1934 Berlin and Astaire had both become major figures in musical theater, they still had never met.

Then, not long after *The Gay Divorcee* became a hit, Pandro Berman contacted Irving and asked if he would like to score an

Astaire-Rogers picture, and Berlin, who "was particularly excited by the prospect of writing for Astaire," instantly agreed.[14]

If, that is, RKO Pictures would agree to his terms. His stock flying high on the continued success of *As Thousands Cheer,* Berlin demanded a dizzying $100,000 to write songs for the picture that would become *Top Hat.* It was a fee he might have been able to extract from one of the major studios, but not from the financially troubled RKO, which could afford not a dime more than $75,000. But Berman offered a compensation: the studio would also pay him ten percent of the film's gross profits should its box-office receipts top $1,250,000. It was an unprecedented deal, yet Berlin accepted reluctantly, since few movies grossed over a million dollars in that era.

Or perhaps, poker player that he was, he was feigning reluctance, for he also came away with two other singular concessions: artistic control over the use of his songs, including participation in script conferences and retention of the rights to his compositions. "Irving Berlin was the toughest trader I've ever met in the film business, the hardest-headed businessman I've ever known," Pandro Berman recalled.[15]

And so, after presenting eight-year-old Mary Ellin and two-year-old Linda with compensatory gifts for the Christmas he'd be missing, Irving Berlin boarded a plane to take the eighteen-hour flight to Los Angeles. It was December 1934 and he was returning to Hollywood, victorious.

* * *

More Cheers fell through, but the cruise to Italy had not been in vain, for it inspired a song which, though instantly forgotten, led Berlin to write another tune destined for posterity. "Moon over Napoli" was further proof that Irving Berlin had to turn out a good deal of dross before he could get to the gold. Its lyric—

> Moon over Napoli,
> I am thinking of the night I spent so happily . . .

was a throwback in quality to 1907's "Marie from Sunny Italy"; its melody was equally unmemorable. But according to Philip Furia,

> Berlin [became] intrigued by a rising, step-wise sequence of notes for the lyric phrase, "When a dark-eyed maid invited me to 'See—Naples and Die.'" Subtly changing some of the intervals, he reworked the first eleven notes of the phrase to what became the music for "And my heart beats so that I can hardly speak" in "Cheek to Cheek."[16]

Furia claims that Berlin wrote the music and lyrics to "Cheek to Cheek" in New York, before he left for the West Coast, "in a single intense day of labor, which, given his work habits, probably meant more night than day."[17] Other accounts have him making substantial revisions to the song after arriving in Hollywood, working with Fred Astaire's rehearsal pianist Hal Borne.[18]

Wherever Berlin created it, it is an extraordinary piece of work, the longest song he ever wrote: verseless, with no fewer than seventy-two measures as opposed to the standard thirty-two, with a *double* chorus ("Heaven, / I'm in heaven . . .," a melodic phrase inspired by Chopin's Polonaise Number 6), followed by a *double* bridge ("Oh! I love to climb a mountain / And to reach the highest peak. . . . / Oh! I love to go out fishing / In a river or a creek . . ."), followed by a soaring outlier section ("Dance with me—/ I want my arm about you . . ."), impassioned and minor, that is virtually its own song. The ambitious strangeness of "Cheek to Cheek" cries out that Berlin was both paying tribute to and pitting himself against Cole Porter's paradigm-breaking "Night and Day."

He had brought some ten or twelve new songs with him to Hollywood, yet director Mark Sandrich found them, apart from "Cheek to Cheek," more suited to the random scheme of a revue than to moving along the plot of a movie musical.[19] So

Berlin rolled up his sleeves and set up shop in his suite at the Beverly Wilshire—then, because fellow guests complained about the nighttime piano-pounding, moved to the hotel's penthouse. In time-honored fashion, he turned luxurious accommodations into a den of hard labor, toiling through the night in pajamas and slippers for weeks on end, tapping out tunes on the Buick and lyrics on a typewriter, in between pacing, smoking, and chewing gum.

Then he brought the new songs in to RKO. Many years later, Hermes Pan recalled his shock at hearing them: "I was so thrilled to meet Irving Berlin," Pan said, "so I was surprised . . . because he was just a lousy pianist. He played the entire score with his transposing piano, and his bass was clunk-clunk-clunk. And then he would sing the song, and we were all asking ourselves, Is this any good? I remember 'Cheek to Cheek,' especially; the way he sang and played, it sounded so awful."[20]

Well, it makes for a good story, even if the truth falls between his daughters' loving memories of their father's singing and playing and the similar accounts of Pan and others. In any case, once the five songs were orchestrated, they transformed into sheer brilliance. All five would all land on NBC's *Your Hit Parade*, which debuted in April and quickly become an institution and popular-culture arbiter. Two of the tunes stood above the others: "Cheek to Cheek," once again featuring Astaire with the Leo Reisman Orchestra, was a best seller; and "Top Hat, White Tie and Tails," Astaire's greatest tap number and in Berlin's opinion the best of the songs he wrote for the Astaire-Rogers films.

Two of the other three—the quintessentially jaunty Astaire song-and-dance number "No Strings" and the gorgeous love ballad "Isn't This a Lovely Day (To Be Caught in the Rain)?"—were also great. And the irresistibly campy climactic production number "The Piccolino" was just sheer fun (and, predictably enough, had been backbreakingly hard for Berlin to write).

Pandro Berman told Barrett decades afterward that, once the tough trading was through, hiring Berlin made his life easy: "There wasn't anything I needed to do," he said. "We talked, sure. Talked over the script. You could tell him this or that was needed. But you couldn't tell him how to do things. You wouldn't. . . . Nothing more you had to do than hire him and let him alone."[21]

* * *

There was always a summer rental, in Long Island, the Adirondacks, or Westchester, but in the spring and summer of 1935 it was a stucco house with teal-blue shutters and a red tile roof on the beach at Santa Monica.

There by the Pacific, which sometimes rolled right up to the beach wall, Berlin was right at home in his home away from home, swimming in the surf or the pool, taking a late breakfast in the sun. Mary Ellin's friend and playmate Sammy Goldwyn remembered Irving as "a happy person. Your mother had a little quality of sadness. Your father was accessible. One of the most accessible adults I remember."[22]

Berlin spent pleasant spare hours playing poker and gin rummy with Sammy's father Sam, Joe Schenck, David Selznick, and Max Winslow, now a producer at Columbia. But his true happiness was the great work he was doing and the great people he was working with. Every morning Irving's longtime chauffeur Jack MacKenzie would drive him to the RKO studios in Culver City, and he would walk through the heavy door and onto the soundstage, where, amid a jumble of lights and wires and equipment, a kind of heaven awaited.

As Hermes Pan recalled, the composer "was constantly on the set, hovering unobtrusively in the background, quietly noticing everything that went on. He often paced, one hand held to his head, the other in his pocket, seeming always to chew gum. Though he said very little, his nervous intensity instantly alerted everyone to his presence." And from the first day of shooting Irving Berlin saw that Fred Astaire's intensity fully matched his. "Throughout the filming the songwriter was constantly heard to comment, softly, 'I love what you're doing, oh, I love it.' "[23]

Berlin and Astaire began what would become a lifelong friendship during the making of *Top Hat*. They not only recognized the genius in each other but the similarities: each man had a mocking sense of humor, a total devotion to his wife, and a keen sense of sartorial style; both were out-and-out perfectionists when it came to work.

"That's why he's so good," Berlin told the *New York Times*'s John S. Wilson in 1976. "I've never seen anyone work as hard as he did to get a certain step. He'd get mad at himself on the set—not at other people, but at himself—when he couldn't get a step to work."

The truth Berlin discovered in writing *Top Hat*'s score was that it had less to do with moving along the slender plot than with writing dance music, more intensely than ever before. Fred Astaire had become his muse.

Though virtually a knockoff of *The Gay Divorcee* in cast, production team, story, and tone, *Top Hat* was the far better picture and, on its release in the late summer of 1935, a far bigger hit, grossing $3.2 million, five times its production budget, in an era when movie tickets cost twenty-five cents.[24] The movie broke records at Radio City Music Hall, was held over for three or four weeks at theaters that usually played a picture for just a week.[25] It wasn't just that Depression audiences wanted more Astaire and Rogers, and more of the spun-sugar escapism RKO was selling, it was that for the first time, Fred and Ginger were making terpsichorean magic, and musical love, to the great songs of Irving Berlin, songs he'd written lovingly to order. "The songs," Ethan Mordden writes, "sound the way Astaire and Rogers act, and, like them, bear highly inflected profiles, genuine character content."[26]

This, of course, was part of Berlin's genius. And a sequel was almost a foregone conclusion.

* * *

But he was barely getting to work on the next picture when he received shocking news: his older sister Sarah had killed herself, jumped off the roof of her Brooklyn apartment building.

Sarah was in her mid-fifties, childless and stuck in a disappointing marriage. She was said to lack her brothers' and sisters' vitality, and to be "sad, always sad."[27] There is no evidence that in his deepest melancholies Irving ever harbored self-destructive thoughts, but his daughter writes that years later her father would commiserate with "a close relative over another tragic suicide," saying, "I know how you feel. . . . Just how you feel."[28]

He flew east for the funeral, then flew back to Hollywood to get back to work, the tonic for all ills.

* * *

Apart from the single blip of the dry spell, Berlin had been at the top of his game for a quarter-century—and would remain there for fifteen years more. *As Thousands Cheer* and now *Top Hat* had given him tremendous momentum, which he and the team of Berman, Sandrich, Pan, Astaire, and Rogers would carry forward with *Follow the Fleet*, albeit to diminished effect.

The movie unwisely took Astaire out of formal attire and put him into a sailor suit, the plot was a lot of hooey revolving around a benefit show put on to salvage an old ship, and the works were gummed up with another couple besides Fred and Ginger: the hulking Randolph Scott and the winsome if less than electrifying Harriet Hilliard, who would go on to greater fame as the radio and TV wife of bandleader Ozzie Nelson in *The Adventures of Ozzie and Harriet.*

But as *Top Hat* had proved, Berlin didn't need a great story to write a great score, and even if *Follow the Fleet*'s songs are a notch below *Top Hat*'s, they're thoroughly delightful, and one and a half of them are immortal.

The half is "Let Yourself Go," an irresistibly sexy fast-dance number that modulates from a hot minor to a joyous major each time the title phrase is sung—and which Ginger Rogers manages to almost completely unsex with her pleasant, pallid vocal. Fortunately, she and Astaire then redeem the tune (reprised as an instrumental) with their sizzling dance-contest duet.

And their exquisite adagio on a moonlit Art Deco terrace at the picture's end, a visual and sonic masterpiece of light and shadow—the seven-and-a-half-minute scene is virtually a movie within the movie—marks the zenith of Astaire and Rogers's art, and of Irving Berlin's.[29] "Let's Face the Music and Dance" is an ode to the urgency of seizing fleeting pleasures with the power of great carpe diem poetry.

> There may be trouble ahead,
> But while there's moonlight and music
> And love and romance,
> Let's face the music and dance . . .[30]

Here the almost inevitable minor-to-major modulation occurs midstream in the lyric, as the thought of future trouble—might as well say it: of death—momentarily dissolves in the elixir of light and life.

Berlin had learned a great deal about trouble in his lifetime, and, no matter how brightly the sun shone, well understood the shadows light always implied.

14

Write Hits Like Irving Berlin

Two WEEKS to the day after *Follow the Fleet*'s February 20, 1936, premiere, the Academy of Motion Picture Arts and Sciences dealt Irving Berlin a stinging blow, giving the Oscar for Best Original Song to Harry Warren and Al Dubin's "Lullaby of Broadway" (from *Gold Diggers of 1935*) over the two other nominees: Berlin's "Cheek to Cheek" and Jerome Kern, Dorothy Fields, and Jimmy McHugh's "Lovely to Look At" (from the Astaire-Rogers film *Roberta*). Irving was "plenty mad," his daughter recalled.[1]

Was he robbed? From the vantage point of eight decades on it's clear that he was. Eighty years on, "Lullaby of Broadway" is merely a period piece, albeit an irresistible one, while "Cheek to Cheek" has the snap, crackle, and pop of the greatest Berlin, and a whiff of immortality.

But it wasn't just the Oscar snub that galled him: Berlin had a burr under his saddle that spring. Though *Follow the Fleet* was an immediate hit, it wasn't quite as big a hit as *Top Hat*, on whose considerable coattails the new picture rode. *Top Hat* had been glorious and transcendent; *Follow the Fleet* was the almost-as-good one that came after it.

Irving Berlin had a favorite phrase about success, borrowed from his friend Cole: *one of those things*. And he had a related saying about the continuation of success: *don't count on it*. The sentiments, wrapped up in the ancient Yiddish *kineahora*, the warding off of the Evil Eye, stemmed from hard experience with loss and failure—as well as, naturally, the wish that good things would continue. Disappointments were inevitable, he knew; at the same time, it would have been less than human not to feel stung by them. *Follow the Fleet* was a disappointment.

He was therefore receptive when one of RKO's rivals came calling—and all the more receptive because the caller was his oldest friend and card-playing pal Joe Schenck. Schenck and his business partner, the supremely ambitious producer Darryl F. Zanuck, had recently merged their successful company 20th Century Pictures with the ailing Fox Film to create 20th Century–Fox, which they were in the process of turning into a major studio. And a major studio in the mid-1930s needed a musical unit, and landing Irving Berlin was a spectacular coup.

Berlin's first project at 20th was *On the Avenue*, which turned the backstage formula of so many thirties musicals on its head: what if a personage satirized in a revue like *As Thousands Cheer*, someone like Woolworth heiress Barbara Hutton, for example, felt injured enough to want to close the show down?

The cool, gorgeous (and nonsinging) British blonde Madeleine Carroll, fresh from Alfred Hitchcock's *The 39 Steps*, played *On the Avenue*'s heiress; from Warner's Zanuck borrowed Dick Powell, the boyish crooning star of *42nd Street* and *Gold Diggers of 1933*, to play the writer and principal player of the show within a show. The multitalented singer Alice Faye, a protégée of Zanuck's, played the girl-next-door cast member who falls for Powell's character, who of course has already fallen for the heiress.

Because the picture *was* a backstager—most of the action took place in the theater where the revue was presented—Berlin didn't need to integrate score with plot. There was one exception: a song Powell's character sings to Carroll's when they go for a nighttime drive, the car radio helpfully providing the instrumental backing. The startlingly strange, rangy, and modern-sounding song, "You're Laughing at Me," was one Berlin said he'd written in 1927 and promptly shelved: "I thought it was so bad," he said, "I wouldn't have it published." Nine years later he changed his mind: "I peddled it to Mr. Zanuck for a great deal of money," he boasted.[2]

As a former screenwriter, Zanuck felt well qualified to weigh in on story matters. Unfortunately, as the lead producer of *On the Avenue* as well as head of the studio, he also felt qualified to weigh in on musical matters. And as the movie was being completed (at the end of 1936), he decreed that one of the nine numbers Berlin had written for the movie would probably have to be cut. The song was "I've Got My Love to Keep Me Warm."

It was a tune Irving had worked especially hard on, and one he felt rightfully passionate about. It would become a much-beloved standard in the years to come, recorded by, among many others, Ella Fitzgerald and Louis Armstrong, Frank Sinatra, and Tony Bennett. To Zanuck, however, "I've Got My Love to Keep Me Warm" was a piece of material, and one that, given the non-plot-driven nature of *On the Avenue*'s score, was expendable.

Berlin conveyed his feelings in an extraordinary "Dear Darryl" letter:

> I again want to tell you how strongly I feel about this number remaining in the picture. To take it out, in my opinion, would be just the same as if they decided to take "Let's Face

the Music and Dance" out of *Follow the Fleet*, which easily could have been done as there were seven numbers in that picture. . . . I consciously constructed [this song] along the same lines, and after the picture is released, I will guarantee that the band leaders will prefer to play it to any other song in the score.[3]

The song stayed in the picture.

The letter smoothly blends Berlin's acknowledgment of Zanuck's chiefdom with his clear sense of his own power and importance, as well as the sharpest possible understanding of the value of his own work. As it turned out, he was absolutely right about "I've Got My Love to Keep Me Warm": though the sweet curio "This Year's Kisses" was all the rage with band-leaders and record buyers after *On the Avenue*'s release in February 1937, true to its title, the tune faded quickly; "Love to Keep Me Warm" has endured.

As *On the Avenue* has not. As appealing as Dick Powell and Alice Faye were, they were no Fred and Ginger—and 20th Century–Fox's musical unit, under the heavy-handed control of Zanuck, was a far cry from RKO's dream team. While Berlin was toiling away at 20th, Jerome Kern and the sublime lyri-cist Dorothy Fields were joining forces with Pandro Berman, Hermes Pan, and the director George Stevens to create *Swing Time*, the picture regarded by many as the peak of the Astaire-Rogers oeuvre. Not only was Stevens the finest craftsman ever to direct Fred and Ginger, not only was Pan in peak form, but Kern and Fields produced a truly great score, highlighted by three masterpieces: "Pick Yourself Up," "A Fine Romance," and the pair's most enduring standard, "The Way You Look Tonight."

* * *

In January 1936 Hollywood feted Irving Berlin with a silver jubilee celebration of "Alexander's Ragtime Band" at the Ambassador Hotel. A ballroom full of the town's power players—including, according to *Variety*'s page one account, "Joe Schenck, Irving Thalberg, Harry Cohn, . . . Pandro Berman, and musical heads of every studio in town"—gathered along with sundry songwriters and musicians (Jerome Kern emceed) to literally sing the praises of the "humble little fellow" who

> was in a trance last night—just as much as he was in 1913 when the Friars gave him a testimonial. . . . He had to gasp and grasp for words and when they came into his esophagus for expression he was just gagged and, as he said, he was having "a hell of a time" saying something.
>
> But in that humble unassuming way he spoke his heart out to his pals in both lyrics and melody . . . interpreted by Hollywood's top notch song composers. Each of them played a chorus from his hits, starting with "Alexander's Rag Time Band," vintage of 1911, and winding up with "Cheek to Cheek," a 1935 sensation. And everyone of the 155 of them there joined in chanting the choruses . . . [as] Irving sat there with head between his hands, dreaming.[4]

A remarkable gathering, it was a well-deserved tribute to a great artist, of course. But also a grand celebration of power by power, and the furtherance of the cult of personality Berlin never did anything to discourage: he was a Chaplinesque figure, camera-ready and seemingly self-effacing, who did possess genuine humility and deep reticence alongside a justifiable arrogance and a sometimes pleased, sometimes resigned acceptance of the fact that he was seen as the public face of his work. He was a national brand, and his brand was still growing.

Darryl F. Zanuck was impressed enough with the event that he decided, virtually the next day, to turn Berlin's life and life work into a singing, dancing biopic. "To Zanuck," Bergreen writes, "Irving Berlin was simply show business incarnate, his life story the history of popular entertainment during the previous twenty-five years, and *Alexander's Ragtime Band* (the movie) was supposed to be an outsized biographical drama of Berlin's life, studded with his hit songs."[5]

There were two problems: first, at age forty-eight, Berlin wasn't ready to sum up and sign out; and second, Zanuck put Berlin in charge of writing his own life story.

In the meantime, real life intruded. Irving spent much of 1936 shuttling back and forth between Hollywood and New York, where in June Ellin gave birth to their third (and last) daughter, Elizabeth. The birth was a joyous occasion, and helped the couple come to a decision they'd been waffling about for a while: the children would be raised in New York, where the private schools were excellent and tradition still held sway. During the school year Ellin would continue to divide her time between Beverly Hills and Manhattan, now and then taking the baby with her, and the family would all be together for summers and holidays. And by and by, of course, Irving would return to Broadway.

Berlin, meanwhile, was firmly planted in Hollywood, with an office and a secretary in the 20th Century Music Building and two projects under way at Fox. Teamed with the screenwriter Richard Sherman, he'd begun working on a scenario for *Alexander's Ragtime Band*—and from the start, the putatively autobiographical story veered off into odd fictional territory, and mostly stayed there.

To begin with, the hero, Alexander, is not a black bandleader but a white clarinetist (Tyrone Power) working in a New Orleans honky-tonk. And to end with, after both he and ragtime itself fall into obscurity, they're both rediscovered, and in a triumphal finale, Alexander conducts a full orchestra at Carnegie Hall in a performance of his great song—and reunites with his spurned first love.[6]

This cobbled-up scenario may have spoken to Berlin's artistic insecurities. But what it revealed most clearly was his ironbound disinclination to let down his formidable guard. After Woollcott's loving if rococo (and frequently creative) tribute,

Irving would firmly resist every authorial entreaty, and there were more than a few, to participate in a Life of Berlin. There was too much sorrow, too much loss, too much conflict. His early widowerhood, the death of Irving Jr.: things that were just too painful to discuss. Why should Berlin ever have helped a would-be biographer to poke at his pain? For Irving, letting Darryl F. Zanuck anywhere near the real Berlin was out of the question.

In an interim note on the script (May 21, 1937) Zanuck wrote:

> This must be a million-dollar picture in every sense of the word. Audiences will expect to see a wow! It must [have] the scope of Ziegfeld and Old Chicago—American music as the background of a human drama of real people. Maybe our trouble is that we are trying to tell a phase of American musical evolution instead of a story about two boys and a girl.[7]

In the end, both Zanuck and Berlin got all that they wanted: a big fat Hollywood hit.

* * *

By mid-1936 the recent commercial failure of their opera *Porgy and Bess* gave George and Ira Gershwin a financial incentive to consider an offer from RKO's Pandro Berman to create the scores for the latest Astaire-Rogers picture, *Shall We Dance*, and Astaire's next film (to be his first without Rogers), *Damsel in Distress.*

Even so, George dragged his feet at first. When his agent wired him that RKO was "afraid you will only do highbrow songs so wire me on this score so I can reassure them," he waited ten days before sending his reply: "Rumors about highbrow music ridiculous stop am out to write hits." (Perhaps what finally decided him was a letter from Berlin, who wrote, "There is no setup in Hollywood that can compare with doing an Astaire picture, and I know you will be very happy with it.")[8]

The Gershwins signed with the studio. In August, George and Ira, and Ira's wife, Leonore (Lee), flew to Los Angeles and moved into a plush rented house in Beverly Hills. The brothers went straight to work on their score, and George Gershwin began mingling with the show people and songwriters he loved. Late that year he wrote to a New York friend: "I've seen a great deal of Irving Berlin and Jerome Kern at poker parties and dinners and the feeling around is very 'gemutlich.' "[9]

In early 1937 Gershwin, an enthusiastic amateur photographer, took a brooding—and in retrospect, haunting—time-exposure portrait of himself with Berlin: George, eyes closed, a pipe in his mouth, holds his right hand on his chest in a pose of theatrical sorrow. His left hand rests lovingly on the shoulder of his friend Irving, who looks up from under his furrowed forehead and dark eyebrows with an indefinable expression that seems something like wariness.

There may be trouble ahead.

During the production of *Shall We Dance*, Gershwin began suffering crippling headaches and a terrible olfactory hallucination: he kept thinking he was smelling burning rubber. The attacks grew worse.

Nor did his work on Sam Goldwyn's Technicolor musical *The Goldwyn Follies* ease his mind. Early on, when the producer imperiously summoned Gershwin to, in effect, audition for the job by playing a selection of prospective tunes for him and his minions, the composer complied—only to be told by Goldwyn that his music, including an early version of "Love Walked In," simply wasn't catchy enough. "Write hits like Irving Berlin," Berlin's gin rummy partner commanded.[10]

Shall We Dance was released in May, and though the picture contained three of the Gershwins' best songs—"They All Laughed," "Let's Call the Whole Thing Off," and the great "They Can't Take That Away from Me"[11]—it also had a convoluted plot and, even worse (and rather inexplicably), no romantic dance number for Fred and Ginger. Critics complained; box-office receipts were only so-so. Word spread that the Astaire-Rogers magic had begun to pall.

One night in early June, Irving and Ellin gave a dinner party at their summer rental, the Santa Monica beach house of Joe Schenck's ex-wife Norma Talmadge. The dinner guests were George, Ira, and Lee, along with George's close friend and ad-mirer the pianist and wit Oscar Levant and Levant's date (and future wife), the actress June Gale.

During the cocktail hour the ten-year-old Mary Ellin played a Mozart sonatina; then George Gershwin sat down at the key-board.

He played, Barrett recalled,

> some of the songs he'd written for Fred Astaire: "They All Laughed," "They Can't Take That Away from Me," and "A Foggy Day," and the song he'd just finished for The Gold-wyn Follies, "Love Walked In." His hands were big on the keys; his playing was precise, with a strong beat and many flourishes. He bent over the piano, looking up now and then with a quick, sweet smile. . . . Then the grown-ups went into dinner and I went to bed.[12]

At the end of the evening, as the guests were leaving, Le-vant and Gale found Gershwin sitting on the running board of his car, holding his head and groaning in pain. A few weeks later, while working on the score of *The Goldwyn Follies*, he col-lapsed and fell into a coma. After emergency surgery on July 11, he died of a brain tumor. He was thirty-eight.

* * *

It was a strange, doomy season: a recession had set in, and FDR's New Deal seemed in peril, along with American opti-mism itself. In quick succession that spring and early summer came the *Hindenburg* disaster, the death of Jean Harlow, and the disappearance of Amelia Earhart. Then Gershwin. Well before his friend's untimely passing, Berlin had planned to spend the last two weeks of August fishing in Alaska—and in the days immediately after the tragedy, getting away from it all seemed more important than ever.

The vacation was a Manhattanite's dream of roughing it: cruising the great territory's inland waterways in a chartered 107-foot yacht with a crew of six, fishing in clear bays for halibut and bass, portaging inland to pristine northern lakes and streams to angle for salmon and trout. Ellin and the two older girls would come along, as well as Mary Ellin's friend Sammy Goldwyn, the burly chauffeur Jack MacKenzie, and Ellin's diminutive French maid Hermine Tripet.

And, of course, a piano.

Berlin had taken nonworking vacations in the past, but two weeks was a long time to be away from his trusty Buick. The instrument had accompanied him to so many places: to Bermuda, where the humidity had played havoc with its tuning; on the *More Cheers* cruise with Moss Hart; to any number of hotel suites. But Irving Berlin's Weser Brothers transposing piano would not go along on his Alaska cruise, for the simple reason that it wouldn't fit onto the boat.

On July 19, 1937, Berlin sent a telegram to the cruise director in Seattle:

> My piano twenty-seven and a-half inches wide and fifty-five inches high. Very important to have it aboard with me so please see if something can't be done about it.[13]

It was as almost though he was talking about an extension of his body—which, of course, the Buick almost was.

The cruise director wired back two days later:

> Irving Berlin
> Care Twentieth Century Fox Studios PFO Hollywood California

Have exhausted every possibility and find it impossible to put your upright aboard. However can accommodate grand of any size by removing legs.

A "Steinway Grand piano [with] a very soft tone," as Berlin had requested, was found, and installed in the yacht's salon.[14] The salon was also where the two ten-year-olds, Mary Ellin and Sammy, hung around amusing themselves as best they could—but from time to time Irving shooed them away and sat down at the piano.

"What are you doing?" Sammy Goldwyn asked him one day.

"I'm working on a new song," Berlin replied.

Much later, Sammy would tell Mary Ellin that this was the first time he realized her father did something other than play cards.[15]

* * *

On the evening of March 10, 1938, Mr. and Mrs. Irving Berlin, by now thoroughly acclimated part-time citizens of Hollywood, attended the tenth Academy Awards at the Biltmore Hotel.[16] There they saw "Sweet Leilani," words and music by the Honolulu bandleader Harry Owens, improbably beat the posthumously nominated "They Can't Take That Away from Me" for Best Song Oscar. "The relatively unknown Owens was the first songwriter to win as composer and lyricist," writes Bing Crosby's biographer Gary Giddins. "No one at the time seemed to find it ironic or farcical that Owens was handed the statuette by a gracious Irving Berlin."[17] Irving may have been seething inside for his late friend George—but then that was Tinsel Town, where business trumped greatness every time. *Waikiki Wedding*, in which Crosby had groaned his way exquisitely through the tropically evocative but hardly great "Sweet Leilani," had done big business; *Shall We Dance*, in which Astaire and Rogers hadn't even danced to the immortal "They Can't Take That Away from Me," hadn't. Too bad.

Yet Berlin's Hollywood business seemed to be on the boil. The following month, 20th Century–Fox ran a full-page roundup of its upcoming pictures in *Variety*. At the top of the roster was the film now officially titled *Irving Berlin's Alexander's Ragtime Band:*

> The dramatic cavalcade of a generation. 20th's first spectacular hit of the new season. A deeply stirring story sweeping through 25 exciting years . . . with three new Irving Berlin songs—probably the greatest he ever wrote—and some of his ever-remembered hits of the past.[18]

Never mind that the three new numbers were very far from the greatest Berlin ever wrote, although "My Walking Stick" (sung by Ethel Merman) was a loopily Freudian delight, and "Now It Can Be Told," all but forgotten today,[19] is a sideways beauty of a love song, not quite major, not quite minor in tonality—much like love itself. The third tune, "Marching Along with Time," was dropped from the score.

Alexander's Ragtime Band opened in August, and its ceaseless parade of Berlin hits, combined with the hard-to-resist charms of its singing and nonsinging stars, made the movie a huge hit with the public, if not, quite, with the critics.[20] Still, as the *New York Times*'s Frank S. Nugent wrote: "The picture simply rides roughshod over minor critical objection and demands recognition as the best musical show of the year."[21]

The picture also rode roughshod over history, astonishingly purporting to tell the story of ragtime without including a single African-American composer or musician. That deep flaw aside, what *Alexander's Ragtime Band* mainly did was recognize Irving Berlin as a living American institution, one whose music was, as Nugent wrote, "remarkably age-resistant"—which Berlin himself both was and wasn't.[22] His hair was still black; his health, apart from the insomnia and songwriter's stomach, excellent; and he was still writing great songs, even if he had just turned fifty, a birthday he'd pointedly left uncelebrated that May.

*　*　*

As early as *Swing Time*, Fred Astaire would later recall, he and Ginger Rogers "wondered how long it would be safe to carry on this cycle of team pictures. We didn't want to run it into the ground."[23]

RKO, by contrast, seemed determined to run it as far as it would go. *Swing Time* had made a tidy profit, and even as production proceeded on the Gershwins' *Shall We Dance* in the spring of 1937, the studio had called Berlin back to score a new script, a screwball comedy called *Carefree*.

The story, such as it was, turned on a love triangle between Astaire, playing, of all things, a psychiatrist, jauntily named Tony Flagg; Rogers, as the patient Tony tries to nudge into marriage with her fiancé, but of course falls in love with himself; and the perpetually hapless Ralph Bellamy as the fiancé. And though Berlin always took his work seriously, the eleven songs he wrote included an unusual number of misfires: forgotten tunes like "You Can Be My Cave Man," "Let's Make the Most of Our Dream," and, amazingly, "Why Do I Love You?," a title Jerry Kern and Oscar Hammerstein had already used in 1927 for one of *Show Boat*'s great numbers.

Quite uncharacteristically, Irving Berlin had disappointed RKO. "Frankly, Irving, as you may have felt, there was no great enthusiasm on the lot for this score," Berlin's longtime musical assistant Dave Dreyer, now working as an arranger in Hollywood, wrote him, as production on *Carefree* wound down in July 1938. Dreyer could be this blunt because his letter had led with good news about the score's one smashing success, "Change Partners": "When Fred and Mark [Sandrich] heard the orchestra play it the first time, they jumped up and hugged each other."[24]

The song—

> Must you dance ev'ry dance
> With the same fortunate man?

—is that good. It also contains a wonderfully witty bridge:

> Ask him to sit this one out,
> And while you're alone,
> I'll tell the waiter to tell him
> He's wanted on the telephone . . .[25]

The quirky, difficult-to-please Alec Wilder could also be quite penetrating, as in this observation in the Berlin section of *American Popular Song:*

> I'd like to point out something here that has greatly impressed me—every song written for Fred Astaire seems to bear his [Astaire's] mark. . . . He brought out in [every writer] something a little better than their best—a little more subtlety, flair, sophistication, wit, and style, qualities he himself possesses in generous measure.[26]

But Irving's happy stretch of writing for his friend and muse was almost at an end. *Carefree*, the title ironic in retrospect, was the eighth Astaire-Rogers film, and, though it was the first in which Fred and Ginger actually kissed, it was also the first to lose money. It was the team's second-to-last picture at RKO. After the final one, 1939's *The Story of Vernon and Irene Castle*— Berlin would not be involved—Astaire and Rogers would go their separate ways for ten years.

And Irving would soon go his. Though (or more likely because) he had already started on his next project for Zanuck, a picture ominously titled *Second Fiddle*, starring Tyrone Power and the Olympic ice skater Sonja Henie, he yearned for his native ground and his natural element. "I feel slow in Hollywood," he told a reporter in September 1938. "The tempo there is slow. So I think it is good once in a while to get back to the theater. I have a feeling that if I don't get back, I'll never see Broadway again."[27]

15

While the Storm Clouds Gather

THINGS SEEMED to be coming apart as the Berlins vacationed in Atlantic City in the late summer of 1938. The family dog was run over on Ventnor Avenue. Back in Manhattan, Clarence Mackay lay in a hospital bed, dying of throat cancer, while Irving and Ellin offered their daughters evasive explanations: a tonsillectomy. A throat abscess. An appendectomy. In the meantime, a monster hurricane was barreling up the East Coast—storm warnings crackled over the radio, along with the screaming, staticky voice of Adolf Hitler and the roars of his hysterical followers. This was the month in which Irving Berlin sailed off into the teeth of another, far greater, storm: Europe on the brink of war.

While Berlin met with his English music publisher, Prime Minister Neville Chamberlain was meeting with Hitler. After giving Germany free rein to invade Czechoslovakia, Chamberlain returned to England waving a piece of paper signed by the

Führer and himself, claiming that he'd achieved "peace for our time," even as antiaircraft guns were being mounted in London and schoolchildren evacuated from the British capital.

Sailing back across the Atlantic, Irving Berlin "tried to write a song that I felt at that time," he recalled to *Variety's* editor, Abel Green, in 1954. "I remember finishing a chorus of a song called 'Thanks America' which I tore up because it was very bad. It seemed a bad editorial set to music."

He then remembered the number he'd written twenty years earlier for *Yip! Yip! Yaphank!* and set aside as "just a little sticky." The original lyrics were:

> God Bless America, land that I love
> Stand beside her
> And guide her
> To the right with a light from above
> Make her victorious on land and foam
> God Bless America, my home sweet home

"It is obvious that the word 'right' had to be changed because in 1918 'guide her to the right' meant the right road," Berlin wrote to Green. By 1938 "right" had different connotations altogether. Also, he'd originally written the number as a war song. "In 1938," Berlin said, "I didn't want it to be a war song. I wanted it to be a song of peace."[1]

Throughout October, as Ellin shuttled back and forth between East End Avenue and her father's sickbed—the children weren't allowed to visit—the shadows lengthened. Nazi forces entered the Czech province Sudetenland. Movie newsreels showed German and Italian planes bombing Spanish villages, the Japanese bombardment of Canton. America's nerves were raw. The night before Halloween, when Orson Welles broadcast a radio dramatization of H. G. Wells's *War of the Worlds*, with an all-too-real-sounding news bulletin announcing a Martian invasion of New Jersey, thousands panicked.

A war with Germany seemed inevitable, yet there was a right and a left in America, and prominent isolationists—including such vocal antisemites as Colonel Charles Lindbergh, the U.S. ambassador to Great Britain Joseph P. Kennedy, and the radio demagogue Father Charles Coughlin—claimed that powerful Jewish interests in the United States were pushing for war mainly to protect their coreligionists in Europe. Kristallnacht, the November 9 pogrom in which thousands of synagogues and Jewish businesses in Germany and Austria had their windows smashed or were burned to the ground, dozens of Jews were murdered, and tens of thousands arrested, outraged many Americans, but the most hard-bitten isolationists remained unmoved.

In early November, Ted Collins, the manager of the radio and recording star Kate Smith, the "Songbird of the South," had asked Irving Berlin if he had a patriotic tune for Smith to sing on her weekly broadcast. Berlin gave him "God Bless America," with its revised chorus and a new verse at the beginning:

> While the storm clouds gather
> Far across the sea,
> Let us swear allegiance
> To a land that's free . . .

On the night of November 10, 1938, one day after Kristallnacht and the eve of Armistice Day, Smith spoke the following words on her CBS broadcast:

> And now it's going to be my very great privilege to sing for you a song that's never been sung before by anybody. . . . It's something more than a song—I feel it's one of the most beautiful compositions ever written, a song that will never die. The author—Mr. Irving Berlin. The title—"God Bless America."[2]

The reaction was swift and powerful: America loved "God Bless America."

* * *

Two days later, Clarence Mackay died at sixty-four. Irving Berlin and the man who had once been unalterably opposed to his daughter's marrying a Jew had long since reconciled, at least on the surface. Berlin's "contribution to my grandfather's declining years," Barrett writes, "was to be nice: an affectionate, respectful son-in-law who, whatever his true inner feelings, appeared to hold no grudge."[3]

Mackay had lived in reduced but hardly impoverished circumstances after the Crash. At death he left his widow Anna Case two million dollars in securities, the remainder of his fortune to be shared equally by Ellin, her brother Willie, and sister Katherine. Irving and Ellin's daughters received twenty-five thousand dollars apiece.[4]

Berlin wore a black mourning band after his father-in-law's death, and he was still wearing it on Christmas morning (that morning was also—no one said it—the tenth anniversary of the death of the boy baby, Irving Jr.), when he presented his grieving wife with a large envelope.

"Oh, Irving, what have you done?" Ellin said—though she'd already guessed the envelope's contents.

"I bought it for you," he said. "It's yours."[5]

It was a rural property that Irving and Ellin had seen earlier that year while visiting the upstate retreat of a society friend, Consuelo Vanderbilt: fifty-two acres of woods around a house and a trout stream in the Catskills, near Lew Beach, a hamlet named after a nineteenth-century congressman. The family went to see the place soon after Christmas. The house was strictly a fixer-upper—a dark ruin with peeling paint—but the woods were lovely, the ice-rimmed trout stream was running fresh, and Irving, who loved to fish, could barely contain his enthusiasm. "Are you excited?" he asked his eldest daughter. "*I* am."[6]

It was an immigrant Jew's Chekhovian dream: his very own

place in the country. But it was also very close to what Berlin had had in mind back in 1924, the year before he met Ellin, when he wrote a workaholic's dream of a song called "Lazy":

> I wanna peep
> Through the deep
> Tangled wildwood,
> Counting sheep
> Till I sleep
> Like a child would . . .[7]

* * *

And then it was back into harness at 20th, and all it entailed: more memos from Zanuck, and more songs for *Second Fiddle*, writing for Mary Healy and Rudy Vallee, a far cry from Rogers and Astaire. Next on the agenda was *Say It with Music*, a sequel to *Alexander's Ragtime Band*. With the consolation of summer idylls in the Catskills to come, Berlin planned to move his family to a rented Spanish Mission–style hacienda high above Benedict Canyon, a long way from the Upper East Side.

Then he changed his mind. He was deeply unhappy that spring; Ellin asked him why. "There's no Lindy's in Los Angeles," he said.[8] "No paper at two in the morning. No Broadway. No *city*."[9]

In *Daily Variety* on May 16, 1939, this piquant note: "Irving Berlin and Buddy De Sylva take off for New York tomorrow via American Airlines."[10]

* * *

George Gard DeSylva, aka B. G. or Buddy, was a man of parts: a highly prolific songwriter and lyricist ("Somebody Loves Me," "California, Here I Come"), and, by the mid-thirties, at 20th Century–Fox, the successful producer of a string of Shirley Temple pictures. In the late thirties DeSylva turned his hand to Broadway, cowriting the book to the Cole Porter–scored hit *DuBarry Was a Lady*. As he finished his work on that show, he came up with an idea for a musical, to be based loosely on the freewheeling politics of the charismatic and corrupt late governor of Louisiana, Huey Long. DeSylva found a writer in Morrie Ryskind, who'd written the screenplay for *The Cocoanuts* (and would go on to write three more Marx Brothers movies). All he needed was a composer.

DeSylva had an attorney, Abe Berman, who also happened to represent Irving Berlin—and who would have known well that Berlin was itching to get back to Broadway. So when Buddy DeSylva and Irving Berlin stepped aboard that American Airlines plane on that May Wednesday, they were discussing nothing less than Berlin's escape from Hollywood.

The Berlins spent the anxious summer of 1939 in their now renovated place in the Catskills: as the bad war news from Europe crackled over the radio that was never far from Irving's side, even at the dinner table, he began scoring the musical that would become *Louisiana Purchase*.

He also walked away from Zanuck and 20th Century–Fox—*Second Fiddle* was a flop, and the *Alexander* sequel had fallen apart—and moved the family back east to another rental, a double townhouse on East 78th Street.

Meanwhile, "God Bless America" had become omnipresent. Kate Smith had made it the theme song of her weekly broadcast, replacing "When the Moon Comes Over the Mountain"; thousands of ordinary Americans sang it every day, in schools and churches and at all manner of public gatherings—even at least one meeting of the Daughters of the American Revolution.[11] Solely on the strength of this one tune, sales of Irving Berlin Inc. sheet music boomed, for the first time in years.[12] "When the song was played at Brooklyn's Ebbets Field [on] Memorial Day," the *New York Times* reported, "the crowd rose and uncovered as if for the national anthem."[13]

But it was no longer a matter of *as if*: a serious groundswell was under way. That June, at a concert sponsored by the Mason

City, Iowa, Chamber of Commerce, a contemporary account noted: "First number to be presented by the large chorus will be 'God Bless America' by Irving Berlin. This number, to be offered with band accompaniment, . . . has been frequently mentioned as a likely candidate for a national anthem, because of its tunefulness, easy singing range and effectiveness."[14]

It was an implicit poke at "The Star-Spangled Banner," which had been the official anthem only since 1931, and which, with its rangy tune and difficult lyrics, gave—and still gives—fits to patriotic Americans trying to sing their way through it. But Berlin would have none of it. "A national anthem is something that develops naturally through age, tradition, historic significance, and general recognition," he said. "We've got a good national anthem. You can't have two."[15]

Yet almost as soon as "God Bless America" was introduced, some Americans began taking pokes at Irving Berlin for his presumption, as an immigrant and a Jew, in having written it at all. " 'America-first' patriots," Furia writes, "rallied round 'The Star-Spangled Banner' and began shouting down efforts to sing 'God Bless America' at public gatherings."[16] At the West End Collegiate Reformed Church, right on Berlin's Manhattan home turf, one Rev. Dr. Edgar Franklin Romig deplored the song specifically in a Sunday-morning sermon. "Mingled with much that is good in the spiritual composition of our people, there is a strange and specious substitute for religion held by many in times of crisis like the present," he said.

> It is compounded of excessive emotion, wishful thinking, and a facile evading of the rudimentary disciplines essential to the building of individual and social well-being, and finds its expression in the mawkish iteration of snatches of song like "God Bless America."
>
> The great national anthems that have survived, and that will outlive most contemporary doggerel, came out of the hearts of men who knew what it was to sacrifice for America.[17]

The language was coded but clear: *our people. A strange and specious substitute for religion. Excessive emotion.* Even the sneering *doggerel* hinted at *mongrel.* The Reverend Doctor Romig might as well have put it in plain English: *the nerve of this Jew songwriter!*

It was a frightening time. A time when—again, right in Berlin's hometown—Fritz Kuhn's German-American Bund could draw a crowd of twenty thousand homegrown Nazi sympathizers to a rally in Madison Square Garden. A rally where, in between "The Star-Spangled Banner" and "The Stars and Stripes Forever," Kuhn blamed "the Brandeises, the Baruchs and the Untermeyers" and "Jewish financiers" for getting America into the Great War; where the Bund's national public-relations counsel, G. W. Kunze, declaimed, "If Franklin Rosenfeld takes the place of George Washington, so in the cultural life Beethoven is replaced by Irving Berlin and the like."[18]

This was the fringe, but the fringe was scarily close to the main fabric of American life in those prewar years. It was a time when Jews, as Philip Roth wrote in his dystopian novel *The Plot against America,* were "a small minority of citizens vastly outnumbered by our Christian countrymen, by and large obstructed by religious prejudice from attaining public power."[19] A time when Jews, even wealthy and famous Jews like Irving Berlin, had to watch their step—and soon, worry about the times to come.

* * *

On May 28, 1940, after out-of-town tryouts in New Haven, Washington, D.C., and Philadelphia, *Louisiana Purchase* opened at the 1,400-seat Imperial Theatre, on West 45th Street, the Music Box being in the midst of a 739-performance siege by Kaufman and Hart's *The Man Who Came to Dinner.* Berlin's Babylonian Exile was over; at long last he was back on Broadway where he belonged.

And the critics were welcoming, if not ecstatic. "Mr. Berlin and Mr. Ryskind have been associated with more brilliant shows than this," Brooks Atkinson wrote. "But after an absence of seven years, Mr. Berlin has returned to remind us that he still can write songs without bursting into a fever of perspiration. . . . 'Louisiana Purchase' is a gay, simple, friendly musical comedy with the accomplished ease of a thoroughbred."[20]

It was faintish praise, yet theater audiences were glad enough about Berlin's homecoming—and needful enough of escape from the relentless drumbeat of bad overseas news—to make the show a solid hit: *Louisiana Purchase* would run until mid-June 1941, for a total of 444 performances, making it the longest-running book musical since *Show Boat* in 1927.[21]

It was the book musical Berlin had long been looking for. And the score was better than ingratiating: it was charming. "Without seeming immodest I think I have the best collection of songs I've had in a long time," Berlin said—and, always a keen judge of his own work, he had grounds for saying it.[22] He had written great songs for Rogers and Astaire, but no movie score was as challenging as the score for a two-act Broadway musical.

With the fourth wall–breaking "Apologia" at the top of the show, in the form of a letter dictated by Liebowitz, an entertainment attorney not unlike Abe Berman, to Buddy DeSylva, Berlin merrily signaled that he was very much up to the challenge. The number harked back to the clever opening recitativos of the *Music Box Revue*s and *As Thousands Cheer*:

> Take a letter to Mr. B. G. DeSylva.
> My dear Mr. DeSylva,
> I've read the book of your show,
> And as your legal adviser,
> I'm writing to let you know
> That you're skating on very thin ice. . . .
> You can't write a book or a play
> Based on characters living today . . .[23]

Of course, *As Thousands Cheer* had done precisely this, to great effect, while *Louisiana Purchase* merely danced around the subject of that state's colorful politics: it was an entertainment rather than pointed satire.

And the score was consistently entertaining, from the title number, written in up-to-the-moment Swing Era style—a new key for Berlin—to the winsome, "Let's Call the Whole Thing Off"–style "Outside of That I Love You" ("I hate the ground you walk upon / I hate the phone you talk upon . . ."[24]), to theracy "Latins Know How," to the sweet ballad "Fools Fall in Love," about which Alec Wilder wrote thirty years later, "Why it never became a standard is beyond me. It's simply delicious."[25]

The fact is—it must be noted—that unlike *Top Hat, Follow the Fleet,* and even *Carefree, Louisiana Purchase* didn't produce a single standard. Since *As Thousands Cheer* in 1933, Berlin had been writing almost exclusively for Hollywood, which seemed, during this period, to draw hits from him in a unique way. Maybe he was simply out of practice where Broadway was concerned. Much of his theater music after World War II would go on to achieve popular success, but *Louisiana Purchase*—however charming—was just a warmup.

* * *

While he was in London back in September 1938, Berlin had discussed the depressing news from Europe with a friend, the Hungarian-born film producer Alexander Korda; their talk later inspired him to write a song of uplift:

> It's a lovely day tomorrow;
> Tomorrow is a lovely day.
> Come and feast your tear-dimmed eyes
> On tomorrow's clear blue skies. . . .
> Just forget your troubles and learn to say,
> Tomorrow is a lovely day.

A year later Berlin interpolated "It's a Lovely Day Tomorrow" into *Louisiana Purchase*. In the spring of 1940, as Nazi tanks rolled down the Champs-Élysées, "the great Gallic musical star Irene Bordoni, for many Americans the embodiment of France, stood on the stage of New York's Imperial Theatre," Robert Kimball writes. "Her voice breaking, her eyes filled with tears, night after night Bordoni sang Berlin's poignant song of hope 'It's a Lovely Day Tomorrow' while friends and family—their fate uncertain—were trapped behind enemy lines."[26]

The frightening times were getting more frightening by the day: all at once, far across the sea didn't feel far enough. Years later, Barrett writes, her mother told her that she and Irving "genuinely believed, in the summer and fall of 1940 and well into the next year, that the Germans would win. . . . Eventually, so went their worst imaginings, [Hitler] would conquer England, then Canada, then 'make an arrangement' with the United States that would amount to conquest. And if that happened, how would they protect their half-Jewish children? Flee to South America?"[27]

It is the precise scenario of *The Plot against America*. Only then it seemed all too real a possibility.

* * *

"I think that 'God Bless America' is the most important song I've ever written," Berlin told a reporter that July, adding prophetically, "I'll tell you more about it in five years."[28]

He was speaking personally as well as artistically. It was a song he had written from the heart, one he felt intensely protective about. As the tune's popularity skyrocketed, "I was grateful beyond words that it had the quality it seemed to have," Berlin said, "but I wanted to make sure it kept that quality."[29] With the help of ASCAP, he barred the use of "God Bless America" "by all swing arrangers, by all cabarets and night clubs."[30] Only Kate Smith was allowed to sing it on the radio.

(She also made a best-selling recording of the song, as did Bing Crosby.) On July 10 Berlin took his high-mindedness even farther, eschewing all profits from "God Bless America" in perpetuity by establishing a trust fund for the distribution of the song's royalties—$43,646.66 as of that date—with the Boy Scouts and Girl Scouts of America named as beneficiaries.[31]

That summer "God Bless America" was performed, with its composer's evenhanded approval, at both the Republican and Democratic National Conventions. Through the summer and fall Berlin and his wife campaigned hard for FDR; Irving sang "God Bless America" at civic events around the country. Barrett recalled hearing her father perform his composition at a Boy Scout rally in the Catskills: "No other singer, not Crosby, not Judy Garland, not Kate Smith herself, or a long procession of opera stars performing it on state occasions, could give it quite that conviction," she writes. "He meant every word. . . . It *was* the land he loved. It *was* his home sweet home. He, the immigrant who had made good, was saying thank you."[32]

On September 24, 1940, at the Golden Gate International Exposition on Treasure Island, San Francisco, ASCAP brought together more than forty of its most distinguished members, including George M. Cohan, W. C. Handy, Jerome Kern, Harold Arlen, Hoagy Carmichael, Johnny Mercer, and Irving Berlin, to perform their most famous works to an audience of thousands. In an evening concert in the California Coliseum, Cohan sang a medley of his hits, including "You're a Grand Old Flag," and "Over There"; Kern played "Smoke Gets in Your Eyes"; Handy took a cornet solo on his "St. Louis Blues."

"But the most rapturous applause," an account of the evening read, "is saved for Irving Berlin, who sings his own 'God Bless America.' Berlin's tenor voice is frail and has a limited range, but it is a moving performance." A very young Herb Caen, writing for the *San Francisco Chronicle*, described audience members standing, without prompting, and joining Berlin: "Hundreds started to sing with him. Then thousands. And when he came to the end of his song, 15,000 Americans were on their feet singing with him."[33]

16

◆◆◆◆◆

What Is a War Song?

IN HIS BOOK about the song "White Christmas," Jody Rosen
describes a chance encounter between Irving Berlin and Mark
Sandrich in Washington, D.C., in April 1940, while Berlin was
in town "for a film premiere."[1] The source for the story—the
subject file for the movie *Holiday Inn* in the Irving Berlin Collection at the Library of Congress—is impeccable, but something about the account feels off. For one thing, film premieres
in Washington were and are about as common an occurrence as
Senate subcommittee meetings in Culver City, and it's hard to
imagine any such event, let alone one that would have brought
two such consummate show-business creatures as Berlin and
Sandrich to the nation's capital at the same time—with the
possible exception of the gala premiere of Frank Capra's great
comedy-drama *Mr. Smith Goes to Washington*, held in Washington on October 17, 1939: the biggest thing to hit D.C.,

Capra recalled in his memoir, "since the British sacked the White House."² It seems far likelier that their chance meeting occurred in the autumn of 1939 than in the spring of 1940, for reasons that will soon become clear.

Irving would have been happy to see Sandrich, with whom he had clicked from the start of their work together at RKO; he would have known that the director had recently left that studio and was now producing and directing musicals at Paramount. In the course of their conversation, Berlin mentioned his idea for a revue based on holidays—an idea, Sandrich instantly replied, that would make a perfect movie for Bing Crosby.

There is no indication in Berlin's February outline for a holiday show that he'd had anything in mind but Broadway. But Sandrich's mention of Crosby, a superstar of movies, records, and radio, would have stirred Irving's interest, despite his recent disenchantment with Hollywood. Irving and Mark Sandrich "parted with a handshake agreement to undertake the [holiday movie]," writes Rosen.³ And Berlin would soon set to work on writing Bing Crosby another hit song.

The origins of "White Christmas" are more than a little murky, probably because Irving Berlin wanted it that way—he preferred, at all times, to be the one in control of his backstory. *The Complete Lyrics* dates the tune's composition to 1938 or 1939, "either in New York or possibly at the Arizona Biltmore Hotel in Phoenix or perhaps in both places"—but then quotes the Hollywood columnist Erskine Johnson, who interviewed Berlin while he was publicizing the movie *White Christmas* in 1954, stating flatly that "the melody was written in August 1938."⁴

This timing makes a certain amount of sense. It was the summer of Berlin's (latest) discontent with Hollywood, the *Carefree* summer. The song's seldom-sung verse (Crosby would omit it from his megaselling recording) captures perfectly the silky-seductive monotony of Lotus Land:

> The sun is shining,
> The grass is green,
> The orange and palm trees sway.
> There's never been such a day
> In Beverly Hills, L.A.
> But it's December the twenty-fourth,
> And I am longing to be up north . . .[5]

And yet a lead sheet for "White Christmas" didn't exist until 1940—January 8, 1940, to be precise, when Berlin bustled into his 799 Seventh Avenue offices first thing on a Monday morning, startling his staff, and announced to his longtime musical secretary Helmy Kresa: "I want you to take down a song I wrote over the weekend. Not only is it the best song I ever wrote, it's the best song *anybody* ever wrote."[6]

The story comes from an interview Kresa gave some forty-five years after the fact. But Berlin himself seemed to confirm the account, at least partially, when he told a reporter in 1954: "Much as I'd like to take a bow and say I anticipated [the tune's] future success, I must admit I didn't. Maybe because it was so easy, comparatively, to write I didn't realize its potential. I wrote it in two rather brief sessions and that's fast for a song. Some take a lot more work."[7]

Never one to resist burnishing his legend, he made it sound as if "White Christmas" all but leaped fully formed from his brow. But as Rosen writes:

> Berlin was a fanatical tinkerer whose songs often gestated for months, or even years, undergoing several revisions before taking final shape; for every song that he completed, there were dozens of false starts and half-songs, snatches of song lyrics and piles of hastily scrawled angles [song ideas] that he stored for future use.[8]

In all likelihood Berlin *completed* "White Christmas" over that weekend in January 1940. As he later told a reporter, "I wrote it for a revue I intended producing, changed my mind and put it away until it was used in a Bing Crosby picture."[9] Making Berlin and Sandrich's chance Washington meeting far more likely to have happened in the fall of 1939 than in spring of 1940.

By January 1940 Berlin would have finished most if not all of the score for *Louisiana Purchase*. The dread Christmas season, the time of mourning for his lost son, had come and gone. He would have been eager to turn the calendar page, to move on to the next thing. And if by January 1940 he had already had that fateful encounter with Sandrich, the next thing would have been the holiday movie, and a big new song for Crosby—the kind of thing that would have propelled him through a blazing bout of weekend work.

Berlin spent much of the spring and summer occupied with "a slew of phone calls, cables, and face-to-face meetings" about the movie project that would come to be called *Holiday Inn*.[10] On September 3, he wrote his Hollywood lawyer George Cohen, with pride and barely concealed excitement: "There is already one song done for the picture. It is called WHITE CHRISTMAS and it is to be a main part of the contract."[11]

But he still hadn't signed his contract with Paramount, nor had the studio come to terms with Crosby. Wrangling proceeded through the fall. Then, on December 4, *Variety* reported, "Irving Berlin has postponed his movie project, because he is planning a Broadway review [*sic*] entitled *Crystal Ball* . . . for projected Spring 1941 opening."[12] Perhaps Berlin was trying to force Paramount's hand. On January 14, 1941, he wrote tensely to Cohen, "I am not willing to sign any contract before they have signed Crosby."[13]

Paramount finally signed Crosby, though Berlin continued to dicker with the studio. But there would be no opening for

Crystal Ball, in spring 1941 or at any other time, though Irving's dream of mounting another *Music Box Revue* would linger for years.

* * *

The headlines grew bigger and blacker by the day: even inside Fortress America, 1941 was a terrifying year. While the Nazi war machine kept rolling across Europe and North Africa and raining bombs on England, a battle of words between isolationists and interventionists raged inside the United States. Charles Lindbergh, the leading proponent of America First, continued to proclaim that neither rescuing Britain nor saving Europe's Jews from German aggression was worth a drop of American blood or a dime of its money. His wife, Anne Morrow Lindbergh, claimed in her best-selling anti-interventionist tract *The Wave of the Future* that democracy was on the way out and fascism, or something very much like it, was the inevitable next step. And Ellin Berlin, though so reticent by nature that the effort nearly undid her, made a series of network radio speeches sharply criticizing the isolationists in general and the Lindberghs in particular.

For his part, Irving kept touring "God Bless America," most prominently at FDR's unexampled third inaugural in January, where he led the singing of the song some twenty times over two days of festivities.[14] "God Bless America" would continue to be sung all over the country—but neither it nor any of the rest of Berlin's oeuvre would be heard on most U.S. radios for ten long months in 1941, due to a boycott by NBC and CBS of all ASCAP composers—the cream of American songwriting—as a result of the performance-rights organization's demand for a large hike in license fees. The boycott fostered the rise of a competing organization, Broadcast Music, Inc.—BMI—which sought out artists in genres that ASCAP shunned: blues, rhythm and blues, gospel, country, folk, and Latin. BMI's rise would lead to changes in the music business that would shake ASCAP and its writers to the core.

The boycott was just one of several headaches for Berlin in the hectic winter and spring of his fifty-fourth year. Though he and Crosby had committed to *Holiday Inn,* Paramount still hadn't signed the male and female costars. He also faced growing discord with his longtime business partner Saul Bornstein over Berlin's largess in the matter of the "God Bless America" trust fund—Bornstein didn't mind that his partner had given away his own royalties from the song, but he bitterly resented the lost publishing revenues. And then there was a truly serious worry, much closer to home: the trial of Joe Schenck.

In his role as 20th Century–Fox's chairman, Irving's oldest friend had been making payoffs for years to the heads of Hollywood's powerful stagehands' union, the International Alliance of Theatrical Stage Employees, or IATSE. All the studio heads did it: the bribes were simply a cost of doing business. But the union was run by the Chicago mob, and when a copy of a $100,000 check Joe Schenck had written to a racketeer mysteriously found its way to federal investigators, the feds, beginning what would become a major investigation of gangland involvement in Hollywood labor practices, brought Schenck in on the catchall charge of tax evasion. Though Irving (along with Charlie Chaplin and the chief justice of the California Supreme Court) gave a passionate character defense of his friend at his New York trial, Schenck was convicted that April and sentenced to three years in prison.

* * *

In May, Berlin hunkered down with Mark Sandrich to hammer out the story of *Holiday Inn.* As all concerned knew well, a movie musical needed only the barest wisp of narrative to propel the action from one song to the next, but there had to be *something,* "since the revue format was considered unsuitable for the screen," Berlin's notes on the project indicate, with a hint of disappointment. At first, he wrote, there was "just a thread of a story about an easygoing fellow who works only on holidays." What seemed more important than story at the start, besides the songs, was casting—a matter of keen interest to Berlin as a profit participant in the project. He and Sandrich, Berlin recalled, "thought it would be a great opportunity to co-star the screen's number one male singer with the screen's number one male dancer, Fred Astaire."[15]

Paramount brass thought differently, as Berlin and Sandrich quickly discovered when they met with the studio's head, Y. Frank Freeman, and its production chief—who happened to be the omnipresent Buddy DeSylva, back from Broadway and no longer at 20th. And in this matter, the man who had so recently been Berlin's professional ally was now his adversary. "When Mark proposed co-starring [Crosby] with Fred, DeSylva shook his head," Berlin remembered. "I can get George Murphy for $50,000," he said. "Why do I need Astaire for $100,000?"

"If we don't get Fred Astaire," Sandrich said simply, "we don't do the picture."[16]

They got him, and work on *Holiday Inn*'s story, such as it was, proceeded. The plot revolved around Crosby's laid-back character, a retired trouper who buys a farm, and when farming doesn't work out, turns the farm into an inn that's open only on holidays. Astaire's character, an old show-business pal of Crosby's, stops by and tells Bing his idea is crazy. Enter the daughter of a rich family with a nearby estate.

"It will obviously be a two boys and a girl setup," Berlin wrote in his notes that spring. The goal, he continued, was to work as many holidays as possible into the story, with Bing the innkeeper devising an angle for each as an attraction to guests: "For instance, on New Year's everyone has to make a resolution, but of course will not keep. Washington's Birthday everyone has to tell the truth. Mother's Day everyone brings his mother. Etc."

It wasn't Shakespeare.

Irving planned, he said, to repurpose two old songs in the film—"Lazy" ("more or less Bing's theme song") and "Easter Parade"—and had written four new ones: "Happy New Year Blues," "White Christmas," "Plenty to Be Thankful For," and "This Is a Great Country," for the Fourth of July. And he had two new numbers in the planning stages: "The Wedding of Capital and Labor," for Labor Day, and "Abraham," for Lincoln's birthday.[17]

Then it was over and out and back to New York.

* * *

By August he was in Hollywood again, having "completed 10 songs for the picture," according to *Variety*—though one of them, the best of them by far, continued to demand his attentions.[18] As Berlin later told Erskine Johnson, "I took it off the shelf and polished the lyrics a little, and went to Bing's dressing room . . . to get his okay on all the songs for the picture. I was nervous as a rabbit smelling stew. I sang several melodies and Bing nodded quiet approval. But when I did 'White Christmas' he came to life and said 'Irving, you won't have to worry about that one.'"[19]

That's the story Berlin told while plugging the movie *White Christmas* in 1954, and it's a good one—Berlin, as always, expertly spinning his own history. But the testimony of Walter Scharf, the Paramount house arranger who was in charge of orchestrating Irving's score for *Holiday Inn*, widens the view and broadens the narrative.

As Scharf recalled to Jody Rosen, Berlin was fixated to the point of obsession on "White Christmas" from the moment he walked onto the Paramount lot that August, and the arranger was "the man who faced the brunt of Berlin's anxieties." And his anxieties were on full display when he first performed the tune for Scharf, Sandrich, and a group of studio executives, whose reaction was the same as that described again and again by those listening to Irving Berlin demonstrating a new song: confusion and disappointment. "It was almost like a child playing with three fingers," Scharf remembered. "Nobody knew what to make of it."[20]

And while Crosby's initial reaction to "White Christmas" may have been as positive as Berlin described, his response when Scharf said he thought the song would turn out well was something else again: "I *hope* so," the singer said, rolling his eyes.[21]

The job of orchestrating "White Christmas" was a process of hard labor and false starts, undertaken over a period of weeks in Scharf's office, where the arranger discovered what a succession of previous orchestrators and musical secretaries had found: though Berlin lacked the technical skill to describe the harmonies he wanted, he knew precisely what they were when he heard them.

Even when their work together was done—"when Scharf was making final transcriptions of the orchestrations that the pair had decided upon—Berlin couldn't tear himself away," Rosen writes. "Rather than go back to his hotel, the songwriter camped out in Scharf's office, catching the odd hour of sleep on the sofa while Scharf toiled at the nearby piano."

When the time came for Crosby to prerecord the song (which he would lip-sync in the movie), Sandrich and Scharf were eager for a respite from Berlin. Go back to your hotel and get some rest, they told him. Technical preparations and rehearsals would take hours.

"The session was speedy," Rosen writes. "Crosby stepped to the microphone and finished 'White Christmas' in his usual two takes." But when Scharf happened to walk over to the far corner of Stage 5, he spied Berlin, crouched timidly behind a couple of soundproofing flats. "I'm sorry," Berlin said sheepishly. "I couldn't bring myself to go. . . . So when are you going to start the recording?" He thought he had been listening to a rehearsal. Crosby had already left to play golf.[22]

* * *

At the beginning of the war in Europe, Berlin's songwriting had taken the conflict into account only metaphorically: in the cloud-gathering verse of "God Bless America," the tear-dimmed chorus of "It's a Lovely Day Tomorrow." These were followed by some head-on (and less successful) attempts: an undated set of lyrics (no music is known to survive) called "Hitler and Mussolini," for a projected vaudeville-style dance number in the *Crystal Ball* revue; October 1940's "A Little Old Church in England," about a London church destroyed in the Blitz ("A pile of mortar and brick appears / Where it had peacefully stood for years"); February 1941's "When That Man Is Dead and Gone" ("Some fine day the news will flash: / Satan with a small mustache / Is asleep beneath the lawn"); and June's "Any Bonds Today?" ("The tall man with the high hat / And the whiskers on his chin / Will soon be knocking at your door / And you ought to be in"). And on June 20, 1941, in Massey Hall, Toronto, over the airwaves of the Canadian Broadcasting Corporation, Berlin himself introduced a number called "When This Crazy World Is Sane Again":

> Someday we'll all be in clover,
> Someday we'll all be in tune,
> Someday our fears will be over,
> Someday—let's hope it is soon.[23]

But the Berlin song that would have the greatest impact on America and Americans as the United States entered the global conflict was one that, on the face of it, had nothing whatever to do with war: the great and strange holiday song he'd first conceived of years earlier and had been obsessing over ever since.

What makes "White Christmas" so great, and so strange? Dozens of writers have poured thousands of words into analyz-

ing the bridgeless fifty-four-word chorus of this seemingly simple tune. "People read a lot of things into that song," Berlin
himself said, "that I didn't put there."[24]

When the *Washington Post* asked him about the song's origins in 1954, Berlin harked back nostalgically to his tenement
past: "I was a little Russian-born kid, son of an Orthodox rabbi,
living on the lower East Side of New York City. I did not have
a Christmas. But I bounded across the street to my friendly
neighbors, the O'Haras, and shared their goodies. Not only
that, this was my first sight of a Christmas tree. The O'Haras
were very poor and later, as I grew used to their annual tree, I
realized they had to buy one with broken branches and small
height, but to me that first tree seemed to tower to heaven."[25]

Nostalgia is certainly essential to "White Christmas"—
Jody Rosen links the tune to the great tradition of wistfully
reminiscing songs such as Stephen Foster's "The Old Folks
at Home"—as is something else: secularity. In the 1930s and
1940s, when the United States was unquestioningly a Christian
nation, the vast majority of Christmas songs sung and heard
by Americans, including the two Bing Crosby had recorded in
1935, "Adeste Fideles" and "Silent Night," were, quite appropriately, concerned with the essence of the holiday: the birth
of Jesus Christ. (Three notable exceptions were "Jingle Bells,"
first published—as a Thanksgiving song!—in 1857, and "Santa
Claus Is Coming to Town" and "Winter Wonderland," both
debuting in 1934.) Strikingly, Tin Pan Alley had largely failed
to capitalize on the holiday—perhaps because so many of its
songwriters and publishers were Jews.

Irving Berlin clearly planned to redress this omission with
"the best song anybody ever wrote." And since it wouldn't have
been authentic for him as a Jew to write about Christ, he chose
to universalize his lyric. And herein lies a first clue to the deep
strangeness of "White Christmas." For what could be stranger

than a Jew out of the shtetl and the Lower East Side creating what is arguably the most influential Christmas song of all time? No less an observer than Philip Roth considers the question (along with "Easter Parade") in his brilliant dissection of antisemitism, the novel *Operation Shylock:*

> The radio was playing "Easter Parade" and I thought, But this is Jewish genius on a par with the Ten Commandments. God gave Moses the Ten Commandments and then He gave to Irving Berlin "Easter Parade" and "White Christmas." The two holidays that celebrate the divinity of Christ . . . and what does Irving Berlin brilliantly do? He de-Christs them both! . . . Is anyone really dishonored by this? If schlockified Christianity is Christianity cleansed of Jew hatred, then three cheers for schlock.[26]

The only person dishonored in the formulation is Berlin himself, with Roth's peremptory dismissal of "White Christmas" as schlock. *Is* "White Christmas" schlock? Even as fervent and articulate an admirer of the Berlin canon as Jody Rosen has his doubts. " 'White Christmas' isn't my favorite song; it isn't even my favorite Irving Berlin song," he writes. Rather, it is, he continues,

> about as good a summary as we have of the contradictions that make pop music fascinating: it is beautiful and grotesque, tacky and transcendent. Revisiting the song's story, listening for the thousandth time to its maudlin, immemorial strains, we are reminded of a trick in which Berlin and Crosby both specialized: how, time and again, they proved that art and schlock could be one and the same.[27]

Of course, there are estimable commentators enough to certify "White Christmas" as real art. Alec Wilder writes with a certain wonderment of "the truly daring succession of notes in the chromatic phrase of the main strain" of the song.[28] Philip

Furia calls the tune "the counterpart to Robert Frost's great modern poem, 'Stopping by Woods on a Snowy Evening,' which uses the simplest of rhymes and the barest of imagery to evoke a beautiful but melancholy scene."[29] And a year after America's entry into World War II, when the song had become a touchstone for hundreds of thousands of homesick U.S. soldiers and sailors stationed overseas, Carl Sandburg would write:

> Away down under, this latest hit of Irving Berlin catches us where we love peace. The Nazi theory and doctrine that man in his blood is naturally warlike, so much so that he should call war a blessing, we don't like it. . . . The hopes and prayers are that we will see the beginnings of a hundred years of white Christmases—with no blood-spots of needless agony and death on the snow.[30]

But we are getting ahead of ourselves. When we left off, sometime in the last week of November or the first week of December 1941, Bing Crosby was headed out for that round of golf after prerecording "White Christmas," Fortress America was still secure, and only a handful of people connected professionally or familially to Irving Berlin had ever heard the song.

On Sunday morning, December 7, a lovely day in Los Angeles, Irving and Ellin were relaxing in Beverly Hills when the news from Pearl Harbor hit with the force of a bomb. Soon they would head back to New York to spend a more somber holiday than usual with their daughters. On the night of December 24, on his *Kraft Music Hall* broadcast, Crosby sang "White Christmas" to America for the first time.[31] Still staggered by the unprecedented surprise attack, America barely took notice.

17

This Is the Army, Mr. Jones

As a bruised and reeling USA jumped into war mode at the dawn of 1942, so did Irving Berlin. All at once, history had given him permission to alchemize the anxiety of the past three years into a big idea, and one came to him quickly: an updated revival of his World War I all-soldier revue *Yip! Yip! Yaphank*— as a Broadway fund-raiser for the entire U.S. Army. In late February, Berlin phoned the army chief of staff, General George C. Marshall, to pitch the idea, and on March 11 he received an official go-ahead on War Department stationery. Berlin's stilted reply reflected both his exaltation and his slight discomfort before high-Wasp military authority. "I am delighted to accede to your request," he wrote. "I need not assure you that I will give this all my time because nothing is closer to my heart."[1] He was speaking with utter honesty about his powerful feelings of patriotism, but whether consciously or unconsciously, was also expressing another of his heart's desires: here, at long last, was the chance to do another revue.

He went to work immediately, setting up shop in early April at his old stomping ground, Camp Upton, and like a commanding general himself, throwing together a staff: a copyright manager for the new songs he would write (all the profits from which—more than six million dollars in the end[2]—would go to the Army Emergency Relief Fund), stage and music directors, costume and set designers, and a first sergeant to make sure the three hundred cast members the War Department promised him would maintain army spit and polish.

He decided to call the new show *This Is the Army*. And thanks to his new friends in the War Department, Berlin had the luxury of cherry-picking its cast—a number of them professional entertainers in civilian life—from combat divisions around the country. Freed from the need to negotiate with the Musicians Union, he was also able to assemble a full orchestra of forty-four pieces, many more than would be found in the pit of a standard Broadway musical.[3]

Moreover, Berlin's troupe wasn't varied only geographically: at his insistence, the army permitted him to recruit some two dozen black soldiers for his company. At a time when the armed forces were still segregated, the choice was revolutionary, but also, given the centrality of African Americans in American show business, thoroughly practical. Just like that, the cast of *This Is the Army* became the only integrated unit in the armed forces in World War II.

The revival as Berlin conceived it, Jablonski writes, would have the same basic structure as *Yip! Yip! Yaphank*, "opening with a minstrel show that led into a vaudeville segment (with acrobats, jugglers, and a magician), interspersed throughout with musical numbers and dances. Once again, impersonations of celebrities peppered the second act, set in New York's by-then-famous Stage Door Canteen."[4]

And in the next-to-last number on the bill Irving cast himself, back in his World War I uniform, complete with wide-brimmed campaign hat and puttees, reprising "Oh, How I Hate to Get Up in the Morning."

The gala premiere was set for the significant date of July 4, 1942, at the two thousand–seat Broadway Theatre, on Broadway and 53rd, and time was short. But Berlin knew how to write under pressure: working at a furious pace—in other words, like Irving Berlin—he produced a score of twenty numbers in an astounding three weeks, a song a day. The tunes struck familiar chords: patriotic ("Some Dough for the Army Relief"), humorous ("My Sergeant and I Are Buddies"; "Ladies of the Chorus," a drag number), and romantic ("I Left My Heart at the Stage Door Canteen"). As usual, Berlin's wry humor predominated. The show's title song, for all practical purposes, and the tune that would ultimately have the most staying power, was a stirring march with a comic twist, "This Is the Army, Mister Jones":

> No private rooms or telephones;
> You had your breakfast in bed before,
> But you won't have it there anymore.[5]

But there were also new, tough notes. Pearl Harbor had darkened Americans' optimistic worldview. "The boys are different from those who served in 1918," Berlin told the *New York Times* in May. "They have seen many of [their] ideals shattered. They are more serious and grim. They know what they are up against."[6]

* * *

Things didn't look good for America at the outset of the war. In the first few months of 1942 the Japanese scored a series of crushing victories against Allied forces in the Pacific. (U.S. forces wouldn't engage with Germany until the end of the year.) Americans at home were brave on the surface but terrified beneath: nobody knew how long this awful conflict might last or how much sacrifice it would demand. All the while, at Camp Upton and then in rehearsals at the Broadway Theatre, Irving Berlin was trying to construct a peppy, uplifting, coherent army show, and take full command of his sizable and talented staff and company.

His stage director was twenty-four-year-old Sergeant Ezra Stone, a professional stage actor since the age of fourteen and Henry Aldrich on the nationally beloved radio serial *The Aldrich Family*. On the radio Stone sounded like a Middle American adolescent, but in real life he was a sharp-witted, opinionated Jew from New Bedford, Massachusetts (born Ezra Chaim Feinstone) who resembled a chubby Oscar Levant.

Though Stone was initially awed by Berlin ("I got the full blast of his charm—very warm, very enthusiastic, very gracious," he recalled), the two men quickly locked horns.[7] The first disagreement occurred when Irving informed Stone that he wanted *This Is the Army* to begin as *Yip! Yip! Yaphank* had: with a minstrel show, the company in blackface. Stone found the idea repugnant, and said so—only to find himself up against a man who not only didn't seem to realize that the convention was outdated but did not like his authority to be questioned. The director was able to change Berlin's mind only with a diversion, arguing the impracticality of getting all those men out of blackface in time for the next scene.[8]

The composer's initial intransigence about a minstrel-show opening could well have stemmed from the fact that he had recently written just such a scene, now committed to celluloid in the soon-to-be-released *Holiday Inn*. In Berlin's Lincoln's-birthday number, "Abraham," celebrating the sixteenth president's emancipation of the slaves, not only Bing Crosby, but all the rest of the scene's white performers, performed in blackface. Crosby's getup, complete with stovepipe hat and shaggy white Uncle Ben sideburns, was a grotesque imagining of black imaginings about Abraham Lincoln.

What's more, the song contained the couplet

When black folks lived in slavery
Who was it set the darky free?

But after an editorial in the *Baltimore Afro-American* objected, Berlin had his office change the offending word to "negro" (uncapitalized) in all future sheet music of "Abraham." "No song is important enough to offend a whole race," Berlin told *Time.*[9]

* * *

Circumstances threw Berlin and Ezra Stone into each other's company at length as they prepared *This Is the Army.* As he had not been able to do in *Yaphank* days, Irving went home every weekend, as did Stone; each Monday he and Stone would make the two-hour drive back to Camp Upton together. "The small talk quickly ran out," Stone recalled. To relieve the silence, the young sergeant would turn on the car radio.

"He hated that," Stone remembered. When he asked Berlin why, Berlin answered, quite simply, that he didn't like to hear other people's music. "He was half-joking, half-serious," Stone said.

Once, George Gershwin's "Mine" happened to come on the radio, and the young director blurted, "That's my favorite song." He instantly realized he had committed a faux pas: "I could feel the blast and the chill," he recalled.

"Why is it your favorite song, Ezra?" Berlin asked.

"Well," Stone stammered, "I guess because it has two melodies and two sets of lyrics, and it's unique."

"It's an old trick," Berlin replied, clippily. "I've used it many times."[10]

Irving also came up against his twenty-three-year-old music director, the Juilliard-educated Private Milton Rosenstock. When Rosenstock had the audacity to question Berlin on a musical point, Rosenstock recalled many years later, Berlin fixed him with a dark stare and said, "You never did a show. What do you know about show business?

"In the business," Berlin told Rosenstock, "I'm a certain kind of man. When I go home, I'm another man. One doesn't interfere with the other. The businessman is hard. If somebody can't do something, and I love him, he won't have the job. If somebody I hate, who disgusts me, can do the job, he's got it."[11]

When his confidence in Rosenstock failed to rally, Irving summoned a longtime collaborator, the sixty-four-year-old conductor Frank Tours, from retirement in California. After watching young Rosenstock lead the orchestra through a rehearsal of *This Is the Army*'s overture, Tours told Berlin, "I'm going back to California, Irving. You don't need me. This man knows much more about it."[12]

Meanwhile, Ezra Stone continued to get under Berlin's skin—to the point that Berlin decided to bring in a new director, the thirty-three-year-old Joshua Logan, a Broadway wunderkind whose rising career had been sidetracked when he was drafted. Arriving in the midst of rehearsals, Logan was elated to meet the living legend: "Berlin was at once excitement, glitter, comedy and melody," he wrote in his memoir. "I fell for him immediately. But at that moment he was in a black panic. The show, he said, had good things, but it was a badly arranged jumble. He gave me nine days to take it apart and put it back together into a hit."[13]

Logan watched rehearsals, expecting chaos. Instead he saw ten rows of bleachers filled with highly talented soldiers; he witnessed "song after song . . . jokes, big choruses, acrobatic acts . . ." He was thrilled. But "when I turned to Irving, overcome with enthusiasm, he said, 'It's not right, it's not right. You've got to fix it.'"[14]

This was the seldom-seen Berlin, the one prey to bouts of self-doubt, the one who covered his agonizing uncertainties with toughness and jauntiness and ceaseless nervous activity. This was the man the generals and the three hundred talented, sometimes fractious men under his command were all looking to for nothing short of brilliance.

This Is the Army premiered at the Broadway Theatre on the warm Saturday night of July 4. "I remember the special vibration at the fourth row center where we sat," Mary Ellin Barrett writes, "embedded in generals to the front, generals to the back, generals to the right and left. . . . The word from people who had seen a dress rehearsal was that something wonderful was about to unfold."[15]

And then the show was off and running, the dozen first-act songs—from "This Is the Army, Mister Jones" to "My Sergeant and I Are Buddies" to "The Army's Made a Man Out of Me," sung by Ezra Stone himself ("I used to be a tenor/But now I'm a baritone"[16]), to the black soldiers' number, "That's What the Well-Dressed Man in Harlem Will Wear," to "How about a Cheer for the Navy?"—interspersed with juggling, acrobatics, magic, a comedy routine by Private Julie Oshins, a Catskills tummler in civilian life. The audience roared with delight, and during intermission, buzzed with surprise that these young soldiers, amateurs, most of them, were not only performing competently but putting on a superb revue. Once again Irving Berlin, America's top songwriter, had delivered the goods.

The second-act curtain went up. After a salute to the air corps and a skit in which the GIs hilariously impersonated such Stage Door Canteen stars as Alfred Lunt and Lynn Fontanne and Gypsy Rose Lee, the spotlight focused on the short, dark-haired man in his old doughboy's uniform, yawning and swinging his legs over the side of a cot, then standing up, solo, at center stage. Berlin opened his mouth to sing, and the roof fell in. The audience roared and rose to its feet, applauding furiously for a full ten minutes.

Finally he was able to croon, in his high, hoarse, Lower East Side–accented tones, his old song, that lilting throwback to a sweeter time, when all a soldier had had to worry about was having to get up too early in the morning. And there was no question of modesty, false or true, on the part of Irving Berlin, whom even his wife called "a ham at heart."[17]

The crowd, of course, went wild once more when he finished. Even the critics stood and cheered. But when *This Is the Army*, which continued to draw packed houses and generate hundreds of thousands for the Emergency Relief Fund, went past its originally scheduled four-week run to eight weeks, then twelve, there were those who were eager to charge Berlin with vanity and even exploitation.

The songwriting community was scarcely less envious and backbiting than it had been when the young phenom and his "Alexander's Ragtime Band" had conquered the world in 1911. Three decades on, between "God Bless America," *Louisiana Purchase*, and now *This Is the Army*, Irving Berlin was on a major roll, and some of his competition didn't like it a bit. "Amid the huge popularity of the army show," Jablonski writes, "word soon began circulating around Tin Pan Alley: it was all a scam. Berlin was exploiting the war for his own benefit, effectively mounting a massive publicity campaign that cost him nothing."[18]

Cole Porter, whose own (for-profit) army show *Let's Face It!*, starring Danny Kaye and Eve Arden, was a big Broadway hit, got wind of the sniping and wrote his old friend a sympathetic letter, using the affectionate nicknames the two geniuses had bestowed upon each other:

> I can't understand all this resentment of my old friend, "The Little Gray Mouse." It seems to me he has every right to go to the limits towards publishing the music of his Army show, as every cent earned will help us win the war. . . . It's really distressing in these days of so much trouble to know that

envy still runs rampant even on that supposed lane, Tin Pan
Alley.

Rat Porter[19]

* * *

On August 4, 1942, a month to the day after *This Is the
Army*'s opening, *Holiday Inn* premiered, in a benefit for Navy
Relief, at the Paramount in Times Square. The movie's screen-
ing was preceded by a thirty-minute stage show celebrating
Irving Berlin's thirty-fifth year in show business. The show,
broadcast live on NBC radio, featured, among others, the bands
of Benny Goodman, Xavier Cugat, and Kay Kyser performing
Berlin songs—and Berlin himself, who, Rosen writes, "made a
brief appearance on the Paramount stage before racing out the
side door, jumping on his bicycle . . . and pedaling ten blocks
north to the Broadway Theatre, where he threw on his costume
in time for his *This Is the Army* star turn."[20]

Everybody seemed to love *Holiday Inn*, from the Hollywood *machers* who saw the picture in early screenings to ticket-
buying audiences to the major critics. And the movie's real star
was its score. "The plot is not taken too seriously," one columnist wrote, "for there is no doubt that Crosby will win the girl,
even from the start, and that Astaire, a scheming gold-digger,
will be justly served. What really holds 'Holiday Inn' together
is its songs and dances, and there is no letdown in them."[21]

But as for the score's centerpiece, the tune in which Berlin
had invested so much hope, the collective silence was deafening. The *Times*'s review mentioned "White Christmas" only in
passing, calling it "tender"; the *Herald Tribune* called it "tuneful"; and *Variety* failed to mention it at all.[22]

Some members of Berlin's inner circle had worried aloud
that the song was too schmaltzy; even Berlin, despite his boast
to Helmy Kresa, was uncertain early on about the song's prospects.[23] The number he was betting on at first was the film's

Valentine's Day number, "Be Careful, It's My Heart"—a workmanlike ballad that began with the arrestingly weird lines

> Be careful, it's my heart
> It's not my watch you're holding,
> It's my heart.[24]

The tune was nice, Bing Crosby's gorgeous reading made the hokum halfway believable (though the twenty-six-year-old Frank Sinatra, on his recording with the Tommy Dorsey Orchestra, sounded infinitely more vulnerable and therefore actually credible), and by the time of *Holiday Inn*'s premiere, after Berlin's hardworking staff "had stroked, cajoled, threatened, and charmed bandleaders, radio executives, and sheet music jobbers," Crosby's Decca recording was number ten on the Lucky Strike Hit Parade.[25] It soon rose to number two—and then stalled.[26]

Then something amazing began to happen.

"White Christmas," which Berlin had deliberately chosen *not* to promote at the outset, preferring to wait until the commencement of the holiday season (in those sweetly innocent times, after Thanksgiving), started to sell like crazy, on record and in sheet music. In August. By mid-September it was, Irving wired triumphantly to Mark Sandrich, "our number one song without any plugs." By the first week of October it stood at the top of the Hit Parade, and—with recordings by the Freddy Martin Orchestra and Dinah Shore joining Crosby's—*Billboard* proclaimed "White Christmas" "one of the most phenomenal hits in the history of the music business."[27]

At the end of November *Time* reported that the song had sold 600,000 units, outpacing "any previous hit in Irving Berlin's hit-studded career," and, all by itself, sparking hopes on Tin Pan Alley for a revival of the fading sheet-music business. Then the magazine noted the reason why: "With thousands of U.S. servicemen facing snowless Christmases from North Africa to Guadalcanal, White Christmas has unexpectedly become the first big sentimental song hit of World War II."[28]

Families at home listened to it longingly; soldiers and sailors far from home listened longingly too. "There was," Jablonski writes, "hardly a Post Exchange (PX) coin-operated jukebox anywhere that did not feature Bing Crosby's recording of the song."[29]

Soon the war would be taking the song's composer far from home, too.

*　*　*

On September 26, after 113 standing-room-only performances at the Broadway, Berlin closed in New York and took his show on the road aboard a special train, stopping first in Washington, D.C., where President Roosevelt watched the production from a box at the National Theatre, then threw the cast a party at the White House. On another night Ellin and Irving dined alone with just the president and FDR's friend and adviser Harry Hopkins and Hopkins's wife. Berlin also lunched in the Senate dining room and heard Senator Alben Barkley give a speech about him before a full session of the upper house. "Irving is having a wonderful time," Ellin wrote to Alexander Woollcott from Washington. "He is getting through this show the rewards of all the shows and all the years."[30]

But the years also exacted penalties. Woollcott would die the following January, of a heart attack, during a radio panel discussion on Nazi Germany. And his death was, Mary Ellin Barrett writes, the latest in "a year of losses": Max Winslow in June, Alice Duer Miller in August, and George M. Cohan in November. (Sam Harris had died in July 1941.)

Woollcott was just fifty-six, only a year older than Berlin. "I was really depressed by Alec's death," Berlin wrote to the Broadway columnist Irving Hoffman—depressed, in all likelihood, not only by the loss of a close friend and adoring biographer, but by the death of a near contemporary.[31]

The show went on. *This Is the Army* proceeded from Washington to Philadelphia, Chicago, St. Louis. At Christmas the tour stopped in Detroit, where Ellin and the girls had also traveled to spend the holiday with Berlin. A photographer snapped the family in their suite at the Book-Cadillac, with their hotel Christmas tree, and after the show they met backstage with some of Berlin's "boys": Sergeant Alan Anderson, his stage manager; Corporal Milton Rosenstock, the conductor, and Sergeant Ezra Stone, with whom the songwriter had apparently had a falling out, which Berlin never discussed afterward.

Stone, who as a Broadway veteran and a national radio star had his own ego, "was outspokenly bitter," Alan Anderson recalled years afterward, about Berlin's replacing him with Josh Logan at the last minute.[32]

And then there had been an incident.

There was a piece of stage business at the end of the show, as the company was making its bows: Berlin would appear from the wings at stage left and Sergeant Stone would order the men to turn left face and present arms to acknowledge the author. But at the Washington performance, at the moment Berlin appeared at stage left, Stone gave the company a right-face order instead, to acknowledge FDR, who was sitting in a box to the side of the stage. Thus the company's three hundred men appeared to be simultaneously turning their backs on Irving Berlin. In front of the president.

Berlin was furious. Stone claimed he'd made an error in the pressure of the moment. "I can't really believe that Ezra acted in innocence," Anderson later said.[33]

Two and a half months later, at the Municipal Auditorium in St. Louis, the tension simmering between Berlin and Stone finally came to a boil. After a performance one evening, Berlin summoned Anderson, Milton Rosenstock, and Stone to his dressing room and charged Stone "with having gotten a whole lot of his cronies on the show who added nothing to the show and that many of them were Jewish." Berlin, Anderson recalled, "said something like, 'I've heard criticism that we have a lot of Jews in the show who are avoiding the real war.'"

Stone reacted angrily. "What about your friends?" he said, accusing Berlin of loading the show with song pluggers he knew from the music-publishing business. In a book Anderson later wrote about the *This Is the Army* tour, he claimed Stone used the phrase "kikes in the music division."[34]

Berlin's response is unrecorded.

His discomfort about the show's ethnic composition didn't come out of left field. Adolf Hitler had been raving antisemitic slanders and threats for years, and Lindbergh and Coughlin et al. had been fanning the flames in the United States. And though Irving Berlin was *Irving Berlin*, who could de-Christ Christmas and Easter and command wealth and respect, Wasps ruled America, and he was worried there were too many Jews in the show.

* * *

The touring company reached its final stop, San Francisco's War Memorial Opera House, on February 1, 1943. After two weeks of performances there—*This Is the Army* had by now earned two million dollars for the Army Emergency Relief Fund[35]—the 359 members of the cast and crew boarded their train and headed down to Los Angeles, where a tent city had been built for them near the Warner Brothers studio lot, to prepare to shoot the movie adaptation of the show.

Jack Warner had paid $250,000, a huge sum, for the screen rights—this too went to Army Emergency Relief—and tapped Michael Curtiz, the director of *Casablanca*, to helm the picture. Two screenwriters, Claude Binyon and Casey Robinson, were assigned to transform Berlin's narrative-free revue into a three-act story that America could love. This they did—and in the process completely desemitized *This Is the Army*.

The movie's plot revolves around a song-and-dance man

named Jerry Jones (played by veteran song-and-dance man George Murphy) who, after being drafted into the army in World War I, creates a revue called *Yip! Yip! Yaphank* and is then sent to fight in France, where a shrapnel wound ends his dancing career. A quarter-century passes. After Pearl Harbor is attacked, Jerry's singing and dancing son Johnny (played by Ronald Reagan) enlists and prepares to go into battle—when he's ordered to sidetrack himself and stage a new army revue. Reluctantly he puts together a show called *This Is the Army* and takes it on tour. After a climactic performance for President Roosevelt, Johnny and the cast are sent off, happily, into combat.

Much as Berlin had whitened up his own true story for the plot of the movie *Alexander's Ragtime Band*, *This Is the Army* subtracted Berlin as artistic genius and reinserted him, playing himself, sort of, as the cute old guy in a World War I uniform who reluctantly gets out of bed to sing "Oh, How I Hate to Get Up in the Morning." Which was written by . . . Jerry Jones?

But this was the terror of Jews at the top of show business in those times: that white Christian America, which of course was the way America defined itself then, would also feel that there were *too many Jews in the show*. This was the reason the Jewish founders and presiding moguls of Hollywood, Goldwyn and Mayer and Zukor and the Warner brothers, so vigorously promoted a white-picket-fence, Andy Hardy vision of America, even allowing their films to be purged of Jewish references so they could be exhibited in Nazi Germany in the years leading up to World War II.

Abel Green outdid himself with his *Variety* review of *This Is the Army*, the movie:

> After the history of World War II is written, the Warner Bros. filmization will stand out like the Empire State Bldg. amidst the many other highlights in the motion picture industry's contributions to the home front and war front. . . .

It's democracy in action to the hilt. It's showmanship and patriotism combined to a super-duper Yankee Doodle degree.[36]

Viewed today, the movie is sheer camp, pure propaganda, its humor elephantine and its tone of patriotic uplift treacly and unrelenting.[37] But—and this is the key thing—viewed then, as Allied forces were locked in a life-or-death struggle against fascism on two fronts, and American boys were fighting and dying overseas, *This Is the Army* was stirring, even thrilling, stuff.

And America went for it, big-time. The picture, released in August, would be, in *Variety*'s words, a "box-office tornado,"[38] putting more than eight and a half million dollars into the coffers of the Army Emergency Relief Fund. As the summer of 1943 turned to fall, Allied victories in Europe and Pacific were turning the tide of the war. And Irving Berlin was back home in New York, though not for long.

18

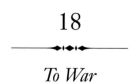

To War

The home he returned to was a new one. Ever practical, Berlin had moved his family from the plush double townhouse on East 78th to a penthouse apartment a third the size at 1 Gracie Square. On the one hand, the smaller digs were appropriate for a breadwinner earning no bread at all—not even expenses—from *This Is the Army*. On the other hand, his other all-consuming enterprise, Irving Berlin Inc., was doing very well indeed: *Holiday Inn* had enjoyed a triumphant run and "White Christmas" had become a business in itself, by now having sold more than two million copies of Bing Crosby's Decca recording and more than one million units of sheet music.[1] At the Academy Awards in March, standing on the stage at the Cocoanut Grove to present the Oscar for Best Song, Berlin had opened the envelope to find he was presenting it to himself for "White Christmas."[2]

He was rich and colossally successful, yet there was a part of him that would never leave the Lower East Side, would never find any security secure enough. And Ellin, remembering her father's financial downfall all too clearly, would have been his willing partner in frugality.

He could have stayed at home, counted his receipts, and written a new show, some escapist fun perhaps, to take Broadway's mind off America's troubles. But there was a war on, and what *This Is the Army* had stirred in him stirred in him still. He was a national figure, with national responsibilities. So he elected to cross the German-patrolled Atlantic to London, where Nazi bombs were still falling, to take the army show on a tour of the British Isles. All proceeds would go to British War Relief. Berlin had always had a soft spot for England, and the feeling was mutual.

He flew over by army plane in mid-October, checked into his favorite hotel, Claridge's, and set straight to work writing new material for English audiences. The cast and crew sailed a week later aboard the *Monarch of Bermuda*, part of a convoy of some hundred vessels plying the U-boat-infested waters. Of necessity, given wartime travel restrictions and security concerns, the company had been trimmed to half its original size. Before leaving, Irving had sat down with Sergeant Alan Anderson, his stage manager, and "selected out a hundred and fifty names," Anderson recalled, "using the whole roster and saying, 'This guy's a fuck-up' and 'This guy I don't think can physically hack it' and 'This one's personality is difficult.' We knew we were going to have to live in close quarters overseas. . . . It would take considerable cooperation from everybody."[3]

The culling carried enormous significance: many of those removed would wind up in combat units and in mortal danger. Anderson himself made the cut, as did the comedian Julie Oshins, and music director Milton Rosenstock. Corporal (later Warrant Officer) Ben Washer, the show's publicist and Berlin's travel facilitator and general fixer, remained essential. Not surprisingly, Ezra Stone had fallen into the difficult-personality category, and thus by the wayside. By coincidence, Josh Logan had been posted to London; pulling strings, Berlin had Logan's commanding officer release him to polish the staging of the show.

In tweaking *This Is the Army* for British audiences, Berlin felt a strong need for a new song, one that would emphasize the solidarity of the American and British armed forces—a solidarity that was by no means easy or natural, given English ambivalence about the United States in general, and in particular about the massive amounts of military and financial aid the younger country had been extending to England since the beginning of the war. And then there was the thorny issue of soldier's pay—considerably higher for the Yanks than for their British counterparts. Since America's entry into the conflict, GIs arriving in Great Britain had found themselves the objects of fascination, envy, and resentment: "overpaid, oversexed, and over here," as the joke went.

"Aware of such tensions," Jablonski writes, "Berlin returned to his London hotel one night . . . and soaked in a hot tub. Meanwhile, he pondered the song, and 'by the time I was through with the bath, I had it all worked out.'"[4]

This was the story he told later. The less-colorful truth is that he'd had made a stab at a song of solidarity before leaving for England, and, as was often the case when he was trying to set noble sentiments to music, had come up with a lyric (no music survives) that was both earnest and deadly dull:

> England and America
> Standing side by side,
> Bound together with ancient ties
> That the oceans can't divide . . .[5]

The lyrics he worked out in the bathtub at Claridge's, seasoned with just the right dash of gentle humor, were much better:

My British buddy,
We're as diff'rent as can be;
He thinks he's winning the war,
And I think it's me . . .[6]

Clad in his trusty doughboy's uniform, Berlin himself performed the charming tune at the gala premiere, at the Palladium on the night of November 10, 1943. He may have been a
ham at heart, but his theatrical acumen also told him that he
was the man to put this all-important number over. His instinct
was correct. "London Wild Over 'This Is the Army,'" the Associated Press reported the next day.

> Irving Berlin "said it with music" Wednesday night at the
> British premiere of "This Is the Army" and enthusiastic Lon-
> doners were saying Thursday that he and the army cast [have]
> "done more for Anglo-American unity than all the lend-lease
> from Washington."
>
> The audience at the Palladium already was warmed and
> applauding when the dark-haired slim composer pranced out
> of the wings and went into the hit song he had composed
> especially for the British performance.[7]

The applause kept coming. After the curtain on the fourteenth, Noël Coward visited backstage, screamed "I love you
all!" to the cast, and embraced Berlin.[8] And on the sixteenth
King George and Queen Elizabeth themselves attended, with
their daughters the princesses Elizabeth and Margaret. When
the royal family went backstage afterward to meet Berlin, the
queen told him, "I've never seen anything like it. 'My British
Buddy' brought tears to my eyes."

"Thank you, Ma'am," Irving said. "I wrote the song in a
bathtub."[9]

*   *   *

After two weeks at the Palladium, the show struck out for
the provinces: Glasgow, Manchester, Liverpool, Birmingham,

Bristol, and then across the Irish Sea to Belfast. In early February the company returned to London, and on the sixth gave a special matinee performance at His Majesty's Theatre for the new Supreme Allied Commander, General Dwight D. Eisenhower.

Irving Berlin seldom kept a journal, but he did jot down some impressions of the latter part of the British tour, and took particular note of that afternoon. "I was brought to General Eisenhower's box during intermission," he wrote,

> and met him for the first time. He wanted to know all about the show and the boys and told me how much he liked the first act. . . . After the second act, General Eisenhower was so enthusiastic that he asked to come back and speak to the boys.[10]

The boys were mightily impressed by Eisenhower. "What a dynamic personality!" a company member named Max Showalter wrote in his journal.[11] And Alan Manson recalled: "He had this Kansas voice; if you closed your eyes you'd think it was Clark Gable. He said, 'I know you think you're just doing a show and that you feel maybe you're not really soldiers, but don't ever think for one minute that you're not doing a job. This thing is so important.'"[12]

Four months later to the day, the invasion of Europe from whose secret planning Eisenhower took an afternoon to see *This Is the Army* would begin the final stage of the war. And the day after he met Eisenhower, Irving Berlin learned that the supreme commander had recommended to Army Chief of Staff Marshall that Berlin should take *This Is the Army* to North Africa and Italy.

* * *

For many years the story has persisted that Prime Minister Winston Churchill met with Irving Berlin during World War II under the impression that he was meeting with the philosopher and Oxford don Isaiah Berlin. The story is amusing; the facts are confusing. During the war Isaiah Berlin worked in Washington for the British Information Services, sending his Foreign Office confidential, wittily worded dispatches on the doings of the U.S. government. The story goes that Churchill had enjoyed the letters and, hearing Isaiah Berlin was going to be in London, had him invited to lunch, but that wires were crossed and Irving Berlin was invited instead.

Berlin's account of the afternoon doesn't clarify matters:

> *Wednesday, February 9th:* I arrived at 10 Downing Street at one-twenty-five. . . . I was ushered into the Prime Minister's private sitting room on the ground floor. Mrs. Churchill received me. The guests had not arrived. Soon they all came— I think about ten of them.
>
> Mrs. Churchill introduced me to her guests, but, as usual, I failed to get their names. There was a British officer (a General I think), a Lady Somebody, a young girl, her cousin, and two other men, one of them a member of the Cabinet, and another woman.
>
> Mr. Churchill soon came in, dressed in his "zipper" suit. We were served some Sherry and then went in to lunch. The British Officer sat at Mrs. Churchill's right, and I sat between her cousin and the Lady Somebody. Mr. Churchill sat on the other side of her.

The scene is set for confusion. Churchill does most of the talking at lunch, holding forth wittily on early British history; Berlin speaks with Mrs. Churchill's cousin about *This Is the Army*'s tour of Great Britain. Then the prime minister turns to Berlin and asks what reaction he got during the tour through the provinces.

> I made a general answer about how well we were received, etc. We discussed the amount of money earned for British Service Charities. He heard the figure wrong. I told him of

the song I had written, "My British Buddy." He thought I said "My British Brother."

The question arises: if Churchill truly believes the Berlin lunching with him to be an Oxford don assigned to British Information Services, how does the PM suppose him to be earning sums for British Service Charities, not to mention writing songs? After lunch the women leave the dining room and the men stay behind for coffee. The plot thickens. "Mr. Churchill asked me to move over next to him," Berlin continues.

> He turned and very abruptly asked what I thought of the political situation in America. I was fussed and told him very frankly that I knew little about politics. . . . I told him that if Mr. Roosevelt wanted to be our next president, he would be elected; that instinctively I felt that most people would vote for him. I turned and asked him whether he didn't think so, and he said, quite seriously, "I'm not allowed to say."

Churchill then asks Berlin "whether they still felt that the war would be over in 1944. I didn't realize [Berlin writes] he meant the American people and thought he was asking me that question. I looked at him and said, 'This is something for my grandchildren—to have the Prime Minister of Britain ask me when the war will be over.' He smiled at this."

Churchill asks Berlin how he feels about the Zionist movement; Berlin pleads ignorance and instead tells Churchill an amusing story about a "Jewish gentleman . . . with an Irish brogue" whom he met in Belfast.

"All in all, [the prime minister] was very pleasant," Berlin writes.

> After we joined the ladies in the sitting room, Mr. Churchill left. In saying goodbye to me he said, "Well, you didn't answer any of my questions and I don't think you had the chance to ask any." He said this with a twinkle.[13]

* * *

As his company prepared to leave for Algiers, the first stop on the extended tour, Berlin was sailing back across the Atlantic with serious business to attend to. His relationship with his partner Saul Bornstein had been worsening for a long time, and the 1942 death of Max Winslow, who'd also had a one-third interest in the firm, had brought matters to a crisis, as had the battles over the publishing revenues from "God Bless America" and *This Is the Army.*

Berlin was eager to split with Bornstein and, by extension, Irving Berlin Inc. But was the songwriter free to take his enormously valuable catalogue with him? Did Berlin own his songs, or did the company?

There was also the matter, never discussed publicly by Berlin then or later, of Bornstein's stealing from the firm. Berlin's secretary Mynna Granat had discovered years earlier that the business manager was writing contracts to nonexistent songwriters for nonexistent songs, advancing funds to the imaginary composers from the firm's account, and pocketing the money himself, a practice apparently widespread in music publishing. Bornstein, little thinking that Granat would be interested in such things, had stored the dummy contracts in the company safe, to which she had access.[14] The loyal secretary had alerted Berlin to Bornstein's misdeeds, yet at the time Berlin had been unwilling or unable to take decisive action, perhaps in part because, apart from his larceny, Bornstein was running the firm so successfully. Now, amid the pitched battles over "God Bless America" and *This Is the Army,* Irving had to do something.

But on this trip he failed. "I not [only] wasn't able to get anywhere with [Bornstein]," he later wrote to a friend, "but I left my affairs in serious condition. The copyrights of all my songs are involved."[15] In the third week of March he left matters to the lawyers and rejoined his traveling show in Naples.

* * *

The venue was the San Carlo Opera House, miraculously untouched by German bombs even as much of the city lay in ruins. And the Luftwaffe was still bombing: the partially destroyed palace of Victor Emmanuel, on the waterfront, had received twenty-two direct hits before *This Is the Army*'s cast and crew moved in, and took a twenty-third while they were there, though no one was injured.

Showalter's journals bring to vivid life the experience of being in the war zone that was southern Italy in the spring of 1944: the terror of being awakened in the middle of the night by air-raid sirens and the deafening boom of antiaircraft guns and bombs; the pity of seeing starved Italian children begging for cigarettes and chocolate among the ruins; the strangeness of happening upon swastika-emblazoned wrecks of German planes lying among the blooming fruit trees and eternal cypresses of the lush countryside.

In Naples audiences were trucked in from the front just north of Caserta. "The men were brought down in relays to see the show," Alan Manson remembered. "They didn't know what they were getting. They thought they were going to see an accordion player and a broad shaking her ass. But we gave them an enormous show, with 150 men."[16]

A hundred fifty men, and Irving Berlin himself. And he wasn't just singing "Oh, How I Hate to Get Up in the Morning" anymore. While on the tour Berlin wrote some dozen occasional songs, not just because the circumstances inspired him but also knowing that nothing would so please the soldiers who came to the shows as material fresh from the great man, tailored specifically to them, and sung to them by him. "Mr. Berlin introduced a new number he'd just written," Showalter noted, on April 15, 1944, while the company was still in Naples.[17] The song was called "The Fifth Army's Where My Heart Is." One imagines Berlin, in his tour outfit of insignia-less fatigues, demonstrating the tune—block chords on the keyboard; reedy, hoarse voice—while his boys listened carefully:

> We landed in Salerno
> And kept right on the go
> As we fought our way through Napoli
> Into Anzio . . .[18]

The Fifth Army, under the command of General Mark W. Clark, was in the process of battling its way up the west side of the Italian peninsula to Rome. German defenses were heavy and deeply entrenched; Allied casualties were high. And just a few days after Berlin played the new song for his troupe, he was performing it for a Fifth Army audience, at the Teatro Garibaldi, a provincial opera house in the little town of Santa Maria Capua Vetere, some fifteen miles north of Naples and that much closer to the front.

"We're playing now for the people we were meant for all along: the front-line soldiers," Lieutenant John Koenig, the show's scene and costume designer, wrote to a friend in New York.

> They come, literally, from their foxholes, are piled into trucks and are driven sometimes two hours to get here. They're in helmets and mud; they come early and sit quietly waiting for the show. Some chew gum, some just stare ahead of them in a daze of unfamiliar relaxation. . . .
>
> The curtains part, the show begins and today's worries —the only tangibles over here—vanish. . . . And twice a thousand-odd hands clap in hysterical appreciation. The GI's are not timid with applause; they whistle, yell and roar approval. . . .
>
> But there's something almost too concentrated and frantic about their enjoyment, something too hysterical in their laughter. This show must be the only real pleasure they've had in a long, long, time.[19]

In his upbeat letters to Ellin, Berlin made Santa Maria seem like a safe haven from the war. He didn't mention the thunder of battle rolling down the valley, the ubiquitous land mines, the nightly air raids. Rather, he wrote of the comfortable apartment he and Ben Washer shared: its sunny balcony, its well-tuned piano, the delectable pasta cooked by the attentive landlady Signora Polito.[20]

The other side, the side "most satisfying for me," he wrote to his wife, was making visits with a few of the boys every other day to army field hospitals, closer still to the fighting, to put on brief entertainments for the wounded and the dying. "The shows are mostly outdoors on an improvised platform," Berlin wrote, with determined cheerfulness. "The stunt lasts about a half hour and is very informal and different every time. It's all ad lib and sometimes when the mike is good I play for myself."[21]

Yet as Ben Washer's diary made plain, it pained the Old Man deeply to see these hurt or maimed young soldiers, some not much older than Mary Ellin. On one visit Berlin leaned down to talk to a gravely wounded young GI, who asked him in a weak voice to write to his wife. Moved, Berlin jotted down her name and address and promised he would write to her. But by the time he did, the young woman was a widow.[22]

*   *   *

By early May, the Allies were mounting their fourth and final assault against the heavily fortified town of Monte Cassino, some forty miles to the northwest of Santa Maria and the last bastion before Rome. On the eighteenth Monte Cassino fell at last: the four-month struggle to capture the pivotal objective had resulted in fifty-five thousand Allied casualties. On June 4 General Clark and the Fifth Army marched into Rome.

Two days later, over American Forces Radio, came the electrifying news of the Allied invasion of Normandy. The next day, Showalter wrote,

rumors were flying thick and fast . . . about the show breaking up—that we were going to Egypt—that we were going
home, etc. Mr. Berlin had had a company formation after the
evening show—he read several letters from Gen. Eisenhower
and Gen. Marshall commending us, and then told us that
from Italy we go to Egypt, India, Australia, Hawaii, etc.—in
short, we're going around the world! It was wonderful news
for me, but the older fellows with wives and children were
disappointed and I can't blame them.[23]

Rome, in distinct contrast to Naples, seemed barely touched
by the war. The Royal Opera House was a clean, beautiful,
modern theater in a still-vibrant city. But the capital was really
two cities: the poor and middle class were suffering grave food
shortages, while the rich, many of whom had collaborated with
the Nazis, lived as they always had.

Wealthy Romans made up much of the audience at *This
Is the Army*'s one performance for civilians during the Italian
tour, a benefit for the city's orphaned children. At the end of
the show Berlin asked for requests, and obligingly performed
"Always," "Cheek to Cheek," and "Alexander's Ragtime Band."
Then, speaking through an interpreter, he told the crowd how
his family had come from Russia and settled in an Italian neighborhood on the Lower East Side.[24] And then he got the audience to sing along with him on one of the songs he'd learned
there, the old Neapolitan street melody "Oi Marie."

He later said that he'd planned the sing-along from the
start, just to be able to hear "all those well-dressed, upper-class
people, Fascists among them, singing this song of the streets as
if it were the Italian national anthem."[25]

* * *

In July the company flew south to entertain at the complex
of army air force bases around Foggia and Bari, near the heel
of the Italian peninsula's boot. It was a far cry from Rome: the

region was sweltering and dusty, the accommodations were rugged, and the air corps food miserable. The troupe was plagued by mosquitoes and dysentery. Yet Berlin wrote Ellin in his usual upbeat key: "Playing for the Air Corps is thrilling and they can't do enough for us. . . . It's blistering hot here but I brave it every day so I can come home with a healthy tan."[26]

But he had been touring for four months, and his fifty-seven years were wearing on him—as was the still-unresolved Bornstein business. He needed a rest, and he needed to get his affairs in order. "After supper, we had a meeting in the Mess Hall," Showalter noted in his journal,

> and Mr. Berlin got up to give us his farewell speech—said he hated to leave us but he wasn't well, his business was in a muddle, and he had to go to his dentist in Hollywood to have two more teeth pulled out, which wouldn't leave him very many of his own. . . . Just how much longer we'll be gone, he didn't know, but he hopes to join us in the Pacific because "I'm a ham, I might as well admit—I enjoy playing those shows, and I'm crazy about you guys—you're wonderful."[27]

Then he boarded a military plane to begin the long flight home.

19

And Back

"I CAN SEE HIM STILL at the Lew Beach dinner table, just back from Italy, his deep tan camouflaging the weariness," Mary Ellin Barrett writes. "He is animated with his stories, his souvenirs. But I knew, watching him walk up the path to the cottage with my mother, that this was a man badly in need of a break."[1]

His wife, too, was weary: from the grinding, unending anxiety about her husband's safety, and from the constant effort of putting on a brave face for her daughters. "She wouldn't have shown to the children how worried she was. But I know she was worried," her oldest daughter remembered.[2] Ellin tried to keep as busy as possible with wartime volunteer work, and she continued her writing career, finishing her first novel, a romance with an anti-Nazi theme called *Land I Have Chosen.* (There had been a flurry of distracting activity that spring when, in a deal Berlin himself negotiated from England, Warner Brothers bought the rights to the book for what even *Variety* conceded was a "somewhat extraordinary" $150,000, a record for a first novel.)[3]

But she fretted ceaselessly that Irving's natural curiosity, the boyish capacity for wonder that was so key to his brilliance, would put him in harm's way. He had written her, after the fact, about a hair-raising flight he'd taken, just for the fun of it, with an air corps flyboy: straight up for thousands of feet in a P-38, power dives and barrel rolls. And all she had to do was read the newspapers to know that he was too close to the front lines. And then there were the phone calls from Irving's older sister Gussie, more than once saying the same thing: "'Ellin, I had a terrible dream last night—I dreamt Irving was killed.'"[4]

The sweet respite in the Catskills wouldn't last long. Soon Berlin was off once more, to the city, to attend to very complicated business having to do with Saul Bornstein and the office, business that he preferred not to talk about.

It was a mess that had to be cleaned up once and for all, and negotiations went on through Labor Day. In the end, Berlin got to keep his precious copyrights, free and clear, and Bornstein got $400,000 and, under a new company named Bourne Inc., the entire non-Berlin catalogue, including such standards as "Moon over Miami" and "My Mammy" and all the songs from Disney's *Snow White, Pinocchio*, and *Three Little Pigs*, including Ann Ronell and Frank Churchill's huge hit "Who's Afraid of the Big Bad Wolf?"[5]

Irving Berlin Inc. was no more. But the phoenix that rose from the ashes, Irving Berlin Music Company— the 1914 name reborn—would continue to prosper mightily, from new (and still endearingly messy) offices at 1650 Broadway, next to the Winter Garden Theatre and just a block and a half from the old offices at 799 Seventh.

And what of Bornstein's larceny, never mentioned in the many *Variety* accounts of the divorce? "With proof in hand that

Bornstein had been accumulating an illegal income from their firm," Jablonski asks, "why didn't Berlin sue him or have him prosecuted?"[6] In the end, he writes, Berlin decided to sweep the matter under the rug, apparently wishing to avoid bad publicity and let go any vindictiveness he may have felt toward the man who, while lining his own pockets, had, after all, run the business for so many years, basically very successfully.

* * *

"On Saturday, December 30th we disembarked with Berlin on the pier to greet us," Max Showalter wrote in his journal, laconically acknowledging that *This Is the Army*'s creator had rejoined his traveling troupe in Milne Bay, New Guinea, after an absence of five months.[7] In the interim, Irving Berlin had briefly rested with his family, resolved his legal issues, and gone to Hollywood to see his dentist and do some movie business— he and Mark Sandrich had signed with Paramount to make a new Bing Crosby musical, *Blue Skies*. Meanwhile the company had taken the show to American bases in Egypt, Iran, and India, raising the morale of thousands of GIs while braving heat, sandstorms, insects of all varieties, and terrible food, but also getting to see places and meet people such as they had never imagined back home.

From Milne Bay, Irving Berlin and his troupe commenced the final portion of their tour, traveling along the north coast of New Guinea from army base to naval base to air corps base, playing wherever they were asked, including, Showalter noted, "a colored quartermaster camp." Then, boarding an old Dutch freighter called *El Libertador*, the company sailed north, taking the show to the Admiralty Islands and the Philippines. Danger —Japanese bombers still flying missions, holdout pockets of Japanese troops in the jungle—was always close by. If the contrasts of war-racked Italy had been jarring to Berlin, his time in the southwest Pacific must have felt almost surreal: the overpowering heat and humidity, the crack of rifle fire and the boom of artillery all too close at hand, the one-night stands in remote camps on improvised outdoor stages, for huge audiences, under tropical downpours.

Yet as former members of the troupe recalled, "Berlin flourished in these strenuous conditions. He relished the camaraderie among the men. Their youth and unquenchable enthusiasm proved infectious, and he himself exhibited remarkable physical stamina."[8]

For exercise, he would dive off the ship and swim in the sparkling Pacific. And on New Year's Eve, Max Showalter wrote,

> after doing a show at the Navy Base across the bay . . . Mr. Berlin threw a beer party for us in the officer's club at Camp —it was a thatched hut—the band played—we sang. . . . Mr. Berlin even turned cartwheels—in addition to plenty of beer we had sandwiches and a wonderful time![9]

Cartwheels!

Along with the fellowship of the enthusiastic young troupe, there was the pleasure, day after day and night after night, of witnessing military audiences' reaction to his creation. Showalter, on a performance at Oro Bay: "It rained during the show but none of the audience budged—I climbed to the top of the hill after ['Mandy'] and what a thrill it was to see approximately ten thousand faces laughing and enjoying the show—really a wonderful sight!"[10]

Early in the tour, in response to audience demand, Berlin had begun closing the show by leading a sing-along of "God Bless America." One night in New Guinea, he devised a remarkable piece of business to go along with the tune: "During the finale when we all sing 'God Bless America' with Mr. Berlin," Showalter writes, "he asked to have a complete blackout, then asked everyone in the audience to light a match or turn on their flashlights—the whole hill was ablaze with twinkling lights and it was really a thrilling sight to see!"[11]

Berlin echoed the sentiment in a letter to Ellin: "To see an audience of 17,000 light up like so many flickering stars would even impress Hassard Short. Every new place we played I told you was the most thrilling . . . well this is really it."[12]

In another letter from the Pacific he wrote,

> I feel . . . I will have done a harder and better job here than anywhere else. . . . The show continues to tremendous audiences—at different bases and of course different theatres. This is tough on the boys but the result is terrific. . . . I have come in for much personal praise and attention. I wouldn't say this to anyone but you, but I am greatly pleased with the dividends here.[13]

I am greatly pleased with the dividends here. An admission of forgivable pride from a great artist who had not only done his country a great service by creating *This Is the Army* but shown remarkable bravery in touring with it in two theaters of war.

On March 23, 1945, aboard the ship, Berlin gathered the company and told them the next evening's performance would be his last: he was headed back to the States. The tour would continue without him, he said, for several more months. What he didn't say was that on March 5 Mark Sandrich had died of a heart attack at age forty-four—another tragic personal loss for Berlin, as well as a professional one—and that Paramount had sent him an urgent request to return to Hollywood to determine the fate of *Blue Skies.*

* * *

This he did, but only after taking care of even more important matters first: flying home to see his family, then traveling to Washington to brief the War Department on his Pacific tour. On April 12 President Roosevelt died. The nation reeled; the war, and life, went on. Four days later *Variety* reported: "Irving Berlin flies west Tuesday to stay all summer working on Paramount's 'Blue Skies.' Mrs. Berlin follows with the family as soon as a house is obtainable. First essential on Berlin's studio business will be a producer-director replacement for the late Mark Sandrich."[14]

For much of the last eighteen months he had been in motion, with little respite, and for the past four months he had traveled thousands of hard miles, performing in tropical rainstorms, sailing to far-flung ports aboard a rusty freighter, flying endless hours on military planes. He had reaped considerable personal dividends, he had experienced much exhilaration, but he had also seen the terrible effects of war, in Europe and in the Pacific. He was nearing sixty, and he was tired, far more tired than he let on.

"He was totally exhausted," Mary Ellin Barrett told me in 2011, with the perspective of her years, though as a self-involved eighteen-year old in the summer of 1945, what she saw was a man "none the worse for wear, though too thin, his face under the jet-black hair deeply creased. He wore glasses a lot of the time now, but if anything, the glasses made him look younger, covering the circles under his eyes."[15]

Like *Holiday Inn*, *Blue Skies* was to be a showcase for an array of old and new Berlin songs, its love-triangle plot—again Berlin's idea—more or less a paraphrase of the earlier movie's. Once again Bing Crosby would play his devil-may-care character, in this case a nightclub owner rather than an innkeeper, who got the girl, lost the girl, got the girl back. The twenty-three-year-old Joan Caulfield, a discovery of Mark Sandrich's, was to play the girl. And Fred Astaire was once again to costar as Crosby's rival—but then he changed his mind. At forty-six, after almost forty years in show business, the great dancer was seriously considering retirement. So Paramount, hoping for movie magic, made a curious casting choice, hiring Paul Draper, a brilliant dancer who combined tap and ballet but had next to no motion-picture experience, as the second lead.

Not only had Draper never really acted in a movie (he had

danced, but not spoken, in 1936's *Colleen*), but Sandrich's replacement, Stuart Heisler, a competent-enough director, had never made a musical before. And Joan Caulfield, who was to sing and dance in *Blue Skies*, was quite beautiful but could neither sing nor dance. For this reason, Heisler wanted her replaced—but Crosby, Catholic and in the throes of a troubled marriage to an alcoholic, had begun an affair with the young actress and fallen deeply in love. And Crosby, Paramount's superstar, vetoed Heisler's decision.

Then, as Paul Draper's first scene was filmed, it turned out that he stuttered. (Had Paramount never thought to screen-test him?)

Dividing his days between songwriting for the picture and visiting the troubled set, Berlin was more than earning his big money. "You can't imagine the headaches," he told his family.[16]

Matters improved markedly when Astaire changed his mind about retiring and signed on to replace Draper. And the non-filmmaking part of the Hollywood summer proceeded pleasantly if not surreally after the jungles of New Guinea and the Philippines: setting up house in a bungalow on the verdant grounds of the Beverly Hills Hotel, Irving and his family entertained Joe Schenck, Fred and Phyllis Astaire, the Levants, the Frank Capras, and George Cukor and his houseguest Somerset Maugham. While Irving played gin rummy with Astaire and dined with Charlie Chaplin and Kate Hepburn, the *This Is the Army* troupe continued across the South Pacific, taking the show to one dot on the map after another: Iwo Jima, Eniwetok, Kwajalein. In Guam, a few days after the horrific bombing of Hiroshima and Nagasaki, the company changed ships to the far more luxurious S.S. *Haleakala* and steamed east toward Hawaii.

And part of her father was still overseas with them, Berlin's oldest daughter recalled. He corresponded with several members of the troupe that summer, and was in continual touch with people in Washington, "about getting his 'boys' promotions, home leave, discharges, or reassignments, about winding up the show and the possibility of his rejoining the company for a final performance in Honolulu. That he was having a hard time winding down was not apparent, however, except in conversations I'd hear between him and other men, the exchange of war stories that I found boring, not having been there, not knowing, not really understanding."[17]

For his wife and children it was enough that he had come home safely. But Berlin was suffering a form of dislocation similar to that felt by millions of other men who returned from combat zones overseas to placid American lives. He had been to many places in his fifty-eight years, but mainly he had worked, and the work had taken place in his mind, inside "my shell," as he confessed in a letter home: at the piano and the typewriter, around the same ambits on Broadway and in Hollywood.[18] Then, for the better part of eighteen months, he had gone so far outside his ambit that nobody who hadn't been through it could ever understand.

Depression set in. And with it, worsening insomnia. When his niece Katherine, who was staying with the family that summer, would innocently ask, "How did you sleep, Uncle Irving?" he would say, "Not a wink, Katie, not a wink."

He was joking, his family observed; but he really was exhausted.

"My doctors tell me when I finish this picture [*Blue Skies*] I should take six months off, a complete rest," he wrote his Hollywood lawyer, George Cohen. "But you know me, I'm better off keeping going."[19] He then went on to describe his next project, one last Music Box Revue.

* * *

The *Blue Skies* score contained a lot of Berlin songs—old Berlin songs. From "A Pretty Girl Is Like a Melody" and "You'd Be Surprised" (1919) to "Everybody Step" and "All By Myself" (1921) to "Blue Skies" (1926) and "How Deep Is the Ocean?"

(1932). The film's two big production numbers were 1930's "Puttin' on the Ritz," in which, thanks to trick photography, nine Fred Astaires sang and danced at once, and 1933's "Heat Wave," performed by Astaire and the "Puerto Rican Pepperpot," Olga San Juan. A baker's dozen other Berlin tunes, none newer than 1933, were used as background music.

The wealth of nostalgic numbers was justified by the span of the film's story, which extended from just after World War I to a decade or so thereafter. And the sheer bulk of Berlin material in the picture justified the songwriter's rich deal with Paramount. But only one new number, the wistful ballad "You Keep Coming Back Like a Song," had any staying power, remaining on the Hit Parade for eleven weeks yet more or less vanishing thereafter. The lack of strong new tunes was a disconcerting sign: of the movie's troubled production, and perhaps of something else.

Blue Skies' headaches certainly hadn't helped Berlin's creativity. Nor had the dislocating effects of his return from war. Nor had his worries, mostly kept to himself, about being, at fifty-eight, "no chicken," as he wrote to Ellin. And during the three exhausting years he had devoted to *This Is the Army*, younger songwriters had flourished. The forty-three-year-old Richard Rodgers, in the prime of his working career, had "composed the scores to *By Jupiter* with Lorenz Hart and, with Oscar Hammerstein II, the historic *Oklahoma!* and *Carousel*," Jablonski writes. "Three full musical scores, and all of them major hits."[20]

Maybe it was time to yield the stage to younger men. "I am looking forward to the end of my end of *This Is the Army*," he wrote home from the Pacific, "and the beginning of a peaceful older age—after *Blue Skies* and the *Music Box Revue*."[21]

A week after Berlin finished his work on *Blue Skies*, General Marshall invited him to Washington for a "meeting," subject undisclosed. Berlin walked into the chief of staff's office to find a roomful: not just the chief of staff but Ellin, plus two of the generals he'd known overseas, plus his old friend and fellow Algonquin Round Tabler the playwright Robert Sherwood. In a surprise ceremony, Marshall conferred upon Berlin the Medal for Merit, the nation's highest civilian honor, "for the performance of extraordinary service to the United States Army" in creating and producing *This Is the Army*, and for "building and maintaining morale among soldiers and civilians"—not to mention netting the Army Emergency Relief Fund more than nine million dollars.[22] Berlin was deeply touched.

In the third week of October, aboard a military plane commandeered for him by Eastern Airlines head Eddie Rickenbacker, he flew to Honolulu to make an end of his end of *This Is the Army*, and of *This Is the Army* itself. "Mon. (Last Benefit Performance—Honolulu Stadium)," Max Showalter noted laconically, on October 22. "Steak for lunch.—Mr. B."[23]

Before a cheering crowd of seven thousand, Berlin and his troupe performed his show together one last time. One last time, handsome, square-jawed Sergeant Bob Shanley sang the finale, "This Time," in his stirring baritone:

> For this time
> We are out to finish
> The job we started then,
> Clean it up for all time this time,
> So we don't have to do it again.[24]

Then Mr. B., wearing a light-colored suit and tie, stepped to center stage and sang "Oh, How I Hate to Get Up in the Morning," "God Bless America," and "White Christmas," before making a curtain speech. "I hope to God that I never have to write another war song," he told the audience.[25]

Later, aboard the *Haleakala*, he blew out the candles on a huge cake inscribed s.s. HALEAKALA/ALOHA/T.I.T.A. A black-and-white snapshot, faded to sepia, shows Berlin standing over the cake just afterward, bidding his boys farewell. Slim and animated, with his arms spread and eyeglasses held in his left hand, he looks amazingly youthful. The men around him, in fatigue pants and undershirts, are smiling delightedly.

The next day all would disperse, Berlin flying back home and the cast and crew of *This Is the Army* reporting to the Oahu Army Personnel Center for processing and shipment aboard the aircraft carrier *Petrof Bay.* "When the carrier reaches the West Coast," the *Stars and Stripes* reported, "the troupe will split up for the first time since rehearsals began in May, 1942."[26]

The years in between, Berlin later said, "were the most exciting, the most valuable, the most extraordinary of his life . . . were the great divide . . . before . . . after."[27]

Irving Berlin had already seen how strange the after could be. But then it turned stranger still.

20

There Is America's Folk Song Writer

On November 2, 1945, Jerome Kern, having traveled from his home in Beverly Hills to New York to work with Oscar Hammerstein on a revival of *Show Boat,* and with Hammerstein and Richard Rodgers on a musical about the turn-of-the-century sharpshooter Annie Oakley, suffered a stroke as he walked up Park Avenue. He never regained consciousness, and died nine days later. He was just sixty.

"Shortly after Mr. Kern's death Irving Berlin called at the hospital," the *New York Times*'s obituary read the next day.[1]

Berlin was crushed by the death of the man he esteemed most among the great American songwriters, his friend since 1912. "I loved Kern," he said.[2] And then there was the sobering fact that Kern had been just three years older than he was.

The whole business was rocked by Kern's passing. "That was the worst week of my life," recalled Dorothy Fields, who with her brother Herbert had already written the libretto for the Annie Oakley show, in which Ethel Merman was to star. "The worst week of everybody's life."[3] After the funeral, Fields remembered, she and her brother were sitting at a restaurant with Rodgers and Hammerstein (who were producing the musical),

> and we started discussing whom we could get who could possibly replace somebody as gifted as Kern. And Dick [Rodgers] finally said, "Well, I know somebody, but it means that Dorothy can't do the lyrics." I said, "I have enough to do with the book. I don't care, who is it?" And he said, "Irving."[4]

"We all thought that was fabulous," Fields said, though Rodgers wrote in his memoir that he had immediate misgivings about the idea. "We're aiming awfully high to try to get Berlin," he said to Hammerstein.

"What can we lose?" Hammerstein answered. "The worst that can happen is that he'll refuse."

All of them, Rodgers remembered, were afraid Berlin would be miffed at being their second choice. But "apparently this never played any part in Berlin's thinking," he wrote.[5] More worrisome was the other concern Rodgers voiced about the great man: "He's a boss. It's got to be his show all the way—his money, his ideas, his songs. He doesn't work for other people."

And according to Dorothy Fields, when she phoned Berlin with the idea he did demur, for precisely this reason. "Well, I don't know whether I'd want to do a show that isn't 'Irving Berlin's' whatsoever,'" he said. But Fields held her ground. "Irving, sorry," she told him, "but this is our idea, our play, and it can't be 'Irving Berlin's Annie Oakley.'" "Let me think about it over the weekend," Berlin said. "And if I decide I want to relinquish the billing that I've always had, then we'll talk about it."[6]

Always was saying a lot: in Hollywood the possessory credit had been his only since 1937, when he cannily negotiated it into his first project with 20th Century–Fox, *Irving Berlin's On the*

Avenue. And on Broadway, the rules were simply different—he had declined, after all, to put his name on his theater, the Music Box, nor had it appeared above the titles of his two most recent shows, *As Thousands Cheer* and *Louisiana Purchase.*

Yet *billing* was just shorthand for what Berlin really meant. And then there was the thing he wasn't saying: in his heart of hearts he still wanted to do one more *Music Box Revue.* The form was still the one he loved best, even if, while he'd been on tour with *This Is the Army,* the art of the Broadway musical had changed considerably. An October report in *Variety* had mentioned the existence of a new *Revue,* even noting its *Crystal Ball*–like title, *Tea Leaves,* but said that the show's "originally planned" fall opening had been bumped back to spring—by S.R.O. audiences for Rodgers and Hammerstein's *I Remember Mama* at the Music Box.[7]

The producers made an enthusiastic pitch for *Annie Oakley,* but Berlin told them he just wasn't interested in writing the score for a book show. As a result of *Oklahoma!,* Rodgers wrote in his memoir,

> everyone was upholding the importance of "integration" in creating musicals, and he feared that sticking closely to the story line would inhibit him. We argued that just the opposite would be true: a good libretto could offer tremendous help in stimulating ideas for songs and in showing exactly where they would be the most effective. Still, Berlin remained unconvinced.[8]

"Why don't you read Dorothy and Herb's script, Irving?" Hammerstein said.[9]

Berlin read it. There was what he later described as a "very skinny first act." Act one served mainly as an introduction of the performers in Buffalo Bill Cody's Wild West Show, and Annie Oakley and her four younger siblings, described in the stage directions as an "unwashed brood of ragamuffins." In the open-

ing scene, a marksmanship contest, Annie shows up the traveling circus's vain and handsome sharpshooter, Frank Butler, setting the stage for a rivalry and a love affair.

"This is up your alley," Irving told Hammerstein. "Why
don't you and Dick do it?"

"It's not up our alley," Hammerstein said—and Berlin took
this to mean that the show was a conventional one, a star vehicle.[10] True enough.

Then he thought of another objection. "I can't do hillbilly
lyrics," he told Oscar.

"Don't be silly, Irving," Hammerstein answered. "All you
have to do is to drop the final *g* from most of the verbs." The
method was one the master lyricist had used to such effect that
other writers said he'd created a special language called Apostrophe.[11]

The line was good for a laugh, but finally Berlin told a
"very understanding" Hammerstein that he was going to pass.
"I thought that was the end of it," Berlin recalled in 1966. It
wasn't.

> That week on a Friday, Dick Rodgers telephoned and said,
> "If you will do the score, I can get Josh Logan to direct it."
> . . . I still was reluctant but Dick said, "Why don't you think
> about it over the weekend?"[12]

Another weekend. This time, though, Berlin went into
action. He reread the first act, then he corralled Helmy Kresa
and, harking back to the old days, headed down to Atlantic
City—probably over the weekend of November 17–18, just a
week after Kern's death[13]—where, in the thick late-night hush
of a grand hotel in the off season, the Muse might be expected
to appear.

She appeared. "The songs for the score came quickly and
easily," Berlin would recall years later. "I think the reason was
because of the possibilities in the Fields' script, my association

with Rodgers and Hammerstein and above all, writing songs for Ethel Merman."

Merman, a former stenographer from Queens, had made her Broadway debut in 1930, when George and Ira Gershwin cast her as a nightclub singer in *Girl Crazy:* her breakout performance of "I Got Rhythm" made her an instant star. She bounced back and forth between Hollywood and Broadway during the thirties, but the musical theater, where her phenomenal belting alto could reach the back of the second balcony (and sometimes, legend had it, through the walls of the adjoining playhouse), was her natural home. After *Girl Crazy* she starred in five Cole Porter shows, beginning with *Anything Goes,* and Berlin had become a fan.

Over the course of two nights he wrote "They Say It's Wonderful" and, mastering Apostrophe himself, "Doin' What Comes Natur'lly." Two nights, two perfect songs.[14] But when Berlin returned to the Rodgers and Hammerstein office the following Monday he was in a cautious frame of mind. "Give me another week," he said.

Rodgers was losing patience. "Either you want to do it or you don't!" he snapped. "Which is it?"[15]

"I want to do it," Berlin conceded.[16]

Jablonski posits that his caution stemmed from the fact that he had completed only two—or three, or five—songs so far and wanted to be able to demonstrate at least a half dozen to the producers.[17] This makes sense, but Berlin's general hesitancy about the project also bespeaks a deeper insecurity, as he would later confirm in a letter to Harry Ruby: "Everytime I start with a show," he wrote, "I wonder if this is the time I'll reach for it and find it isn't there."[18]

And this wasn't just any every time. He was feeling his age, and he'd just closed *This Is the Army* three weeks before. He had spent the six months before that enduring *Blue Skies,* the two and a half years before that taking the army show across America and then to war. His doctors had ordered him to take a complete rest, not write a new musical. And along with his age and fatigue and the terror of the blank page, plus the dual challenges of writing in a new idiom and hewing to the story line, there was this: he had never before had to inhabit a protagonist over the course of a show. And not just any protagonist, but a female one.

* * *

Before Berlin read the Fieldses' script, his former musical assistant Dave Dreyer remembered, he had never even heard of Annie Oakley. "He thought Annie Oakley was something you punched holes in, a free ticket."[19]

Yet as he learned about the real Annie Oakley, Berlin found qualities in her that got him where he lived. Like him, she was "a poor, uneducated, feisty, and enormously talented performer."[20] She was a battler; he was a battler too.

As she was preparing her memoir in 1990, the year after her father's death, Mary Ellin Barrett interviewed a number of people who had been important to Irving Berlin, among them Jay Blackton, the conductor of the musical that, as it came together, took on the title *Annie Get Your Gun*. By then an old man, Blackton summoned up the gestation of the show forty-five years earlier: "Here is the picture, if I could put it into words," he told Barrett.

> Rodgers and Hammerstein with two huge hits, *Oklahoma!* and *Carousel*, both setting a new style; Irving [had] been away from Broadway for a while. . . . And you know, Dick and Irving never really meshed. They had great mutual respect— Irving called Dick a musical genius, and I remember Dick one day onstage during a rehearsal, looking at Irving pacing below, saying, "There is America's folk song writer." But they were not soul mates. . . . There were those so well behaved, respectable other two and this street fighter, taking the place of Jerome Kern. Irving was a fighter you know, still

the young fellow from the streets. And I would say Irving
Berlin wrote this tremendous score not just for himself but
for Richard Rodgers. The extra reach, again and again and
again, to show he still had it in him.[21]

America's folk song writer: a curiously pallid encomium,
double-edged, even. Was it part putdown? The sublimely gifted
Rodgers could be a dark and angry man. Did his failure to mesh
with Berlin have anything to do with a still-festering resentment at the show-stealing interpolation of "Blue Skies" into
Rodgers and Hart's *Betsy*, all those years ago?

Perhaps. "Blue Skies" wasn't a folk song; nor were "Let's
Face the Music and Dance" and "Cheek to Cheek." But there
was also truth in what Rodgers said. "White Christmas" and
"God Bless America" arguably *were* folk songs: as Kern put it
in his famous formulation, Berlin had the ability to "honestly
[absorb] the vibrations emanating from the people, manners,
and life of his time, and in turn, [give] these impressions back
to the world—simplified—clarified—glorified." He *was* American music. Who knows what gorgeous melodies Kern might
have composed, and what sparkling lyrics Dorothy Fields might
have written, for *Annie Get Your Gun*? Kern and Fields were
great artists: it might have been a wonderful show.

Kern and Fields were great artists, but they weren't Irving
Berlin. Alone of all the writers of the American Songbook, he
could tap into something simply and profoundly American,
something that would make *Annie Get Your Gun* a great show,
and one unlike anything he had done before.

And whatever his mixed feelings about Irving Berlin, Dick
Rodgers the producer was thrilled at the wealth of brilliant
new material his "folk song" writer turned out in astonishingly
short order. "At a conference with Rodgers and Hammerstein
in my office," Berlin recalled, "I sang for them for the first time
'Doin' What Comes Natur'lly,' 'The Girl That I Marry,' 'They
Say It's Wonderful,' 'You Can't Get a Man with a Gun,' 'I Got

Lost in His Arms,' 'I'm an Indian Too,' and I think one other. They were very enthusiastic."[22]

He wrote the bulk of the sixteen-song score in eighteen days.[23] It was as though all his exhaustion and self-doubt had collapsed upon itself and spontaneously combusted in a late-period blaze of glory. And he wasn't just writing for himself and his muse. He had something to prove: to Rodgers and Hammerstein, to the Fieldses and Josh Logan. In return, he depended on their enthusiasm.

Because of *Annie Get Your Gun*'s eventual triumph, and the starry cast of characters involved in its creation, the show's genesis has passed into Broadway folklore. But in the case of *Annie*, almost all the stories have to do with Irving Berlin, and the most famous one shows another instance of his lifelong insecurity.

A number was needed for Frank Butler, Buffalo Bill, and the Wild West Show's manager Charlie Davenport to sing to persuade Annie to join the show. One day that December, Irving phoned Hammerstein and told him he had an idea for the song: it would be called "There's No Business Like Show Business."[24] "He was crazy about it, which of course encouraged me to write it up," Berlin recalled.[25]

But the approval process didn't stop there. A few days later he played "Show Business" for Rodgers, Hammerstein, and Logan. "Naturally, we all thought it was simply marvelous," Josh Logan wrote in his memoir.

> Berlin was very proud of it. You know, when Irving sings a song in that tiny voice—there's a famous crack somebody once made: "You have to hug him to hear him."[26] But when he sings right into your face, he's *reading* you, studying you every second for your reactions.

A couple of days later Berlin returned to demonstrate "Who Do You Love, I Hope?," a number he'd written for the show's two juveniles. The director and producers reacted enthusiastically. As Berlin started to leave, he turned and said, "Oh, by the way, I brought the second chorus of 'Show Business.'"

He sang it for them. Having already heard the song once, and "gone quite crazy about [it]," they smiled and said the second chorus was fine.

> "What's the matter?" he said. "Don't you like the song? Have you gone cold on it?"
>
> "No, no," we said. "It's fine, great. But that song's already a smash. And this chorus wraps it up. Get after those new songs."
>
> "Yes, but the way you looked, so skittish like." And he left the office, worrying.[27]

Berlin's habit of singing right into a listener's face, watching closely for reactions, stemmed, as the theater critic Jesse Green has noted, from "his days as a busker, a music plugger and a singing waiter. If he didn't make an impression, he didn't make a dime."[28] And his worries about "Show Business" may have stemmed from his secretary's response to the number. "You call that a song, Mr. Berlin?" Mynna Granat said when Berlin dictated the lyrics to her. "This isn't a song. This is nothing." He crisply advised her to keep typing and leave the songwriting to songwriters, but she later felt her remarks had gotten under his skin.[29]

Every afternoon Berlin would sing *Annie*'s score (Helmy Kresa accompanied) for a different professional friend, to further test reactions. One day it was Hugh Martin, the writer of "The Trolley Song" and "Have Yourself a Merry Little Christmas," from *Meet Me in St. Louis*. "After a lot of songs," Logan recalled,

> Berlin said, "Well, that's it." Martin was most impressed but I was astounded.
>
> "Irving, you didn't sing 'Show Business.'"

"No, no, that's out," he said. "I can take a hint. I've thrown it away."

"What!" I yelled. "That's one of the greatest songs ever written!"

"I didn't like the way you three reacted."

"We had heard the song before. We yelled our heads off the first time. We can't scream louder every time we hear it. You've got to play it for Hugh. He's got to hear it."

"I don't think I could find it now. It's in a pile. My girl would need quite awhile to dig it up."

"Go try, please."[30]

Mynna Granat riffled through the stacks of paper lining Berlin's chaotic office, finding nothing. Berlin, Logan, and Martin joined the search, to no avail. At long last, Granat located the lead sheet of the song she hadn't much cared for, the song that would become the immortal anthem of show business, right where she'd put it: under a phone book.[31]

* * *

Two or three days before the show went into rehearsal Josh Logan realized that another song was needed for the two main characters. Annie and Frank Butler (to be played by Ray Middleton) had a duet, "They Say It's Wonderful," in the first act, but sang nothing together, apart from a reprise, in the second. At an all-hands-on-deck production meeting in the living room of Hammerstein's East 63rd Street townhouse, Logan recalled, he and Hammerstein agreed that the number should take place just before the shooting contest in the second act.

"Listen, Josh, don't bother Irving with that now," Hammerstein said. "It'll worry him, and he won't be able to finish his work. . . . We'll bring it up when the time is right."

And just then Berlin, who had suddenly appeared behind Oscar's shoulder, leaned over the two of us and asked, "Another song?"

How he knew it, I do not know. Maybe he simply smelled it in the air.

He said, "Just a minute, please, everybody quiet. A discussion has just come up about a new song. They think there's got to be one for Annie and Frank. Let's have a conference right now. If I'm going to write a song, I have to know what *kind* of song."

So there was some discussion—everybody pitched in. Finally Berlin said, "The only thing that I can possibly think is that if it's before a shooting contest, it has to be some sort of a challenge song. Okay, challenge song. Right?"[32]

At this point, Logan said, everyone was exhausted and headed home. He and his wife took a cab from Hammerstein's place to their hotel on 56th near Park. As he put his key in the door to their room, he heard the phone ringing inside. He ran to pick it up. "It was Irving," Logan wrote.

"Hello, Josh? How's this?" And he started singing:

> Anything you can do, I can do better,
> I can do anything better than you. . . .

"That's perfect!" I shouted incredulously. "When in hell did you write that?"

"In the taxicab. I had to, didn't I? We go into rehearsal Monday."[33]

There was nobody like him. And perhaps this was precisely what, at age fifty-eight, he wanted to demonstrate. "In rising to a challenge of his own," Furia writes, "Berlin had crafted an extraordinary song that proved he could do anything his rival songwriters on Broadway could do. On the one hand, 'Anything You Can Do' is a witty catalog duet like Cole Porter's 'You're the Top,' but it also is rooted in character and dramatic situation as are the songs of Oscar Hammerstein."[34]

And now the amazing score, "probably his greatest," in

Alec Wilder's judgment, was complete.[35] It ran the gamut from the delectable comedy of "Anything You Can Do," "Doin' What Comes Natur'lly," and "You Can't Get a Man with a Gun" to the tenderness of "I Got Lost in His Arms," "The Girl That I Marry," and "They Say It's Wonderful," to the loping, beguiling whimsy of "Moonshine Lullaby," a perfect hillbilly lyric if ever there was one—and one unlike any other number Berlin had ever written.

"Where does this man find these tunes?" Wilder asked, wonderingly.

> One may say that he practiced up for this one with *Louisiana Purchase*, but surely that's no answer. For this song sounds as if he had been writing in this vein all his life. And from the record of the published songs it's obvious that he hadn't.
>
> There is a curious absence of ego implicit in all this. For most writers have been very concerned about writing songs which were recognizably their own and no one else's. But if one is to judge Berlin from his published work, all he is concerned with is the best possible song for the occasion, for the situation, for the lyric, or for the current fashion.[36]

And Berlin said it himself! "I hate that term 'integrated score,'" he told the *Herald Tribune*'s John Crosby in 1962. "If you have a great song, you can always integrate it into any show."[37]

He had proved it again and again, in Hollywood and on Broadway. At the same time, he *had* produced an integrated score for *Annie Get Your Gun*, and his muse had helped him. For in writing songs of surpassing tenderness for Ethel Merman along with the usual brass, he had taken both her art and his to new heights.

The show opened on May 16, 1946, at the Imperial, and despite curiously ambivalent reviews (the *Daily News*'s John Chapman: "*Annie* is a good, standard, lavish, big musical . . . but it isn't the greatest show in the world. . . . Mr. Berlin's music is okay"), audiences couldn't get enough of the show.[38] *Annie* ran for three years on Broadway with Merman, toured the United States with Mary Martin for a year and a half, and played at London's Coliseum, with Dolores Gray in the lead role, for 1,304 performances.

As another riposte to the critics ("Critics, what do the critics know," Berlin was fond of saying),[39] that integrated score produced a profusion of stand-alone hits, eight certified standards: "Wonderful," "Natur'lly," "Get a Man with a Gun," "Girl That I Marry," "Sun in the Morning," "Lost in His Arms," along with the written-in-a-cab "Anything You Can Do" and the almost lost "Show Business." Perry Como's recording of "They Say It's Wonderful" hit the Hit Parade a week after the show opened and stayed there for six months.[40] Frank Sinatra's "Girl That I Marry" and Dinah Shore's "Doin' What Comes Natur'lly" followed quickly.

The critics showered Ethel Merman with the plaudits they withheld from Irving Berlin. On opening night she sent him a one-word telegram: THANKS.[41]

The all-star team behind the show all prospered—and prospered as equitably as possible, thanks to Berlin. His royalty had initially been set at five percent of the gross and Herbert and Dorothy Fields's at four percent, yet as he began to write the score, he realized he was drawing inspiration not just from the Fieldses' richly textured and exuberant libretto but from their song ideas, which in seven instances bore titles identical or almost identical to the ones he would eventually use: "That Comes Naturally!," "The Girl That I Marry," "I Cain't Git A Man With A Gun!," "They Tell Me It's Wonderful!," "Moonshine Lullaby," "I'm An Indian Too!" and "Lost In His Arms."[42] As soon as he returned from Atlantic City with the beginning of the score, Berlin insisted to the astonished Rodgers and Hammerstein that his royalty be lowered by a half percent and the Fieldses' raised by the same amount.

"You know you don't have to do it," Hammerstein told him.[43]

Berlin knew, but he did it anyway. Also at his suggestion, his name and the names of Rodgers and Hammerstein and Dorothy and Herbert Fields were all printed in the same type size in the advertising, playbill, and sheet music for *Annie Get Your Gun.*

"Generosity such as this," Rodgers later said, "is an exceedingly rare commodity."[44] But Berlin plainly saw it as fairness, not generosity. Tough trader though he was, taking what wasn't his had never been his style.

And he could afford to be fair. For all its production problems, *Blue Skies* was also a box-office hit that fall. "Irving Berlin, still vacationing in Bermuda, has decided not to do a new 'Music Box Revue' this season," Radie Harris wrote in her *Variety* column that September. "With his twin hits, 'Annie Get Your Gun' and 'Blue Skies,' he has enough income to help support the U.S. Treasury for quite an interlude."[45]

"Naturally I am delighted with *Annie Get Your Gun,*" Berlin wrote to Harry Ruby. "I might add I am also very grateful. At my age, 'over twenty one,' this seems like a second helping."[46]

That winter he and Ellin bought an elegant five-story Georgian townhouse on Beekman Place at 50th Street, with a small garden and an unimpeded view of the East River. They'd admired the place since before the war; now they could more than afford it. Irving Berlin would live there for forty-two years, the rest of his very long life.

21

I've Never Been in a Tougher Spot

ONE NIGHT in February 1947 Irving Berlin took Ward Morehouse, the *New York Sun*'s Broadway after Dark columnist and theater critic, on a sentimental journey—and a publicity opportunity: a ride downtown to visit some of his old Lower East Side haunts. After dining on wild duck and crabmeat crepes at Le Pavillon, New York's fanciest French restaurant ("When I was a kid," Berlin said, "I never knew there was food like this in the world"), they were off, in a chauffeured car— down Fifth Avenue, south on Broadway, east on Chambers, and on into the heart of what, twoscore years earlier, had been the young Berlin's stomping ground.

As they headed north on Madison Street, then east on Montgomery, Berlin, fidgety and excited, leaned toward the driver. "That's Cherry Street at the corner. Stop there. We'll get out."

They got out. Berlin looked around. "This was my corner," he said. "This was my street."

The two men walked, and the memories rushed in. Berlin pointed out what used to be there and what still was: the pier at the foot of Montgomery Street where he and his pals had swum in the East River; the junk shop to which young Izzy had sold pieces of the family samovar; the tenement on Cherry Street he'd left at fourteen to go on the bum.

They got back in the car and proceeded to the Bowery. Banks and antique stores now occupied the buildings that had once been hole-in-the-wall bars: "Diamond Lottie's place— she had a diamond in her tooth," Berlin said, "and this place—" number 57—"was the Saranac, run by Biggie Donovan, a bar with a back room. I sang in there, too. Beer was five cents a glass. Wilson whisky cost ten cents. Whisky was called a stack of reds and gin a stack of whites."

Soon they were in Chinatown, at 12 Pell Street. "Now this, Mr. M.," Berlin said quietly, pointing to a vacant storefront that had until recently been the Sun Wah Curiosity Shop, "really brings back memories. This was the Pelham Café—Nigger Mike's. I worked right in there forty years ago."

After an eventful stop at a Doyers Street mission (Berlin sang and played "White Christmas" to a chapel full of homeless men), the songwriter and the columnist repaired to Jimmy Kelly's, long since relocated from East 14th Street to Greenwich Village. Berlin drank a brandy and reminisced.

"Fourteenth Street was very swell for me," he said. "I was quite a big shot there. I was an entertainer for about a year and then I went uptown and before long I was writing songs with a drawing account of $25 a week. I'd really had an easy time as a kid, honest. My struggles didn't actually begin until after I'd written 'Alexander's Ragtime Band.' It's been a struggle ever since to keep success going.

"I've never been in a tougher spot than I'm in right now. It's easy to do a movie, a package job like *Blue Skies*, but I can't always depend on being able to write the score of an *Annie*

Get Your Gun . . ." His voice trailed off, and he changed the subject.[1]

Back in Chinatown, Berlin and Morehouse had lingered for a few minutes in front of Olliffe's, the drugstore where the sixteen-year-old Izzy Baline had first encountered Joe Schenck in 1904. And a few days after his sentimental journey, Irving Berlin was on his way to Hollywood to sell another package job to his oldest friend.

* * *

The new idea Berlin was peddling to Schenck—now demoted, since his release from prison, from Twentieth Century–Fox's chairman of the board to executive producer—was really a variation on a concept by now established as profitable: a movie compendium of Berlin tunes, some old and some new, with stars to whom the new material would be tailored, and, of necessity, a story. As with *Alexander's Ragtime Band* and *Blue Skies*, a central song would provide the film's unifying theme and title. This time around, the picture would be called *Easter Parade*. To Schenck it sounded like a can't-miss proposition.

Irving stayed at his old friend's Palm Springs place, and the two men talked over a deal—a substantial fee for the songs, plus a share of the gross. They shook on it, and Berlin returned to New York. But after Schenck reported the deal to Fox's production head Darryl F. Zanuck, the shamefaced producer was forced to wire Berlin that while the higher-ups at Fox would pay handsomely for his songs, profit participation was out.

"Dear Joe," Irving wired back, "you and I shook hands on a deal for 'Easter Parade,' [but] let's forget about it."[2]

Meanwhile at MGM, production had just started on a musical called *The Pirate*, with Judy Garland and Gene Kelly and songs by Cole Porter. Garland's husband Vincente Minnelli directed. Eager to keep the Metro machine rolling with another Garland-Kelly picture, studio chief Louis B. Mayer thought a Garland-Kelly picture with a score by Irving Berlin sounded even better. Having got wind of Fox's refusal, Mayer offered Berlin a stratospheric $500,000 for his songs, double what he'd been paid for *Blue Skies*—but without profit participation. "Dear Louis," Berlin wired, "why should I ask one thing from Twentieth and do another for you?" Mayer relented, to the tune of a record $600,000 plus a percentage of the film's profits.[3]

"He was the most fantastic maneuverer for money you ever saw in your life," Dave Dreyer later said of his former boss. "He outmaneuvered all those sharpies in Hollywood as though they were Boy Scouts."[4]

There was more. On February 27 the trade papers announced that Metro-Goldwyn-Mayer had beaten out Paramount, Warner, and 20th Century–Fox for the movie rights to *Annie Get Your Gun.* "Metro's bid of $650,000 is a new high mark for the outright purchase of a Broadway property, dramatic or musical," a front-page story in *Variety* reported. "Determining factor in Metro's outbidding the other studios presumably revolves about company's recent deal with Berlin for 'Easter Parade,' all-star musical."[5]

The money was very nice, but what excited Berlin just as much, if not more, was the prospect of writing songs for Judy Garland. Yet at twenty-four, Garland, MGM's prize possession for over a decade, was entering her period of maximum dysfunction. Addicted to drugs for sleeping and for staying awake, she was usually absent from the set, and when present, often in a barbiturate stupor or an amphetamine frenzy. Soon after she finished shooting her scenes for *The Pirate* in July, she had a nervous breakdown and spent the rest of the summer in psychiatric institutions.

In the meantime Berlin had moved with his family to a beach rental in Santa Monica and begun writing the score for *Easter Parade.* In signing with MGM, Berlin was getting far more than a rich deal: the picture was to be produced under the aegis of Arthur Freed's famed musical unit, with associate pro-

ducer Roger Edens in charge of the music and Vincente Minnelli once more at the helm. The great Johnny Green, composer
of "Body and Soul," would serve as Berlin's musical secretary.
Besides Garland and Kelly, the all-star cast was to include Frank
Sinatra, Kathryn Grayson, and Red Skelton. The veteran screen-
writers Frances Goodrich and Albert Hackett, who had worked
on *The Pirate*, were assigned to create the script.

Over the summer, while Berlin collaborated closely with
Goodrich and Hackett, Edens began picking older Berlin songs
to suit the film's pre–World War I timeframe: the story took
place between two Easters in the early *Ziegfeld Follies* days.
All was proceeding smoothly—and then it wasn't.

As rehearsals began in September, Freed summoned Minnelli into his office and told him that on the advice of her psychiatrist, Garland wanted him off the film. Minnelli's replacement was Charles Walters, who hated Goodrich and Hackett's
script, and brought in a new screenwriter, Sidney Sheldon, to
make the story more upbeat. Sinatra and Skelton's parts fell by
the wayside, and Grayson, primarily a singer, was replaced by
the dancer Cyd Charisse—who promptly injured her knee while
rehearsing a dance sequence, and was replaced by Ann Miller.

Then, early in October, Kelly broke his ankle in a backyard
game of volleyball.

Fred Astaire was persuaded to come out of retirement and
star opposite Garland. He was forty-eight; she had just turned
twenty-five. But by now Berlin was inured to Hollywood Sturm
und Drang, and besides, Astaire was good news.

And so—surprisingly—was Garland.

The damaged young woman and the aging songwriter hit
it off immediately. During recording sessions before the shoot
began, Garland masked her trembling inner state with shows
of mock bravado, growling comments like, "Did I ever tell you
about the first time I went to the nuthouse?"[6] When Berlin

suggested she phrase one of his songs slightly differently, "Judy walked up to him, put her face two inches in front of his, poked a pugnacious finger into his stomach and said: 'Listen, buster, you write 'em, I sing 'em.'" Berlin, who was thrilled to have the great Garland singing his songs—and who knew a thing or two about inner demons himself—loved it.[7]

The shoot went smoothly. Delighted with Walters and buoyed by Astaire's encouraging tutelage, Garland surprised everyone with her professionalism. And the perfectionistic Astaire was delighted with Garland. Looking on from his customary spot behind the cameras, Berlin could have asked for nothing more than Garland and Astaire's magically funny and touching (and superbly synchronized) performance as a pair of tramps, in his great comic number "A Couple of Swells."

And then there was Garland's sizzling rendition of one of his strangest songs.

"Mr. Monotony" is Berlin at his weirdest, a seventy-six-measure musical caricature aimed straight at the heart of every stuffy critic who would decry the use of repeated notes. The melody largely consists of just that, and the lyric tells of the odd love life of a trombonist who plays in precisely this fashion:

> Sometimes he would change the key,
> But the same dull melody
> Would emerge from Mister Monotony.
> Folks for miles would run away;
> Only one preferred to stay:
> She would come around and say,
> "Have you got any monotony today?"[8]

Amphetamine-slim and leggy in a skimpy black costume—just a fedora, tuxedo jacket, silk stockings, and heels—Garland turned the number into a tour de force so blazing that it wound up on the cutting-room floor: as Berlin later explained, it "slowed up the picture. . . . Arthur [Freed] and I were sorry to see it go because we both liked it, a very unusual song based on a phrase. I later used it in the theater."[9]

Not quite true, as Jablonski points out: "In fact, he tried to interpolate it twice more [in *Miss Liberty* and *Call Me Madam*], but each time 'Mr. Monotony' suffered a similar fate: as Berlin recalled, the song stopped the show, 'and everything else,' so it had to go."[10]

* * *

Monotony was not the problem in the Berlin household. The problem in the Berlin household was that the oldest daughter, Mary Ellin, a feisty and headstrong (and by her own subsequent admission, spoiled) twenty-one-year-old, was in the process of falling in love with the young man she would later refer to as Mr. Wrong: the twenty-eight-year-old Dennis Sheedy Burden, a veteran, an ex-navy flyer, a Vanderbilt descendant and, at first glance, a charmer: tall, witty, well turned-out.

He had the right pedigree, but—unknown to Ellin and Irving at first—the wrong everything else: he was impulsive and unfocused, possibly unstable, and he ran with a wild and jaded (and in the time-tested tradition of Old New York, antisemitic) society crowd. He had once crashed a navy plane, not in combat but while joyriding. In short, he was the kind of bad boy many young women find irresistible, and Berlin's overprotected eldest daughter was highly susceptible.

Distance (over the *Easter Parade* Hollywood summer) only sharpened the young lovers' feelings. When the family returned to New York, the relationship accelerated to the point that Ellin told Irving that it might be a good idea for Mary Ellin to travel with them to Mexico for the Christmas holidays. More than that—perhaps she should take a semester off from Barnard and spend the rest of the winter with the family in California (where Irving had to put the finishing touches on *Easter Parade*), "thinking things over."

" 'She is talking marriage,' says my mother, her smile quite faded, 'and I am not sure this is marriage material.' '*What?*' says my father . . ."[11]

The three went to Mexico City (where they were introduced to Diego Rivera, who offered to paint Berlin's portrait: Berlin, too antsy to sit still for that long, turned him down); soon after the New Year they returned to Hollywood. Irving commuted to MGM; Mary Ellin read the galleys of her mother's new novel, *Lace Curtain* (the story of a mixed—Catholic-Protestant—marriage), and racked up hours of long-distance charges talking to Mr. Wrong.

Berlin's sixtieth birthday was approaching fast, and rest was the farthest thing from his mind. The upcoming 1948 presidential election, in which both Dwight Eisenhower and Douglas MacArthur were being pushed as Republican candidates, had given him an idea for a new musical, *Stars on My Shoulders*, about a general returning from the war and being thrust into politics. He began composing songs ("What Can You Do with a General?") and working with the screenwriter and playwright Norman Krasna on a libretto.

In the capable hands of the Freed unit, *Easter Parade* cruised to a finish. Berlin was particularly impressed with the work of the multitalented arranger and composer Edens, who plucked a twenty-year-old number from the Berlin catalogue—"Shaking the Blues Away," from the 1927 *Ziegfeld Follies*—and turned it into a bravura song-and-dance number for Ann Miller.[12] Irving and his family returned to New York at the end of February; Mary Ellin and Dennis Burden announced their engagement a couple of weeks after Berlin's sixtieth.

On the morning of July 3, not long before sixty people were to gather at Beekman Place to celebrate a wedding that her parents dreaded, Mary Ellin sat playing the living-room piano; Irving walked in in his bathrobe and pajamas, haggard after another bad night, unshaven and uncombed. He looked his willful first child in the eye. "It's not too late," he said, in his raspy morning voice. "We can still call it off."[13]

It went on as planned. The couple would be divorced almost exactly a year later.

*　*　*

How could a man who was constantly in motion, who habitually chewed gum, smoked cigarettes, and paced the floor (Joe Schenck once bet him fifty dollars he couldn't sit in a chair for five minutes: after two minutes Berlin was up and pacing),[14] not have feared rest might mean rust? So he kept moving, moving. Just before Christmas, Berlin, the inveterate ham and patriot, flew off with Bob Hope to entertain the troops in West Berlin, which was under blockade by the Soviets and into which the Western Allies were airlifting a steady stream of supplies.

On the way home he stopped in London, to look in on his British publishing office and catch the West End production of *Annie Get Your Gun;* while there he talked with the show's English producer Emile Littler about mounting a new musical. But the more Berlin thought about *Stars on My Shoulders,* the more convinced he became that the subject matter, unlike that of *Annie,* wouldn't work for British audiences. And he cared about British audiences.

Then he got a call from Bob Sherwood.

The playwright, who was living in the English countryside west of London, said he had a great idea for a new show, and Berlin went out to hear what he had to say. Sherwood was not just an old friend; he was the winner of three Pulitzer Prizes for drama and, the previous year, an Academy Award for writing the screenplay of *The Best Years of Our Lives.* During the war, he had worked in London for the Office of War Information. And now he told Irving that aboard a troopship sailing back into New York Harbor after V-E Day, he'd been profoundly moved by the GIs' reactions to seeing the Statue of Liberty: the fifteen thousand soldiers on board had "cheered like schoolboys."[15]

The experience, Sherwood said, had given him the idea for a musical based on the origins of the statue, which had been designed in the mid-1880s by the sculptor Frédéric-Auguste Bartholdi and paid for by subscription among the French people as a gesture of Franco-American friendship. The French funds, however, covered only the work's design, casting, and shipping; the $100,000 cost of building a pedestal for the statue on Bedloe's Island (later Liberty Island) was underwritten by a donation drive conducted by Joseph Pulitzer, the publisher of the *New York World*. His largesse sold a lot of newspapers.

Sherwood's notion was to graft onto the real-life story a fictional circulation war between Pulitzer and his rival James Gordon Bennett, the publisher of the *Herald*. In the playwright's scheme, Bennett would send a reporter to Paris to find the young woman who had modeled for the statue and bring her back to New York as a living symbol of liberty—her every step, of course, covered by the *Herald*.

Berlin liked what he heard: "It had all the qualities of a good musical," he said, "and I told him this was our opportunity to do a show together."[16]

Then he did some research on the statue himself. He phoned Sherwood. "Look, Bob," Berlin said. "His mother posed for it."

"I know," Sherwood said, "but there must have been younger models who posed for the hands."[17]

It didn't sound very convincing to Berlin. Sherwood, who had never written a musical before (nor would again), thus began working up comedic plot machinations, beginning with a mistaken-identity scenario—the lovely young woman whose picture the *Herald* reporter sees in Bartholdi's studio turns out not to have posed for the statue—and a love triangle between the reporter, the French model, and the reporter's girlfriend.

The ungainly plotting was the first symptom of *Miss Liberty*'s problems. The second was that in distinct contrast to Berlin's close and highly successful collaboration with Herbert and Dorothy Fields on *Annie Get Your Gun*, Berlin worked, for the most part, completely apart from Sherwood, writing most of the score before the script was even completed. It was a methodology that went against both reason and the tide of the times.

"In the age of the new integrated musical," Furia writes, "the most successful shows emerged when a single person—" notably, a singular person such as Oscar Hammerstein—"wrote both the book and the lyrics." *Annie Get Your Gun* was an exception, and a great one, "but it required intricate and extensive collaboration." Berlin and the Fieldses were used to fine-tuning their work through rehearsals and out-of-town tryouts; Sherwood, as a distinguished playwright—"too distinguished," Berlin later said, "for this kind of show"—"was accustomed to having his plays produced as he had written them."[18] Sherwood also suffered from crippling bouts of trigeminal neuralgia, a stabbing facial pain also known as tic douloureux, which he treated with bouts of heavy drinking.

And then there was *Miss Liberty*'s subject matter, which touched on Irving Berlin's deepest patriotic feelings. Finding the right balance between comedy and drama was a problem for both Sherwood and Berlin, who was apt to express his heartfelt love for America in heartfelt terms. The results could be awkward. One afternoon in early 1949 the songwriter and arranger Gordon Jenkins accompanied his friend Helmy Kresa to Berlin's offices; as Jenkins recalled years later, the great man himself suddenly appeared and told them he had something he wanted them to listen to.

> Berlin suddenly fell to his knees, arms upraised, in a posture worthy of the vaudeville stage, and began to sing his version

of the Emma Lazarus poem: "Give me your tired, your poor, your huddled masses yearning to breathe free. . . ." He was so moved by his own performance that tears filled his eyes. . . .

When he finished singing, he said, still on his knees, "By God, I'll tell you guys one thing: no one's ever thought of using those lines in a song, and I can tell you it's going to stop 'em cold. . . . The whole house will just sit there in silence. God, what an idea!"

"I hate to tell you this, Mr. Berlin," Jenkins said, "but . . . I used those words in a song three years ago."

Jenkins explained that he had set to music the same lines from Lazarus's sonnet "The New Colossus"—recited at the dedication of the Statue of Liberty in 1886—in his suite *Manhattan Tower*, a song–and–spoken narrative piece that became a surprise hit when Decca released a recording of it in 1946.

"You're a goddamned liar!" Berlin shouted. "Get the fuck out!" He stormed back into his office, slamming the door behind him.[19]

Stealing material was the worst charge that could be directed at a songwriter, and any hint that his work might be anything other than original had always been a hot button with Berlin. But in fairness, he was under enormous stress in the spring of 1949. Mary Ellin's marriage was falling apart. An off-again Judy Garland was barely limping through MGM's adaptation of *Annie Get Your Gun*. And *Miss Liberty*—which Berlin was also coproducing, along with Sherwood and Moss Hart, who had been brought in to direct and iron out the libretto's problems—seemed snake-bit from the beginning.

"Three songs were scrapped after the first run-through, and most of those that remained were well below Berlin's usual standards," writes the Hart biographer Jared Brown. "Much of Sherwood's book was found to be unfunny and talky, and, despite Hart's pleas, Sherwood's approach to the necessary revisions was slow."[20]

Of the early rehearsals, Allyn McLerie, who played the French model Monique, recalled: "Everything was sad; everything was bad."[21]

McLerie was a relative newcomer to the musical stage, as was the show's other female lead, Mary McCarty. Playing Horace Miller, the young *Herald* reporter, was Eddie Albert, who had a skill for light comedy and a nice singing voice; he was also forty-three years old. Hiring a non-all-star cast may have been a money-saving maneuver on the part of the producers, but the show's cast would be the least of its difficulties.

The team of Berlin, Sherwood, and Hart was an impressive one (and a thirty-year-old Jerome Robbins did the choreography), and *Miss Liberty*'s subject matter sounded promising on paper: the musical attracted a huge advance sale of $430,000. The road tour began in Philadelphia on June 13. "Curiosity about the first performance was so great that an unusually large contingent of visitors from Broadway and elsewhere trooped to Philadelphia," Brown writes. But "the final curtain did not descend until 11:40, the second act was in clear need of extensive revision, and the problems were sufficiently severe that a postponement of the New York premiere, originally planned for July 4 . . . was discussed."[22]

The Philadelphia run was extended from three to four weeks—due to popular demand, the producers announced, but actually due to those severe second-act problems. When Robert Sherwood came falling-down drunk to yet another script meeting, Moss Hart said, "There goes the ball game."[23]

The Broadway premiere was on Friday night, July 15; the Saturday-morning papers were withering. "To come right out and say so in public, *Miss Liberty* is a disappointing musical comedy," wrote the *Times*'s Brooks Atkinson. "It is built on an old-fashioned model and is put together without sparkle or originality."[24]

"If 'Miss Liberty' had been written by a couple of guys named Doakes," wrote *Variety*'s Hobe Morrison,

> it would probably have been considered a promising, even an entertaining show. But from such eminent authors as Irving Berlin and Robert E. Sherwood, not to mention stager Moss Hart, it is something of a clinker. . . .
>
> Berlin's songs are certainly better than average, though reminiscent and obviously not up to his best. Probably they'd be better if sung by top stars, with the ability and personality to exploit them.[25]

Premiering at a moment when two musical colossi, Cole Porter's *Kiss Me Kate* and Rodgers and Hammerstein's *South Pacific*, were towering over Broadway, *Miss Liberty* was not just dramatically but musically underpowered—the score had a whiff of quaintness.[26] Harking back to his great successes of the twenties, Berlin had included three waltzes, probably two too many.

The show's one outright hit, the sweet and affecting "Let's Take an Old-Fashioned Walk," was a trunk song, having been bumped from *Easter Parade* by "A Couple of Swells" and then intended for the shelved *Stars on My Shoulders*. The Gallic-flavored "Paris Wakes Up and Smiles" was also sweet, though slight. And "Just One Way to Say I Love You" is lilting and heartfelt, but a little too close for comfort to Frank Loesser's "My Darling," from the then-running hit musical *Where's Charley?* There are recordings, demos made for *Miss Liberty*'s actors, of Berlin himself singing all three numbers to Helmy Kresa's piano accompaniment, and his New York–accented renditions are thoroughly charming and achingly lovely—but all three tunes feel more appropriate to the parlor, and the past, than to the dynamic postwar musical stage.

On the strength of its advance sales, *Miss Liberty* tottered along for 308 performances, "a passable run for most productions," Brown writes, "but a distinct disappointment for a musical that had been so eagerly anticipated—and for a show that had cost so much to produce. Furthermore, the number of empty seats increased dramatically in the latter half of the run."[27] All three producers took heavy losses. The show was Irving Berlin's first out-and-out flop since he'd begun writing for Broadway nearly forty years earlier.

Seven years earlier, in the midst of *This Is the Army*'s national tour, Berlin had mused aloud to a newspaper reporter how the end of his career might play out. "Who is going to tell me that I'm washed up as a songwriter?" he wondered. "That day is sure to come, and I'm always afraid my friends won't have the courage to tell me. I don't want to make my exit in the midst of a bunch of mediocre songs. I want my last one to have just as much merit as the first."[28]

Had the day come? At Lake Tahoe in the summer of 1949, Mary Ellin—in Nevada to get her divorce—was keenly aware of her father's "abrupt temper and haggard look."[29] The failure of her marriage, widely chronicled in the press—even in *Time*, the most public of pillories—had cast a shadow on the family name, and the failure of *Miss Liberty* continued to sting.

22

———◆◈◆———

We'll Never Get Off the Stage

BERLIN'S FAMILY noticed signs of serious depression in him in the fall of 1949. Though he had brushed aside *Miss Liberty*'s failure like the pro he was, he had suffered two other professional setbacks: *Stars on My Shoulders* was postponed indefinitely, its score consigned to the trunk; and, Judy Garland's addictions having overtaken her, MGM had finally cut the troubled star loose from *Annie Get Your Gun* (and her studio contract) and replaced her with the good but not great Betty Hutton. He was also at an impasse with Paramount over terms for *White Christmas*, a Crosby-Astaire sequel to *Holiday Inn:* could his days as the toughest trader in Hollywood be behind him?[1]

The prodigal, his newly divorced oldest daughter, had returned to the family fold at age twenty-three. Each day Mary Ellin reported to her new job—ironically enough, as a researcher at *Time*—and each night she returned to a household filled with barely suppressed gloom and reproach.

"I used to think," Barrett said many years later, "that part of the reason for my father's depression was that I, his wonderful oldest daughter, who had always made him so proud, had made an ass of myself. Then a long time afterwards, my mother said, 'I always thought that was what had triggered his depression, along with his sixtieth birthday.' But she said the doctor said, no, it was the war."[2]

But really it was everything: a combination of exhaustion and the sadness of aging and disappointments both professional and personal. And though now there was new hope—Berlin was "all hot about" the idea of writing another show for Ethel Merman, based on the legendarily vivacious Washington hostess and ambassador to Luxembourg Perle Mesta—the depression had set in, and nothing like the sustained bright burst of *Annie Get Your Gun*'s creation would ever happen again.

The idea for the show that would become *Call Me Madam* seemed on the face of it so natural, so effervescent, that all involved couldn't have been blamed for thinking the thing would practically write itself. The reality couldn't have been more different. The playwrights Howard Lindsay and Russel Crouse labored mightily, and slowly, over the book, and Berlin, who in February of 1950 turned to the warm sun of Nassau for inspiration, quickly hit a wall. "I wrote six songs very quickly," he told a *Boston Post* reporter later that year,

> then I just went blank for two months. I got terribly worried. I couldn't sleep. . . . I like to work under pressure, against a deadline, in New York. But these boys—Lindsay and Crouse —wrote this show like a straight play and then sent it to me, and I had to find a way of getting songs into a play that was strong enough to stand by itself without music, instead of a libretto full of song cues.[3]

Yet while the working process between librettists and composer was far less clear-cut than it had been in the (admittedly

unique) case of *Annie Get Your Gun,* it was far more collaborative than had been the case with *Miss Liberty.* And unlike Robert
Sherwood, Lindsay and Crouse could write comedy.

Then something in Berlin unfroze. After two months,
"suddenly, everything was all right again, and I wrote two or
three songs in one week."[4] He returned to New York and set
about wooing Merman, his slightly reluctant muse, who didn't
want to sing more than a couple of tunes in the whole show.
Merman never had a chance. Jay Blackton, who would conduct
the orchestra for *Call Me Madam,* described what it was like
to be on the receiving end of the Berlin hard sell: "He'd sit me
near the piano, Helmy would be playing, and he'd hover over
me, singing to me, singing right into my ear . . . and constantly
looking at me as if to share the delight of the song which he'd
just written."[5]

A couple of days later, Crouse wrote in his diary, "Irving
calls to say that Ethel loves the songs and she gets on to confirm this in true Merman fashion."[6]

Even if the new score wasn't as brilliant as *Annie Get Your
Gun*'s, it had a similar exuberance, because once again Berlin
was writing for Merman, and once again Merman was essentially playing Merman. With her sunny plainspokenness, Perle
Mesta's fictional stand-in Sally Adams could have been first
cousin to Annie Oakley. Integrated-musical parlance spoke of
the "I am" song: Annie's was "Doin' What Comes Natur'lly";
Sally's, "The Hostess with the Mostes' on the Ball":

> I was born on a thousand acres
> Of Oklahoma land . . .[7]

Another big song for a big personality.

Rather than produce the show themselves, Berlin, Lindsay,
and Crouse enlisted the profusely connected agent and producer Leland Hayward (*State of the Union, South Pacific*), who
quickly found he had to all but beat away potential backers: re-

markably, the theater world was willing to simply overlook the failure of *Miss Liberty*, calculating that Berlin plus Merman would once again equal pay dirt. In short order Hayward scored a coup: convincing RCA and its subsidiary NBC to put up the entire cost ($200,000) of the show in return for the radio and television broadcast rights—as well as permission for RCA Victor Records, which was eager to get into a business then dominated by CBS and Decca, to put out the original-cast album.[8]

Hayward hired the great Broadway director George Abbott (*Pal Joey, On the Town*), and signed Jerome Robbins to stage the dances and musical numbers. Abbott's assistant, a twenty-two-year-old Harold Prince, was assistant stage manager and casting director. One day, while Prince was busy wrangling the throngs of hopefuls who'd lined up outside the Golden Theatre, the backstage phone rang. As Prince remembered years later:

> The voice on the other end said, "This is Irving Berlin, who's this?"
>
> "This is Hal Prince, Mr. Berlin."
>
> "Well, who are you?" And I said, "I'm casting and I'm assistant stage managing; there's a chorus call today."
>
> He asked for George Abbott, the director; he asked for Lindsay and Crouse, the writers, but no one was around . . . whereupon Berlin sang an entire song to me over the phone.
>
> "What do you think of it?" he asked, and I said, "I like it."
>
> He said, "Good, so do I," and hung up.[9]

Rehearsals got off to a slow start. Berlin, always impeccably tailored in a suit and necktie, paced back and forth, eyeing the stage nervously. Sometimes he took off the suit jacket and draped it over his arm while circumnavigating the theater, jingling the change in his pocket and humming.

The show's book continued to be problematic, and the premiere, originally scheduled for the spring, kept getting postponed. The basic story was straightforward enough: Ambassador Sally Adams arrives in the (fictional) Grand Duchy of Lichtenburg, which she had never heard of before her appointment, and charms everyone in sight with her disregard for protocol when she isn't scandalizing them with it. Two parallel love stories develop, one between Sally and the duchy's foreign minister (played by the Academy Award–winning Hungarian actor Paul Lukas), the other between Adams's handsome young attaché (the twenty-six-year-old up-and-comer Russell Nype) and the princess of Lichtenburg (the dancer Galina Talva).

The script had a revuelike jokiness, with Truman-era winks at the audience throughout, including a series of phone calls between Ambassador Adams and "Harry," and sly comments on postwar American power. But by contrast to *Annie Get Your Gun, Call Me Madam* was dramatically underpowered: first and last, a vehicle for Ethel Merman. And in the grand Broadway tradition, the vehicle had a grave mechanical flaw: a gaping hole in the second act.

The first act gave Merman plenty to work with: "The Hostess with the Mostes' "; a satire on D.C. politics called "Washington Square Dance"; the bubbly "Can You Use Any Money Today?"; and "The Best Thing for You," a love-in-the-offing duet for Merman and Lukas. And Russell Nype, goofily handsome with his crew cut and horn-rimmed glasses, stopped the show when he wooed the princess with the delightful (and enduring) "It's a Lovely Day Today."

But things more or less ground to a halt in act two, and the problem was still there when the show opened in New Haven on September 11. The hype the show had generated put enormous pressure on all parties, especially the songwriter. He first tried plugging the second-act hole, against the wishes of Abbott, Lindsay and Crouse, and Merman, with "Mr. Monotony." It landed with a thud, and Merman put her foot down. "I've cooperated, I've sung the song and it doesn't fit," she said. "It's out."[10]

Berlin then tried throwing in an earnest flag-waver about democratic values called "Free" ("Free—/The only thing I want on earth is to be free . . ./To close my door at night and never turn the key . . .").[11] It charmed no one, least of all Merman, who had to try to put it over.

"I want a number with the kid," she told Berlin, meaning Russell Nype, the surprise hit of the show.

Around that time, Bing Crosby and his son Gary had a best-selling single of Berlin's 1914 double song "Play a Simple Melody." "Mr. Berlin said it would be wonderful if he could write a similar song for Merman and Nype," Helmy Kresa recalled.

Berlin borrowed a couple of lines from a tune he'd written for (and dropped from) *Annie Get Your Gun*, "Something Bad's Gonna Happen ('Cause I Feel So Good)." "With that to start on," Kresa said, "he first wrote the sweet melody and I played it over and over again for him as he wrote the rhythmic counter-melody on top of it."[12]

After five days of racking labor simplicity was achieved. With the plaintiveness of love-struck youth, Nype's character sang the first chorus:

> I hear singing and there's no one there;
> I smell blossoms and the trees are bare . . .

Then in the second chorus Merman's character responded with the salty wisdom of middle age:

> You don't need analyzing;
> It is not so surprising
> That you feel very strange but nice . . .[13]

Then the two sang their parts together in countermelody, a sublime juxtaposition of naïveté and experience. When Berlin and Kresa demonstrated it for Merman and Nype, Merman said, "We'll never get off the stage."

She was right. At the Boston premiere on September 19,

the song got seven encores. "At some performances," Ethel Merman's biographer Brian Kellow writes, "Paul Lukas, who appeared in the scene that followed, had to step out onstage and wait while the number was still going, just to cue the audience that the show had to keep moving."[14]

By the time the show premiered on Broadway, on October 12 at the Imperial, *Call Me Madam* had generated a $1 million advance sale—at a time when the top ticket price was $7.20. Scalpers were asking as much as $400 for opening-night seats. Ward Morehouse, in the *New York World-Telegram and Sun*, wrote, "There hasn't been anything with more of a ballyhoo since Sarah Bernhardt trouped the land in tents."[15]

The reality lived up to the hype. Even with a still-shaky second act, the show drew an ecstatic reaction from the first-night audience and from reviewers, who simply bowed to the primal force of Merman singing Berlin, "giving perhaps the greatest performance of her phenomenal career," as *Variety* wrote.[16] "This is one of his most enchanting scores, fresh, light and beguiling; and fitted to lyrics that fall out of it with grace and humor," wrote Brooks Atkinson in the *Times*.[17] "After forty-five years on the sidewalks of Tin Pan Alley, his longevity as a composer is not only amazing but gratifying."[18]

"It's nice after all these years to know that you can still reach up there and find it when you're in trouble," Berlin later wrote to Harry Ruby.[19] But now, in the thick of his seventh decade, he was still in more trouble than he cared to admit.

* * *

Not commercial trouble, by any means. *Call Me Madam* would play 644 performances and gross more than four million dollars, enriching all the principals. It seemed that everything Berlin touched succeeded: even MGM's Judy Garland–less *Annie Get Your Gun* was a big box-office hit in 1950. When it turned out that Ethel Merman had an exclusive recording contract with Decca and couldn't participate in the original-cast album of *Madam*, RCA Victor put out one *Call Me Madam* album, with Dinah Shore trying to fill Merman's very big shoes, and Decca issued another, with Merman but without the rest of the original cast, and Berlin made money from both.

What he needed now wasn't a hit, but—still—a rest, somewhere sunny and quiet. What he got instead was a three-week trip to London, Paris, and Rome with his divorced oldest daughter. They stayed in the best hotels and ate at the finest restaurants, where Irving often gave the headwaiter instructions about what they were to be served, or, taking the more direct approach, barged into the kitchen to inform the chef directly.

In Rome, a *Time* writer who was a colleague of Mary Ellin's, a tall young Midwesterner named Marvin Barrett, showed up in the lobby of the Excelsior Hotel to take her sightseeing. A friend at this point, or perhaps starting to become more than a friend, he had visited Beekman Place while Berlin was in the throes of *Call Me Madam* and passed muster with Ellin, Mary Ellin's sisters, and the girls' longtime Scottish nanny Janet Tennant. Now Berlin, shaking the young man's hand and exchanging a few words with him, took his measure for the first time and apparently liked what he saw: he told the young people there was a car at their disposal and to go have a good time.

Two years later Mary Ellin and Marvin would be married, and would stay married for more than fifty years.

* * *

Just a few weeks after returning from Europe, Berlin and his wife went to Honolulu to celebrate their silver anniversary, January 4, 1951. "We had a lovely time," Ellin later said of the trip, then hesitated. "But." She looked at her eldest daughter— who knew her mother's spirits rose and fell in sync with her father's—and made an up-and-down gesture.[20]

The shadow darkening and lengthening, even under the sun of paradise.

* * *

A poignant item on *Variety*'s January 24, 1951, front page:

With his current legit musical, "Call Me Madam," riding as
another click, Irving Berlin is planning to go on a long rest
from commercial cleffing chores.[21]

But Berlin's resting looked a lot like bustle: plans still afoot
for that final *Music Box Revue;* an NBC-TV adaptation of *Miss
Liberty* in January. The Tony Awards in March, where, though
Frank Loesser's *Guys and Dolls* beat out *Call Me Madam* for Best
Musical, Merman and Nype were named Best Actress and Best
Supporting Actor; Berlin won for Best Original Score. Dicker-
ing with MGM over another package job, to be called *There's
No Business Like Show Business.* Hondeling with 20th Century–
Fox over the movie rights to *Call Me Madam.*

And more travel. To Nassau with the family in February,
and then in June back to France, again with Mary Ellin. The
ostensible occasion for the trip was the wedding of the son of
Albert Willemetz, Berlin's longtime friend and the French
translator of his work (most recently *Annie Get Your Gun,* or as
the smash Paris production was known, *Annie du Far West*). But
then, after the celebration, Irving informed his daughter they
were going down to the Côte d'Azur, to call on Chagall and
Picasso.

Painting was Berlin's new obsession. His good friend the
Broadway columnist and cartoonist Irving Hoffman had given
him a set of artist's materials soon after his sixtieth birthday,
thinking a nice hobby might be therapeutic. But instead of
spending off hours with his oils and brushes, Berlin began using
painting to fill the gap in which songwriting was less and less
often taking place. Increasingly, when family members were
summoned to the top-floor study at Beekman Place, it wasn't
to hear a new number but to look at a freshly finished still life

of brilliantly colored flowers in a bowl: almost always it was flowers in a bowl. "I agree with you that I shouldn't keep painting the same picture," Berlin wrote to Hoffman. "But as I look back on my early songs, I realize I kept writing the same tune."[22] Nor did he have any illusions about his artistic skills: "As a painter I'm a pretty good songwriter," he liked to say.[23]

Father and daughter lunched with Chagall and his family at the artist's home in Vence, and the occasion was genial and easy: Berlin and Chagall were *landsmen*, just a year apart in age and hailing from the same small corner of Belarus, northeast of Minsk. A photograph taken that day shows the two men grinning broadly as the elfin painter, even shorter than Berlin's five foot five and a half, reaches out, in a gesture both intimate and playful, to touch the songwriter's eyeglasses.

The meeting with Picasso, at the artist's hillside compound in Vallauris, was a different story.

Berlin had first met the great man briefly in Cannes, the previous summer, and so now Picasso welcomed him warmly. But it soon became apparent that for the Spaniard the occasion was all about display: his house, his studio, his beautiful young lover Françoise Gilot and their two small children, his paintings, his sculptures, his pottery. He was quick to answer questions— and Berlin was endlessly curious—but asked almost none in return.

Berlin wasn't fazed. He had met many great men—Churchill, Eisenhower, FDR—and, a great man himself after all, and comfortable in his own skin when he wasn't jumping out of it, went on painting flowers anyway.

* * *

Meeting General Eisenhower in wartime London had made a deep and lasting impression on Berlin: when Eisenhower finally decided to run for president in 1952, as a Republican, both Irving and Ellin quickly switched their political affiliation and went all-out for him. At a giant Madison Square Garden campaign rally in February, Berlin—following Ethel Merman trumpeting out "There's No Business Like Show Business," and introduced by Clark Gable—came to the podium and sang, in a voice so small that the din threatened to overwhelm it:

> I like Ike—
> I'll shout it over a mike . . .[24]

It was exhilarating to be waving the flag for his favorite general, but four days later came sad news: his sister Ruth (née Rebecca), who ran a small shop and newspaper distributorship in New Jersey with her husband Abraham Kahn, had died of cancer, at sixty-eight. Of the eight Balines who had arrived at Ellis Island in 1893, only two besides Irving now remained: his older brother Ben, a well-to-do furrier in New London, Connecticut, and his divorced older sister Gussie.

And to a certain extent Berlin was whistling past the graveyard, boasting to *Variety* in late May that "at a period in his life, when most successful men are thinking of retiring," he was looking forward to 1953 as his best year in show business, with three movie musicals in release: at 20th Century–Fox, not just *Call Me Madam* but also *There's No Business Like Show Business*, for which he had closed a $500,000 deal in February, and returning to Paramount after seven years, *White Christmas*.[25]

He spent that summer in Hollywood not writing songs but consulting on the scripts for the package job and the *Holiday Inn* sequel. It all would have felt too familiar: *There's No Business* was yet another cavalcade of Berlin songs over decades, the story of a show-business family rising from vaudeville to Broadway; *White Christmas* was set in the same New England inn, with the same Crosby-Astaire rivalry, only now with the general from the aborted *Stars on My Shoulders* grafted in.

Berlin's mood lightened in August when he returned from the dream factory to his Lew Beach woods and trout stream. The country cleared his head, filled him with energy. "There was a mountain in the Catskills, and at the top was a fire watchtower," his daughter Linda remembered. "We would drive to the bottom of the mountain, and there was a trail to go to the top, which was grueling. But my father would go up and come down the mountain like a gazelle."[26]

One afternoon he sat down at the piano, reached up there, and, wonder of wonders, found it—inspiration—right where he'd left it. On the twenty-seventh he wrote a cheeky note to Irving Hoffman: "I just wrote my first song for the movie *White Christmas*. This will be sung by Bing Crosby and the title is 'Sittin' in the Sun Counting My Money.' See you later."

The note, and the song, were the triumphant sound of an artist remembering just how good he really was. It was as though, having spent much of the previous five years writing for characters, he had returned to himself—some part of his hungry past lived in him still, not just needily but consolingly, as big deal followed big deal even when the songs didn't come. But this song *had* come:

> Sittin' in the sun,
> Countin' my money,
> Fanned by a summer breeze.
> Sweeter than honey
> Is countin' my money,
> Those greenbacks on the trees.[27]

A few days after the note to Hoffman, Berlin wrote to Joe Schenck:

First let me tell you I feel just great. I've had several nights of good sleep without too much help. Also, for the first time in a long time, the work is coming faster and better.

I'm enclosing a lyric of a song I finished here which I am going to publish immediately. . . . You have always said that I commercialized my emotions and many times you were wrong, but this particular song is based on what really happened. The story behind the song is in its verse, which I don't think I will publish. . . .

When I come back to the coast I'll sing the song for you. I think you'll be crazy about it. Personally, I feel it's the best song I have written in a long time and should be a hit.[28]

The song was "Count Your Blessings Instead of Sheep." You may know it:

> When I'm worried and I can't sleep,
> I count my blessings instead of sheep,
> And I fall asleep counting my blessings . . .

What you couldn't know is the unpublished verse:

> Couldn't sleep,
> I was worried,
> Wrapped in problems deep.
> Took a pill,
> Then another;
> Still I couldn't sleep.
> Called a doctor to my bed,
> Asked him what to do.
> Smilingly the doctor said,
> "Did you ever try counting your blessings?"[29]

The line in Berlin's letter to his oldest friend, *You have always said that I commercialized my emotions and many times you were wrong*, is telling: Berlin doesn't say Schenck was always wrong. One's mind goes back to the instances where he was definitely right: *When I lost you. I want to be lazy. I'm so all alone. There may be trouble ahead.*

But the verse of this song is so nakedly autobiographical—Berlin really did have this conversation with his doctor—that it's no wonder he didn't want to publish it. It also raises the question: what were his problems deep? On the face of it, Irving Berlin had everything that humans yearn for: wealth, fame, unparalleled professional success, love, family. What he lacked was control over a perilous world, and over his own mortality, which he would have felt ever more keenly as he approached threescore and ten.

"Count Your Blessings" would be a hit, as Berlin knew it would be; what he didn't know was that though he would live to fivescore and one, it would be his last.

23

———◆◆◆◆◆———

A Worried Old Man on the Hill

IRVING AND ELLIN spent the 1952 Christmas holidays in
Sicily visiting the newly married Mary Ellin and Marvin, who
had quit their jobs at *Time* and, with a generous wedding check
from her father bolstering their bank account, set up house-
keeping as semistruggling writers in the picturesque town of
Taormina.

It was a nice visit, although as Barrett remembered, she
and her husband had at first been appalled by the prospect of
what was clearly an inspection tour by her ever-hovering parents. Berlin and his wife—they also had the twenty-year-old
Linda and Ellin's childhood nurse Mary Finnerty in tow—stayed
in the town's plushest hotel, whose staff fussed over the famous
visitors. Irving bought an expensive emerald necklace for Ellin
and a half dozen pairs of handmade shoes for himself. The
town buzzed; a mandolin concert was given in his honor.

His spirits seemed high. "Whatever was going on with my

father back home (nothing too good in terms of those very ragged nerves and the grim knowledge that Uncle Ben was dying of cancer)," Barrett writes, "he was his enthusiastic-on-the-road self."[1]

He beelined to Hollywood as soon as he returned, to stir his various pots: writing a score for *White Christmas*; meeting with Zanuck for *There's No Business Like Show Business* (the studio chief, impressed by Merman's performance in 20th's *Call Me Madam*, had approved her to star, with Dan Dailey and Donald O'Connor, in the new picture); trying to persuade the producer Jerry Wald to make a movie of *Miss Liberty* (it wouldn't happen).

None of it was very inspiring, though in March there was a shot in the arm: *Call Me Madam*, the movie, premiered, to rave reviews. "A handsome, hilarious, surefire hit movie," said *Time*.[2] Critics were unanimous in their praise for Merman; box office was excellent: it was all very gratifying, but the news from home was bad.

"Irving Berlin flew back to see his very ill brother," Walter Winchell's April 21 column noted tersely.[3] And then, on May 12, a small Associated Press item, datelined New London, Connecticut: "Benjamin M. Baline, brother of the song writer Irving Berlin, died today in Lawrence Memorial Hospital, where he was admitted last Tuesday. He was 72 years old."[4]

It was the day after Irving's sixty-fifth birthday, the official retirement age for most Americans, and an oversignificant landmark for Berlin.

* * *

He still had work to do, but the idea of retirement—voluntary or otherwise—descended on him like a thick cloud through the rest of the year. "Irving Berlin, the multi-millionaire, working hard in the Beverly Hills sun on his next two epics for Zanuck," read a perky Winchell item in July.[5] In reality there was just one project afoot, and it wasn't so epic: the plot of *There's*

No Business Like Show Business, worked up by the veteran screenwriter Lamar Trotti, who died before he could finish, was so pat and formulaic that when Fox reassigned the screenplay to the husband-and-wife team of Phoebe and Henry Ephron, Mrs. Ephron (mother of the eleven-year-old Nora) memorably remarked, "I won't go to see it—why should I write it?"[6]

White Christmas, to be directed by *This Is the Army*'s Michael Curtiz, was a different kind of hell. The story, cobbled together by Norman Krasna and the comedy writers Norman Panama and Melvin Frank, revolved creakily around a crusty but warm-hearted—and frankly Eisenhoweresque—former World War II general (Dean Jagger) who buys the very same Vermont inn featured in *Holiday Inn*, which falls on hard times because there's no snow for the Christmas season, and therefore no guests. Then two of the men formerly under his command, the Crosby and Astaire characters, reunite the 151st Division, which assembles at the inn as snow falls, romantic loose ends are tied up, and the general looks on with misty eyes.

Crosby and Astaire were in, then they bowed out (the screenplay, *Variety* noted, had portrayed the characters to be played by the fiftyish actors as "too young");[7] then Crosby was back in, with Donald O'Connor replacing Astaire—then, in August, O'Connor was hospitalized with a rare fever, and had to bow out. "We were frantic," Berlin later said. "It seemed like a doomed film."[8]

Then a slot was found in the busy schedule of Danny Kaye, who'd just become a massive star with the release of *Hans Christian Andersen*, and all was well again with *White Christmas*. Yet all was not well with Berlin.

When he finished the songs for the score, the *New York Times* reported, "he asked Crosby to drive down to the desert, where he was then living, to listen to them. But in the presence of Bing, Berlin's nerves buckled and he couldn't go on. Crosby quickly rose to the occasion. 'Do you like them, Irving?' he asked. When Berlin nodded, Crosby added, 'Then they're good enough for me.'"[9]

The problem wasn't just Berlin's nerves. The hard fact was that apart from the title tune, by now so huge that it could sell movie tickets all by itself, and "Count Your Blessings," there was nothing to write home about in *White Christmas*'s score, which consisted of retreads from *Stars on My Shoulders* and pleasant but undistinguished numbers like "The Best Things Happen While You're Dancing" and "Love, You Didn't Do Right By Me"—the kind of tunes you might hear a hotel or country club band playing and not think twice about. Always the toughest critic of his own work, Berlin would have known that he was just marking time.

Mary Ellin and Marvin returned from Sicily in September, he with a finished novel, she seven months pregnant. And in November, Irving and Ellin welcomed to the world their first grandchild, Elizabeth Esther Barrett. His frayed nerves notwithstanding, Berlin delighted in being a grandfather, and in the years to come he would continue to take pleasure in his growing family: his daughters would give him nine grandchildren in all.

But something happened that winter.

In February a small item appeared on the front pages of newspapers across the country:

Composer Berlin Enters Rest Home
> HOLLYWOOD, Feb. 13 (UP)—
> Composer Irving Berlin, 65, today denied reports that he is under care in a sanitarium for a nervous condition and fatigue.
> The songwriter admitted he was in a rest home, but said he always lives in a rest home between motion pictures so he can "rest up" and compose songs.[10]

The man who had always been his own best publicist had given the press a statement that would have sounded like a punch line had the matter not been so serious. When the gossip columnist Louella Parsons asked him a set-up question—was he doing better?—Berlin denied once more that he'd been having any trouble at all, telling her, "I've never been better" and, somewhat tangentially, "I've just eaten the biggest lunch."[11]

But in fact Berlin, whose depression and anxiety had worsened sometime over the winter to the point that he was unable to function normally, had been hospitalized for the first time. It wouldn't be the last.

* * *

White Christmas, in gorgeous Technicolor and Paramount's new wide-screen process, VistaVision, premiered in October. The *Times*'s Bosley Crowther was full of praise for the look of the picture, but that was as far as he went. "We wish we could say that the substance of this talent-crammed musical film is as fresh and satisfying as its general appearance on the screen," he wrote.

> But, for the most part, the music is hackneyed, the jokes are flat and slightly sad, and the yarn and locale are wan reminders of the long-ago "Holiday Inn." Its sentimentalizing over a general and the chumminess of Army life is as quaint as its antique endeavor to make Bing out to be a Romeo.[12]

The public bought tickets, though, and kept on buying them: *White Christmas* became a huge box-office hit—which appears to say less about the quality of the movie than about the American public's craving for security in the era of Soviet H-bomb tests and the army-McCarthy hearings. The world had grown relentlessly more complex since World War II, with its clear-cut moral calculations; the whole-hearted team spirit of *This Is the Army*—which after all lay at the military core of *White Christmas*—now seemed like something of a relic. As, more and more, did Irving Berlin.

Nor did *Irving Berlin's There's No Business Like Show Busi-*

ness (the full and official title), released by Fox on December 16 to ride *White Christmas*'s slipstream, add to his luster. The picture was long, plotty, and, despite the best efforts of Merman, O'Connor, Dailey, Mitzi Gaynor, and Marilyn Monroe, inert. The fact that it was chock full of old Berlin tunes simply didn't carry the same kind of charge for the moviegoing public that the long roster of Berlin hits in *Alexander's Ragtime Band* had carried in 1938, a year that suddenly seemed like a very long time ago.

Even Monroe, shimmying and winking her way through "After You Get What You Want You Don't Want It" in a peekaboo white-lace body suit, and slithering and winking her way through "Heat Wave" in a black two-piece (as Merman looks on with patent scorn), couldn't lift the proceedings. She was Gorgeous, yes; Sexy, sure. But her presence was so capitalized and italicized that nothing was left to the imagination, and her breathy singing voice, better used in better films, lent little to Berlin's great songs.

And *Irving Berlin's There's No Business Like Show Business*, which with its elaborate production numbers had been a very expensive picture to make, was a box-office bomb.

* * *

"Sure, I haven't had a hit since I did *Call Me Madam*," Berlin told a reporter from the New York *Herald Tribune* that October. "I put out a couple of songs that I thought were pretty good. One of them, 'For the Very First Time,' was recorded by Tony Martin and I thought it was a good ballad. But it never got off the ground."[13]

"For the Very First Time" was released at a moment when American popular music, and the music business, were changing faster than anyone, including Irving Berlin, could comprehend—changing as profoundly as they had changed when ragtime and phonograph records had come in at the turn of the century.

In April 1954 Decca had released a 45 rpm single called "Rock around the Clock," by Bill Haley and the Comets, and while it was neither a particularly good song nor an especially good performance, this white translation of a black idiom that had existed vibrantly for a decade or more was both a symptom and a harbinger of the doom of the old order, both musically and financially.

"The new music had its roots in the black and country music that had been seeping into the mainstream through BMI since ASCAP's struggle with radio in the early 1940s," Furia writes.

> As Irving Berlin had foreseen many years before, radio was shortening the shelf life of a popular song with its incessant airing of "hits," and the quality of songwriting had suffered from this medium's insatiable appetite for songs. . . . The Top Ten of the old Hit Parade expanded into the Top Forty, and songs had to be turned out by the yard for an ever more youthful audience.[14]

"We don't like rock 'n' roll," an A&R (artists and repertory) man for one of the major labels said. "But we discovered that's what the teenagers want, and that's what we're going to give them. . . . I'm not going to keep recording [Irving] Berlin's old hits, just because they're Berlin's. What some of the old-timers don't realize is that Tin Pan Alley isn't the heart of the music world anymore."[15]

Nor was rock 'n' roll the only culprit. Broadway and Hollywood musicals had once been steady and bounteous sources of dance music, but with Broadway's transition to big, serious musicals like Rodgers and Hammerstein's, and Hollywood's turning out Technicolor spectacles to compete with television, the demand for music couples could dance cheek to cheek by was drying up.

* * *

Irving and Ellin wintered in Haiti that January, staying at the Hotel Oloffson, a picturesque gingerbread mansion in Port-au-Prince, where another illustrious guest, Noël Coward, was thrilled to see them. "Berlin fascinated Noël, who knew *all* his music," Coward's longtime companion Graham Payn wrote, in his memoir.

> One of the few songs Noël ever used that he didn't write himself was Berlin's "Always," which the psychic maid employed to conjure up the ghost of Elvira in *Blithe Spirit.*
>
> One evening, Noël plucked up his courage and performed from memory a medley of Berlin songs on the hotel piano. Berlin was so impressed that he asked Noël who'd written a particular tune he was playing. "Why, *you* did, sir," replied a bewildered Noël. The tune was "White Christmas."[16]

One of Coward's party that night, the dress designer Ginette Spanier, took Berlin in and saw a "little old man who was feeling very, very sad."[17] Only a month later the same man was at the White House, looking very happy.

On February 18, 1955, President Eisenhower presented Berlin with a congressional gold medal with the songwriter's profile on one side and an inscription on the reverse reading, in part, "in national recognition and appreciation of services in composing many patriotic songs, including God Bless America."[18] A photograph taken at the ceremony shows Ike flanked by Ellin and a tanned, beaming, robust-looking Berlin, handsome in a suit and tie with pocket square, delightedly displaying his medal. His hair is still dark. He looks perhaps fifty-five, certainly not about to turn sixty-seven. His wife, genteelly turned-out in white hat, white gloves, and a triple strand of pearls, looks weary.

A Berlin family story: once, when the three girls were young, Ellin had chided Linda for putting her elbows on the dinner table. "Daddy puts his elbows on the table," Linda said.

"Your father is a genius," Ellin replied, ending the conversation.

But living with a genius, she had learned over thirty years, could be as exhausting as being one.

* * *

There was an annoying distraction that spring, though in truth not much work was going on: a would-be songwriter, one Alfred L. Smith, sued Berlin, claiming Berlin had stolen *Call Me Madam*'s "You're Just in Love" from a song Smith claimed to have written in 1947. After a monthlong trial in which Berlin testified at length, and which included, near its climax, a dramatic scene—a piano was wheeled into the courtroom, and the composer sat down at the keys and demonstrated the composition of his great double song—New York State Supreme Court Justice Martin Frank ruled in Berlin's favor.

And then, at the end of November, some more-welcome excitement. "There is some talk about the possibility that Irving Berlin and George S. Kaufman will join S. N. Behrman to make a musical out of 'The Legendary Mizners,'" the *Times* reported. "According to one report, Max Gordon may produce it."[19]

It was more than a possibility: the playwrights Kaufman and Behrman had already signed on, and the noted producer Gordon had committed to the project. And Berlin, anxious for work, and feeling that the story of Addison and Wilson Mizner was the kind of outsized and slightly disreputable Americana he could sink his teeth into, eagerly joined them. The Mizner brothers were adventurers, gamblers, and con men who both turned to more respectable occupations: Addison became a Florida real estate developer and resort architect; Wilson became a playwright and screenwriter—and a friend of Berlin's in New York in the nineteen teens and twenties.

Kaufman and Behrman set to work on the script and Berlin got going on the score. The musical's working title, *Sentimental Guy*, was based on the lead character Wilson Mizner, who, as

Berlin described him, "is as hard as nails—tough on the surface, experienced, caustic, insulting, on the defensive, and thinks he believes his famous crack 'Never give a sucker an even break'— [but] underneath, he is a sentimental slob."[20]

Then, after a month, Kaufman, feeling played out at this stage of his career, withdrew from the project. Berlin and Behrman soldiered on. "Berlin," Robert Kimball writes, "wrote most of the songs for the first act by the spring of 1956." On the evidence of two of them—"You're a Sucker for a Dame" and "You're a Sentimental Guy," both included on the album *Unsung Irving Berlin*—the score, somewhat in the raffish spirit of *Guys and Dolls*, was solid but unexceptional, lacking the fourth dimension, the timelessness, of Berlin's best work.

For a while the show appeared to coalesce: José Ferrer and Mary Martin, Kimball writes, were considered for the leading roles. And then: "Behrman worked on the second act through the fall, but the project remained unfinished."[21]

Jablonski asserts that Behrman gave up because the "book lacked substance."[22] There may have been another factor. On the typed lyric sheet for a number called "Love Is for Boys" ("Love is for boys and not for men, / As sure as the stars above ...")—no music is known to survive—is a poignant notation: "dictated over phone from hospital."[23]

Mary Ellin Barrett writes that the depression that descended on her father in his mid-sixties was "far graver than the walking depression of the 'dry spell'; a nervous breakdown that would last several years, involve periods of hospitalization (at New York Hospital, at Silver Hill in Connecticut), and cause him to say he was retired."[24]

She recalled: "It was 1956 or 1957. Marvin and I and our little growing family were living in Wilton, and Daddy was in New Canaan"—at Silver Hill. "I remember he came over a couple of times to have dinner with us, and . . . said that he was depressed but getting better. But I just remember that it was very nice to see him."

Was his depression not evident?

"No," she said. "But he was hiding a lot in those years. There's no question about it."[25]

"I suffered severe bouts of depression," Berlin would recall years later, of the dark period between his mid-sixties and his early seventies.

> I worried about everything when, really, I had nothing to worry about. . . . There was everything a man could want. Money? It no longer meant anything. It came in, it went out. It would always come in. I decided to quit, to retire. I took up painting. Painting? That's a laugh. Daubs. They were awful. They had no meaning. I wrote no music, I made no songs; I idled, for five years.
>
> Retirement made me sick. I mean that. I got really sick. . . . First, there were health troubles—nerves, vague pains, twitches—then depression. I got to a point I didn't want to leave my room when daylight came.[26]

But he didn't quit, not really. In between the bouts of depression came spurts of inspiration, mostly in the form of lyric sheets without music: several for a planned, but never produced, 1957 NBC-TV spectacular that was to have re-created the spirit of the *Music Box Revues;* some for projected television commercials: for RCA, for Oldsmobile, for Coca-Cola.

Then, more ominously, and even more personally, a limerick entitled "A Worried Old Man," dictated to his secretary Hilda Schneider and sent to Irving Hoffman on April 18, 1958:

> A worried old man on the hill,
> But no one believed he was ill.
> They said, "You'll be sound
> If you just get around"

And one night he was found—
Very still.[27]

Three weeks later he would turn threescore and ten. "It was not," Barrett writes laconically, "a birthday to celebrate."

She remembered taking her small children to visit her parents in Lew Beach, and how, "even in the worst of his depression, [Berlin] could come to life for the children, a nice old grandpa who retreated for part of each day to the tea house, now a studio, to paint. . . . 'If the children didn't come, I knew it would be the end,' my mother said later."[28]

* * *

Yet he seemed perky enough when the *New York Times* interviewed him—at his insistence, over the telephone—for his seventieth. When the writer, Gilbert Millstein, confronted him with Kern's famous formulation—"Irving Berlin . . . *is* American music"—Berlin demurred, sort of. "I know my value, please believe it," he said.

> A man'd be stupid after fifty years not to. Those Hollywood companies made money with me. On the other hand, you'd be amazed how many bad songs I've written. I'm not coy, I don't underestimate or overestimate what I've done, but in my catalogue there are literally hundreds—300 to 350—of the worst songs you ever heard in your life. Oh, my, yes. . . .
>
> Right now, the thing I'd rather do than anything else is a good show. . . . These days, they're difficult, the standards are so high. But if something came along I could fit myself into and contribute something to, I'd start working. You work when you've got something to work on. The springboard for a proposition has to come. At 70, sometimes I feel every minute of it; when I have a good night's sleep, I don't feel more than 30 or 40.[29]

The springboard for a proposition has to come. It was an arresting image, from a writer whose imagery had always been richly, even startlingly, visual. But now there was no springboard, within or without: the high-bounding genius was earthed.

In the year he turned seventy he published not a single song—the first time this had happened since 1907. The following year there was just one: on November 16, 1959, Berlin registered for copyright "Israel":

> Israel,
> With outstretched arms
> You gave hope to your homeless people . . .

Always the sharpest-eyed judge of his own work, he wrote to Irving Hoffman on December 1: "I've reviewed my song 'Israel' and have grown quite cold on it, especially the first half. . . . After going over it a couple of times I felt it was quite heavy."[30]

A heaviness permeated him. In April, when his daughter Linda married the French-American stockbroker Edouard Emmet in New York, it wasn't certain Berlin would be up to giving her away: Ellin's brother Willie was standing by just in case. In the end, the father of the bride made it, but it was a near thing.

* * *

Linda and Edouard Emmet were frequent dinner guests at 17 Beekman Place during the first year and a half of their marriage, and it was clear that "attendance was mandatory as your mother insisted that our presence was beneficial to all concerned," Edouard wrote to Mary Ellin Barrett many years later.

Indeed, the company of his quietly charming French-born son-in-law, who shared Berlin's enthusiasm for painting, seemed to buoy his spirits. "Through long and discursive conversations on any subjects such as Fine Arts, Finance, Food, Fame or lack of it [your father and I] established excellent communications," Emmet recalled. "I knew that he had had a bad case of melancholia and he was still elusive and reclusive towards the world at large with only the immediate family and Irving Hoffman as persona grata. However in the latter part of 1960 and during 1961 . . . his moodiness started to evaporate."[31]

"One night before I went to sleep," Berlin later recalled, "I decided that when I woke up in the morning I would start something and finish it. I was tired of pulling out of everything. Tired of letting people down, letting myself down."[32]

Bonding with his genial son-in-law may have begun the process. But then in the spring of 1961 came that rarest and most hoped-for thing, the springboard for a proposition.

24

What Have You Written Lately?

FEELING BETTER that spring—not all better, but better—
Berlin had come to a decision: "I could do nothing and worry
or do something and worry," he figured. "So I decided to go
back to work. I was scared, but I felt I'd rather be 'unhappy,' in
quotes, doing something than doing nothing."[1]

By work he meant another Broadway show. Amazingly,
Call Me Madam was now over a decade in the past—and though
he'd toiled in Hollywood more recently, he wasn't nostalgic
about it. "Writing movie musicals is for the birds," he later told
an interviewer. "They're just rehashes of old tripe cut to a formula." He needed the stimulation of doing something new for
the theater, he said, but he was scared to death to tackle it.

Several scripts that turned out to be big hits were submit-
ted to Berlin, but he told producers he was too old to commit
to a project.[2] "I was using age as an excuse for my fear of fail-

ure," he said. "And you know what? I practically talked myself into a wheelchair."

In the end the need to feel vital again overcame his fear. He went to Leland Hayward, who'd produced *Call Me Madam*, and told him he wanted to do another show with *Madam's* writers, Howard Lindsay and Russel Crouse.[3]

Since that show Lindsay and Crouse had gone on to write the books of the Ethel Merman musical *Happy Hunting* and Rodgers and Hammerstein's *The Sound of Music*. In the spring of 1961 Hayward arranged a meeting. "[We] told Irving about an idea we'd been kicking around a few years," Crouse remembered. "It dealt with the personal problems facing a President ending his second term and his daughter's love affair with a Secret Service man assigned to guard her. The story was so vague in our minds we didn't know it if would add up to anything."[4]

Nevertheless, Berlin recalled, "I liked the idea and went back to the Catskills and wrote a few ballads." Lindsay and Crouse were enthusiastic enough about what he came back with that they put another project on hold. Then Hayward hired Josh Logan as director, "and we got started," Berlin said. "And once you get started on a show, you just keep going."[5] To maintain creative control, he and his production partners decided to foot the $400,000 cost of the show themselves.

Unlike *Call Me Madam*, the new musical was hung not on a star but on the considerable bona fides of its creative team, all of whom qualified as legitimate Broadway luminaries in 1961. Lindsay and Crouse were Lindsay and Crouse. Leland Hayward, since *Call Me Madam*, had produced *Gypsy* and *The Sound of Music*; Josh Logan, since *Annie Get Your Gun*, had directed *Mister Roberts*, *South Pacific*, and William Inge's *Picnic*.

But it was Irving Berlin's return to the musical theater that lent the new project its biggest charge. From the beginning, the show seems to have been largely propelled by the considerable force of Berlin's reawakened vitality, which gathered momentum as his work progressed: he was having fun. The idea of the first daughter's romance with the Secret Service agent particularly tickled him, and one of the first songs he brought to the playwrights was the showstopper-to-be "The Secret Service":

> The Secret Service
> Makes me nervous—
> When I am dating,
> They are waiting
> To observe us.[6]

Berlin continued writing through the summer, as did Lindsay and Crouse, though the project remained under wraps. As far as the general public was concerned, Irving Berlin was a retired elderly gentleman whose name came up now and then in the press in connection with "White Christmas" or "God Bless America," but no longer in the breathless tones accorded a major influencer of the current culture.

This was not the way Berlin liked it. Nineteen sixty-one marked the fiftieth anniversary of "Alexander's Ragtime Band," and he had tasked Helmy Kresa with making sure the golden occasion and the great song's writer got as much ink as possible. On August 25, in one of the many interviews Kresa had lined up for Berlin, the reporter noticed that the songwriter was in especially lively spirits, "excited by something unmentioned."[7]

Then, on September 1, the beans spilled. " 'Mr. President' is the title of the new musical that is being written to Irving Berlin's songs by Howard Lindsay and Russel Crouse," wrote the *Times*'s Sam Zolotow.

> The pivotal character is a President of the United States as he is finishing his second term and after he has left office. Those concerned insist the concept is not related to any President, living or dead, or to the family of a President. . . .
> It will take at least eight months for the offering to reach

the boards. None of the leading players has been decided upon.[8]

The article was accompanied by a Magnum photograph of Berlin looking severe and alert in his dark suit and tie and black-rimmed eyeglasses, his still mostly dark hair neatly parted. He could have been the head partner of a law firm or the chairman of an investment bank.

But as his son-in-law recalled, the septuagenarian was cheerful, even exuberant, in the closing months of 1961—and this despite two major losses, the death of Joe Schenck, at eighty-two, in October, and the untimely passing of Moss Hart, dead of a heart attack at fifty-seven, in December.

Earlier in the year his daughter Linda and her husband Edouard Emmet had moved to Paris, and Irving and Ellin visited the young couple over the Christmas holidays. The Berlins stayed at the Crillon, the monumental old hotel on the Place de la Concorde, not far from Edouard's office, and father- and son-in-law quickly established a routine: while Ellin and Linda spent the day shopping, Irving and Edouard would go to lunch, then stroll through this plush section of the City of Light.

"Our first walks were along the Rue de Rivoli and the Rue de Castiglionne," Emmet recalled, "and on days when he felt chipper (which was often in 1961) all the way to Rue des Pyramides (the end of the Tuileries Gardens). He really enjoyed passing under the arcades as, he said, it made him feel [like] a 'boulevardier'—his word. He liked the architecture and would tell me about his first visits when he had to wear spats and everyone in that part of town seemed so elegant."

Berlin had first visited Paris in 1911, the year "Alexander" opened the world to him, and his memories of the great city in the time before World War I were vivid and fond. His favorite anecdote, Emmet recalled, was of a late-evening supper at the apartment of Mistinguett, the famed singer-dancer of the Moulin Rouge and Folies Bergère: lobsters were to be cooked, and when young Irving was asked to fetch them, he was delighted to find them on ice in the bidet, waving their antennas and claws.

Emmet also remembered that during their strolls his father-in-law, in the midst of creating *Mr. President*'s score, would sometimes suddenly slip into songwriting mode: "As we walked, the composer lyricist would take over completely and I would watch in fascination your father moving his lips and waving the fingers of his right hand as though keeping time—which is exactly what he was doing."[9]

* * *

The show gradually came together, the book more slowly than the songs. In January the actress Nanette Fabray met with Berlin, Lindsay, and Crouse to discuss playing the first lady (the fact that she somewhat resembled Jacqueline Kennedy was not lost on the authors). To demonstrate their work in progress, the three, Fabray recalled, "began reading jokes and bits of the show off paper napkins, menus, envelopes, all sorts of things. And Irving hummed a couple of tunes—he doesn't hum very well. I was undecided."[10]

Underwhelmed was probably more like it. A plot of sorts evolved. The title character, President Stephen Decatur Henderson, is a patriotic family man with a young and vivacious wife, Nell; a frisky, nubile daughter, Leslie; and a hotheaded son, Larry. In act one, as he finishes his second and final term, Henderson makes a goodwill tour of Europe whose climactic visit to Moscow is derailed when he makes a joke about the Soviet premier that is taken the wrong way; a love story also develops between Leslie and the solid, good-hearted Secret Service agent who guards her. In act two, Henderson leaves office and returns to Ohio to write his memoirs and try to cope with the anticlimax of ordinary life.

But the real story of *Mr. President*, in the months leading up to the first tryout, was the seventy-four-year-old Berlin's miraculous return to Broadway—a storybook comeback instrumental in generating, by the time the *Herald Tribune*'s John Crosby interviewed the songwriter in June, a breathtaking $1.4 million in advance sales, for a show that wasn't to open till October. "I hadn't seen him in years," Crosby wrote, "and he looks absolutely unchanged—still full of that galvanic energy, that gushing, eager, boyish charm I'd remembered."[11]

How many songs had he written for the show? the columnist asked. "Perhaps too many," Berlin said, laughing. He paused for a moment, then brought out a familiar image. "It would have been easy to have gone into the trunk for the songs," he said, "but I wanted to see if I could still reach up and find it there." To illustrate the point he reached over his head for an imaginary melody.

Berlin was thrilled by his renewed productivity, but uneasy about the advance. "This is a new kind of show business," he told Crosby. "In the old days, you had to show what you had before anyone gave you a million dollars. Of course, we have all that money in the box office, but I don't think it makes a hit."[12]

The cast was complete when rehearsals started at the end of July: Fabray had agreed to play First Lady Nell Henderson, and, after the charismatic Robert Preston, of *Music Man* fame, had passed on the role of President Henderson, Berlin and his partners chose the tall, craggy movie actor Robert Ryan, who had a strong presence but a merely pleasant baritone. (Berlin advised him not to take any singing lessons: "If you were any better, you'd be lousy," he said.)[13] The twenty-five-year-old Anita Gillette, who had made her Broadway debut in *Gypsy*, played the third key role, feisty First Daughter Leslie.

On July 23, a hot and humid afternoon in New York, the cast gathered to hear *Mr. President*'s score for the first time. Berlin came out of the wings, took off his suit jacket, and loosened his tie. Helmy Kresa sat down at the upright and looked at the boss for a cue. Berlin nodded, Kresa played the first chords of the opening number, "Mr. President," and the man who had written the song began to sing it:

> Just someone doing the best he can,
> A simple everyday family man. . . .
> Just a simple American,
> Not one of the greats,
> But he happens to be President
> Of these United States.[14]

A photograph taken that day shows Berlin standing by the piano, arms thrown wide, white short-sleeved shirt damp with perspiration, a sheaf of lyric sheets in his left hand, belting out one of the twenty-two tunes from the biggest score he'd ever written, the seventy-four-year-old song plugger selling it for all he's worth. It is an immeasurably touching image. "Irving was as nervous as a cat up a tree," Russel Crouse remembered, "but after he had sung a score or more of numbers in that high, cracked voice, everybody broke into spontaneous applause."[15]

How could they not? It was *Irving Berlin*, singing never-heard Berlin tunes, to *them*.

Though the cast and the score were complete, the book still wasn't. Rehearsals began with a partial script while Lindsay and Crouse continued to hammer away at the inevitably problematic second act. Yet in the eyes of one observer, more than the second act was in trouble. When Nanette Fabray's husband, the screenwriter and director Ranald MacDougall, read the libretto, he said, "Nan, do you really *have* to do this show?"[16]

* * *

The Boston tryout premiered in late August; the reviews were rough. The *Record-American*'s drama critic Elliot Norton, esteemed for his penetrating but judicious assessments of shows bound for Broadway, wrote that while the score had "at least three or four songs with the authentic lilt and magic of Irving Berlin at his ultimate best," many of the other songs were "corny," and the second act didn't work at all. "*Mr. President* is in dreadful shape at the present time," he concluded.[17]

But hadn't *Call Me Madam* also had out-of-town hiccups? The playwrights and the composer got right to work, cutting, rewriting, punching up lines and lyrics. Berlin dropped three songs from the score and added two, "You Need a Hobby" (the title echoing a suggestion he'd heard more than once when he decided to retire), and, trying to duplicate some of *Madam*'s magic, a new double song, "Empty Pockets Filled with Love," to be sung by the regular-guy Secret Service agent Pat to the high-life-loving First Daughter Leslie.

But there was no magic this time around. As Howard Lindsay would later say, "The success or failure of a show is settled when somebody says, 'Wouldn't it be a great idea . . .' Perle Mesta was. This wasn't."[18]

The next stop was Washington, where all two and a half weeks of *Mr. President*'s run were sold out, including standing room. With John F. Kennedy in office, the town had become sexy and glamorous, and the September 25 gala premiere of *Mr. President*, a benefit for two Kennedy charities, had the red-carpet éclat of a Hollywood extravaganza. The *New York Times* found the event important enough to send a reporter.

"President and Mrs. Kennedy joined more than 1,600 of the political and social elite of Washington and New York at the pre-Broadway showing in the National Theater," wrote the paper's Marjorie Hunter. "The theater opening was a high-fashion affair, with holders of $100 tickets entertained royally at pre-theater dinner parties and a champagne supper dance at the British Embassy after the show."[19]

The list of attendees read like a who's who of American power: much of the Kennedy family was present, as were Vice President Johnson and Lady Bird; CBS chairman William Paley; *Time* founder Henry Luce and his wife, Claire Boothe Luce; Alice Roosevelt Longworth; General Maxwell Taylor; Averell

Harriman and his wife, Pamela; Mr. and Mrs. Laurance Rockefeller; Mr. and Mrs. Alfred Gwynne Vanderbilt; and . . . on and on.[20] Berlin found the glittering to-do "flattering, but . . . crazy."[21]

Unfortunately, the offstage show was considerably more impressive than the onstage one. The first embarrassing moment occurred soon after conductor Jay Blackton lifted his baton, when the audience mistook the overture for "The Star-Spangled Banner" and rose to its feet, only to realize its mistake a minute later and awkwardly sit back down. A first-act joke about French President Charles de Gaulle not only fell flat, but generated boos and hisses.[22] The sight of an empty rocking chair in the presidential box distracted the audience throughout the first act—as did the president's arrival fifteen minutes into the second. And Robert Ryan, though a commanding presence, had little idea how to play comedy: he waited until every laugh had died down completely before beginning to speak again, throwing a wrench into the play's rhythm.[23]

Mary Ellin remembered the Washington premiere as "ghastly,"[24] and Nanette Fabray remembered Irving Berlin, at the after-party at the British embassy, sitting in a corner, looking shrunken and miserable. "He knew what a disaster this was," she said, "and he tried to carry on, tried to be kind, gentle, and supportive."[25]

The show itself was far too gentle, betraying an outmoded—or simply imaginary—view of the American presidency in rapidly changing and darkening times. And while the power players watching the Washington premiere of *Mr. President* wouldn't have known every clandestine detail of affairs of state (it was the eve of the Cuban Missile Crisis), or of the affairs of the head of state, they would have been sharply aware that what they were watching and hearing onstage was a fairy tale—and one without even the symbolic force of Lerner and Loewe's hit 1960 musical *Camelot*, whose idealized view of King Arthur's court the president and Mrs. Kennedy had eagerly seized on as a metaphor for his presidency.

The *Washington Post's* Richard L. Coe called the show a "timid bore." Tom Donnelly, of the *Washington News*, wrote, "'Mr. President' is more on the order of 'The Hardy Family Goes to the White House.'" Then he twisted the knife, adding that most of the Berlin songs sounded "suitable for a medley titled 'When It's Cliché Time in Tin Pan Alley.'"[26]

Leland Hayward blamed a familiar American target for *Mr. President's* poor reception: "For some reason—maybe it's the title and the Kennedys' being in the White House—the intellectuals come expecting a cross between 'State of the Union' and 'Of Thee I Sing,'" he said. "Well, we're not doing a satire. We're doing a warm, human, simple story of a man who is President and his family."[27]

In other words, make-believe. But according to Berlin and his coproducers, make-believe was what the public was in the market for: by the producers' lights, *Mr. President* had the potential to become, in the theater term of art, an "audience show": one that the critics deprecate but the mob loves. As proof, they could point to their dizzying advance sale of $2,500,000, the largest in Broadway history.

Yet Berlin, with a half-century's Broadway wisdom, knew the truth was more complicated. "There is a great advantage, of course, in having such heavy insurance," he said, "but there is a disadvantage, too. As all the hoopla built up, so did what the public expected of the show. Nothing less than a miracle would have satisfied those expectations."

Then he too tried to see the bright side. "The New York audiences may not expect the miraculous," he said. "Instead of the built-in resentment that any big pre-sold show is bound to run into, they may be willing to come and judge us on our merits."[28]

Mr. President opened on Saturday night, October 20, at the

St. James Theatre, and Berlin and his colleagues had to wait through a long Sunday for the Monday-morning reviews. The reviews were very bad. Writing in the *New York Journal-American*, John McClain began, "There is just no way to be charitable about *Mr. President*," and concluded by declaring the show "quite simply, an old-fashioned dud."

The *Herald Tribune*'s Walter Kerr went straight at Berlin, whose "hand seems to rise and fall thoughtlessly, as though he weren't looking at the keys," he wrote.

> More seriously, the words—which always were simple, but simply evocative—are prosaic, mere wooden soldiers keeping up with the beat. . . . "It gets lonely in the White House when you're being attacked. And the loyal opposition gets into the act"[29] [*sic*] isn't good Berlin, it is just weak editorial writing. Strangely, the number of harsh, consonant line-endings which are turned into rhymes increases wildly, and against all the old-fashioned rules for song writing.[30]

One can envision Berlin's response to Walter Kerr's teaching him about songwriting. *Critics, what do the critics know.* But in the case of *Mr. President*, they seemed to know a sad truth, and the mob agreed. On June 8, 1963, the show closed after just 265 performances. "The day our advance sales ran out," Nanette Fabray said, "was the day we closed."[31]

The last song the audience heard on that last day was "This Is a Great Country." It concluded:

> Hats off to America,
> The home of the free and the brave—
> If this is flag waving
> Flag waving,
> Do you know of a better flag to wave?[32]

The patriotism Berlin evoked in his finale, with its echoes of "The Star-Spangled Banner" and George M. Cohan's "You're a Grand Old Flag," was real in his heart, and in the hearts of millions of Americans. But it would be sorely tested in the year ahead—the *annus horribilis* of 1963—and in the years ahead.

* * *

Two decades earlier Irving Berlin had wondered aloud who would tell him when he was washed up as a songwriter; he had said he didn't want to make his exit in the midst of a bunch of mediocre songs. This was precisely what *Mr. President* was, but Berlin wasn't ready to exit just yet.

"I was terrified that another depression would follow the bad notices," Edouard Emmet remembered.[33] No doubt the rest of the family was too. "What can you say," Mary Ellin Barrett writes,

> when an old showman's last musical, instead of being, at the least, a good, strong farewell, like Cole Porter's *Silk Stockings* or Kurt Weill's *Lost in the Stars*, is an unprecedented dud? You can say that the old showman took the humiliation with dignity, he shrugged it off, and he didn't sink back into depression, though he would never again be the real "old self" I'd once known. Instead, he wrote a batch of new songs, a score he said was one of his best, for *Say It with Music*.[34]

Reviving the Berlin biopic, which had ground to a halt at Twentieth Century–Fox in 1939 amid insuperable script problems, was Arthur Freed's idea: the old MGM hand, still in place though the studio system had collapsed and movie musicals gone out of style, wanted to make his own exit with a dream project: a final Irving Berlin cavalcade. In March 1963 he lured the songwriter to Los Angeles to receive the Screen Producers Guild's highest honor, the Milestone Award, in a high-Hollywood ceremony at the Beverly Hilton: dozens of stars were present, including Fred Astaire and Ginger Rogers, Groucho Marx, Danny Kaye, and Frank Sinatra. Berlin sang and played "Always," and as a finale, brought the audience to its feet with "God Bless America."

Having softened up the songwriter in grand style, Freed presented his idea to Berlin, who quickly shot it down. For one thing, to date every Hollywood picture purporting to tell the life story of a major songwriter—Kern, Gershwin, Porter—had been tripe, with only one exception, the great *Yankee Doodle Dandy*, starring James Cagney as George M. Cohan. But more important, Berlin simply didn't want his life story, or anything like it, told onscreen while he was still alive.

The crafty producer quickly shifted gears: what about a fictional musical spanning all the decades of Berlin's career, with songs to cover every period? Berlin could tap his catalogue once more and write a few new tunes. Vincente Minnelli would direct and Berlin's old favorite, Roger Edens, would supervise the music.

A package job, yes. But a package job on an epic scale. The deal was announced at the end of April: Berlin got the million dollars he asked for and went to work on the score for *Say It with Music*. Arthur Laurents, a distinguished screenwriter and the librettist of *Gypsy* and *West Side Story*, was assigned to create a script.

Berlin labored through the summer of 1963, producing ten songs, a couple of which—the delightful "Outside of Loving You, I Like You" and the ardent "Whisper It"—can be heard on *Unsung Irving Berlin*. Neither they nor the rest of the score would ever be heard on film.

In September, Irving and Ellin went to London to give a wedding for their youngest daughter, Elizabeth, to the English book editor Edmund Fisher. In his suite at Claridge's Berlin was interviewed by the *Daily Express*'s Herbert Kretzmer, who was surprised and pleased to find a subject he'd expected to be difficult "happy and chatty, . . . giving the lie to the reputation for curmudgeonly reticence that had preceded him to Britain."

Berlin spoke freely about the anguish his temporary retirement had caused him, and the discontents of old age: "I'm not

a kid anymore," he said. "Last May I celebrated, or didn't celebrate, my seventy-fifth birthday." On the other hand, he told
Kretzmer, he was as busy as ever: witness the score for *Say It
with Music.* "I know what I can do," he said. "I know where I
want to go. Age has nothing to do with it. . . . You've got to stay
healthy. That's all."[35]

*   *   *

He stayed healthy, but wrote no songs in 1964, as the advent of the Beatles brought light to the dark aftermath of the
Kennedy assassination and changed the course of popular music
with dizzying speed. Everything was changing with dizzying
speed in the sixties, and the zeitgeist was not kind to the for-
tunes of *Say It with Music.* While MGM went through corpo-
rate turmoil and successive management changes, draft after
draft of the screenplay was rejected and writer after writer replaced: after Laurents came Leonard Gershe (*Funny Face*), who
was followed by the brilliant Betty Comden and Adolph Green
(*Singin' in the Rain, Bells Are Ringing*), who in turn were let go
and replaced by an old Metro musical and comedy hand named
George Wells. The project had come to resemble the boulder
that Sisyphus rolls up the hill.

Wells turned in his first draft of *Say It with Music* on Irving
Berlin's seventy-eighth birthday, May 11, 1966, but by then Berlin was otherwise engaged—and for a change, pleasurably so.

*   *   *

On that day, the seventy-eight-year-old was on the job in
Toronto, working on the tryout of a revival of *Annie Get Your
Gun*, once again starring Ethel Merman, and set to open at Lincoln Center at the end of the month. That day he also dictated
a "Dear Hymie" letter to his old friend Harold Arlen, thanking
Arlen and his wife, Anya, for their birthday greetings and con-
cluding: "Amid all the fuss, somewhere in the background there
is a tiny voice whispering in my ear and repeating one pertinent
phrase—'what have you written lately?' "[36]

He had a ready answer, if a short one: he had composed two new numbers for the revival, "Who Needs the Birds and Bees?"—it would be dropped before the show went to New York—and a new double song, "An Old-Fashioned Wedding."

Like Berlin's other great countermelodies, "Old-Fashioned Wedding" juxtaposed not just contrapuntal tunes but opposing themes. In 1914's "Simple Melody" the contrast had been between traditional music and ragtime; in *Call Me Madam* thirty-six years later, "You're Just in Love" opposed the naïveté of Russel Nype's smitten character and the tough but warm wisdom of Ethel Merman's Sally Adams.

It's striking that Berlin hadn't written a double number for the original *Annie*—perhaps because Herbert and Dorothy Fields's libretto was so rock-solid—but at almost eighty, Berlin wanted to prove to himself and the world that he could still reach up and grab it.

He proved it. The contrast in "Old-Fashioned Wedding" is between the foursquare conventionality of Bruce Yarnell's Frank Butler, who booms out in a rich, turn-of-the-century baritone—

> We'll have an old-fashioned wedding,
> Blessed in the good old-fashioned way . . .

—and Ethel Merman's thoroughly liberated Annie, who tramples roughshod on his square stipulations with a sassy countermelody delivered in that matchlessly ice-cutting voice:

> I wanna wedding in a big church
> With bridesmaids and flower girls . . .[37]

The contrast is delicious, the song is delicious, nobody cared that the ageless Merman was fifty-eight to Yarnell's thirty-one ("She can play it till she's ninety, and I hope she does," Berlin said),[38] and when the revival of *Annie Get Your Gun* opened at Lincoln Center's New York State Theater on May 31, Berlin and Merman (and Richard Rodgers, back as producer) had a triumph on their hands. "New York theatergoers can relax this morning: Ethel Merman and Irving Berlin are collaborating again," wrote the *Times*'s Vincent Canby.[39]

But the triumph was, of necessity, short-lived: *Annie*'s revival was set for a limited run of five weeks. And even if the showstopping number proved that Irving Berlin was still capable of great songwriting, "An Old-Fashioned Wedding" was a hit only in a narrow sense—not, as Berlin hits always used to be, in the broader culture. The Hit Parade was long gone. *Billboard*'s Hot 100 singles roster for 1966 was a mishmash of patriotism (Sergeant Barry Sadler's "Ballad of the Green Berets"), schmaltz (the Association's "Cherish"), Motown (the Four Tops' "Reach Out I'll Be There"), Sinatras (Nancy's "These Boots Are Made for Walkin'"; Frank's "Strangers in the Night"), and plenty of rock 'n' roll by the Beatles, the Beach Boys, the Rolling Stones, and others. Irving Berlin was nowhere in sight.[40]

Twenty years earlier, when someone had had the temerity to call the original *Annie Get Your Gun* "old-fashioned," Berlin had riposted, "Yeah, an old-fashioned smash!"[41] Consciously or unconsciously, "An Old-Fashioned Wedding" was a new riposte to any who might consider him a has-been. Still, some deep part of him was Frank Butler in that song—*was* old-fashioned. In early 1966 he'd written the words for a new number (no music is known to survive), "I Wanna Dance with the Girl in My Arms," for Fred Astaire to sing in the doomed *Say It with Music:*

> Instead of twisting,
> Rock-and-rolling miles apart,
> I wanna dance
> Cheek to cheek and heart to heart.[42]

*   *   *

Say It with Music stumbled on through seismic shifts at MGM, always about to happen, never happening. "Every time they were ready to shoot, the whole management of the studio changed," Arthur Freed's daughter Barbara Freed Saltzman recalled. "The people who made the decisions changed. They became much more business oriented and less artistic."[43]

On January 22, 1968, the *Los Angeles Times* ran a breathless item:

> One of the biggest and most important musicals in the history of M-G-M, Irving Berlin's *Say It with Music* will star Julie Andrews under the direction of Blake Edwards. . . . [It] will go before the cameras at M-G-M's Culver City studios in early 1969 with an all-star cast—one of the largest arrays of musical talents assembled for one motion picture.[44]

But *Say It with Music* would not go before the cameras in early 1969, or at any other time. In the middle of that year the Las Vegas millionaire Kirk Kerkorian would take over MGM and install James T. Aubrey, Jr., the former head of CBS Television, as president. In short order Aubrey would sell off most of the MGM back lot and all the costumes and props that had accumulated over thirty-five years, including Judy Garland's ruby slippers from *The Wizard of Oz*. Metro-Goldwyn-Mayer would cease to exist as a movie studio in 1973, by which time *Say It with Music* had become a distant memory.

* * *

A month before the midpoint of the chaotic year 1968, Ed Sullivan broadcast an eightieth-birthday tribute to Irving Berlin on his CBS-TV variety show. For two decades the Sullivan show had been an American institution, bringing families together on Sunday evenings to watch wholesome entertainment, but by the late sixties it looked as tired as the slumped shoulders of its host.

The Berlin tribute, on the night of May 5, was perfectly tailored to its aging audience. Sullivan's guests were Bing Crosby, Bob Hope, Ethel Merman, Harry James and His Orchestra,

Fred Waring and the Pennsylvanians, Robert Goulet, Peter Gennaro and his dancers, and for the youngsters, Diana Ross and the Supremes.

President Lyndon Johnson, battered by the insoluble problem of the war in Vietnam—five weeks earlier he had announced he would not seek reelection—opened the show with a taped birthday greeting to Berlin. "America is richer for his presence," the president said.

"The rest of the show," wrote the *New York Times*'s George Gent, "was a tuneful demonstration of the truth of that statement. Mr. Berlin has written more than 3,000 songs [*sic*] over the years, and 90 minutes could provide younger viewers with only a sampling of them. But for older viewers, it was a night of nostalgia."[45]

To warm those viewers' hearts, Crosby sang "Marie from Sunny Italy," then went into a medley of early Berlin hits— "Call Me Up Some Rainy Afternoon," "That International Rag," "Alexander"—and wound up, naturally, with "White Christmas." Then Sullivan screened film clips from *Top Hat*, *Easter Parade*, *The Great Ziegfeld*, and *Blue Skies*, climaxing with Berlin's doughboy-uniformed performance of "Oh, How I Hate to Get Up in the Morning" from *This Is the Army*.

Any younger viewers who hadn't already fled the TV room wouldn't have stuck around for much of Diana Ross and the Supremes, who performed a stupefyingly mechanical and perfunctory medley of Berlin hits, singing tiny snippets of songs that did no justice to the material, with which Ross, the reigning diva of Motown, seemed supremely uncomfortable. But then, as if by magic, Ethel Merman wafted out onto the stage, smilingly rescuing "You're Just in Love."

After Robert Goulet sang a number from the soon to be abandoned movie, the lovely "I Used to Play It by Ear"; after Peter Gennaro and his dancers (amusingly) interpreted "This Is the Army, Mr. Jones"; after Merman returned to stop the show with a medley from *Annie Get Your Gun*, Berlin himself stepped up from the audience, where he'd been sitting with Ellin, to sing "God Bless America."

He would be eighty in a week, and in his tuxedo and horn-rims, he looked the best possible version of his age. His hair had only begun to gray; his teeth were his own. His voice was soft—it had always been soft—but he was right on key, and, ham though he was, he played it perfectly, neither over- or underselling the great song, investing it with all the quiet majesty it merited. After the first chorus the curtain parted to reveal two bleachers full of Boy and Girl Scouts, joining in in full-throated accompaniment. The sight of the fresh young faces was as moving as it was meant to be, and as the final chord died down, Ed Sullivan wheeled out a huge birthday cake aflame with eighty candles.

"Schmaltz? Certainly," the *Times'* Gent wrote. "But it was a marvelous party."[46]

And it was, in its way. Yet what was lost in the show's wash of goodwill and haze of nostalgia—what was lost in that moment in general—was only the essence of Berlin: the piercing wit and naughtiness and jarringly deep emotion of his best work, and its timelessness. Nostalgia is not about timelessness but about fixing the past in a specious golden glow of harmlessness. Berlin, whose greatest work was as unsettling as any great artist's, had become America's Grandpa.

* * *

Six days later, on Saturday, May 11, 1968, a cool and cloudy spring afternoon, Irving and Ellin Berlin rode into Central Park's Sheep Meadow in the back of an open convertible, preceded by a children's band from the Bronx, the Silver Beach Fife and Drum Corps, as eight thousand Girl Scouts cheered, squealed, and waved tiny American flags.

The car pulled to a stop near a stage that had been built in the meadow; Berlin got out and climbed the steps to the platform. The small, spry old man stood beaming at the podium, the still center of a world out of balance, in the center of the city he loved. He leaned toward the microphone. "There have been many high spots," Irving Berlin told the crowd, "but this is it."

Then the eight thousand Girl Scouts cheered again, and sang "Happy Birthday, Dear Irving."[47] Berlin smiled as their voices filled the air.

Diminuendo and Coda

AND THEN HE REALLY DID RETIRE. "It was as if I owned a store and people no longer wanted to buy what I had to sell," Berlin would tell Robert Kimball some years later. "Everything changed. The world was a different place. The death of President Kennedy, the Vietnam War, the social protest. Music changed, too. The Beatles and other groups reached audiences. I couldn't. It was time to close up shop."[1]

The shop itself stayed open for business, even if the offices of the Irving Berlin Music Company at Sixth Avenue and 51st, ruled by Berlin's longtime secretary Hilda Schneider, resembled "a time capsule, complete with old switchboard and stockroom."[2] But plenty was still going on: lawyers and accountants handling permissions requests, contracts, and the Berlin real estate holdings; Irving's good friend and entertainment attorney Abe Berman keeping tabs on the "God Bless America"

Fund and Berlin's interest in the Music Box, held in partnership, since the death of Sam Harris's widow, with the Shubert
Organization.

For a few years Berlin went in several days a week to check
on copyrights and sales and the Music Box's receipts, and to
meet colleagues and friends for lunch. But the world was a different place. Lindy's closed in 1969; Dinty Moore's wouldn't be
around much longer. More and more he stayed home.

Though he'd retired, that tiny voice kept whispering in
his ear. So he continued to write, incessantly: it was what he
did, who he was; he couldn't stop any more than he could stop
breathing. New songs, dictated over the phone to Helmy Kresa,
until Kresa lost his hearing; but mostly lyrics, poems, and letters, a vast outpouring of words, read over the telephone to
Schneider, who dutifully typed everything up, filed away copies, and sent the letters over to Beekman Place for the boss's
signature.

The music may have faded, but the vivid, snappy, sometimes stinging writerly voice lingered on, even in the face of
incomprehensible change. A typed lyric sheet from September
1968 commemorates the Soviet invasion of Czechoslovakia:

> Welcome comrades, welcome,
> Welcome to your slaves—
> Thank you for the roses
> On our children's graves . . .[3]

And at the end of the year he wrote the lyric for a song—no
music is known to survive—about an epithet that had become
rife in the protest movement. The number, Berlin wrote, was to
be "done by two pigs—one black and one white":

> Millions of pigs both black and white
> Are being offended day and night
> By folks on the left and folks on the right
> Calling each other pigs . . .[4]

But some events defied even his imagination. In August 1969 he wrote to Harry Ruby about a lyric Ruby had attempted in honor of *Apollo 11:*

> The moon landing is indeed the greatest event that's happened in anybody's lifetime to inspire some kind of a song, but I don't know of any songwriter who can measure up to this occasion. . . .
>
> I remember being in Atlantic City in 1927 when Lindbergh crossed the ocean and landed in Paris. I was there working on the *Ziegfeld Follies* of that year. I was so overcome with emotion and really tried to write some kind of a song. It just didn't work. I could come up with nothing. And looking back, what did Tin Pan Alley come up with? The Lindy Hop and Wolfie Gilbert's "Lucky Lindy."
>
> The best words for a moon song that I've heard so far are those spoken by the three astronauts.[5]

He couldn't give up the idea of writing one more show. He toyed with the notion of a quasi-autobiographical story of the Music Box, perhaps with some of the songs he'd written for *Crystal Ball.*[6] Jerome Robbins, whom he loved, would direct and choreograph; Arthur Laurents would write the book.[7] In the spring of 1970 he spoke with his eldest daughter about it; yet, as she writes, "he hadn't the energy to mount a whole show. 'I'm tired, Mary Ellin,' he said. 'Damn it, your old man has just about had it.'" She put her arms around him a bit awkwardly— they weren't a demonstrative family—and he told her he loved her. She said it back. Then: "Well, darling, I think I'll lie down for a while. You go downstairs to Marvin and your mother. Try to cheer her up. It's not so cheerful always these days being married to your old man."[8]

The telephone became his main link to the outside world, and those he called weren't always happy to hear from him. James T. Maher, Alec Wilder's collaborator on *American Popular Song*, told of a harrowing phone encounter with Berlin after

Wilder had asked permission to use some short passages from Berlin songs as illustrative matter in his book. After seeing an excerpt from the manuscript, Berlin apparently came to feel Wilder was using the passages to accuse him of musical plagiarism. He subjected Maher to an expletive-filled tirade, and summarily withdrew his permission.[9] Wilder's almost worshipful section on Berlin's music thus became the only chapter in the book without musical examples.

Mary Ellin, who knew her adored father almost as well as he knew himself, notes judiciously that

> the character he presented in his eighties and nineties depended to some extent on who was at the other end of the phone. To strangers, or acquaintances who wanted something he didn't want to give, he was a disagreeable, out-of-touch old man who said no and guarded the use of his songs, of everything to do with him, beyond reason. And though some reports of this character are exaggerated, I cannot claim all were (or that I did not have my own experiences, over the phone, of that cranky, difficult old man).[10]

Berlin's archivist Robert Kimball, a telephone friend for the last twenty years of the songwriter's life, wrote that Berlin "got upset when he thought people were trying to take advantage of him or were challenging his right to make artistic and business decisions about his own songs. Yet when artists performed his songs well or individuals wrote books or articles that he enjoyed, he was more than appreciative; his enthusiasm was heartwarming and deeply moving. All of us who were ever thanked by Irving Berlin know how deeply he expressed his gratitude."[11]

In July of his ninety-first year he wrote to one of the most elegant and passionate interpreters of his music.

> Dear Tony:
> This is a thank you note from a great fan of yours.
> I saw you on the Mike Douglas show yesterday, also the

Johnny Carson show some weeks ago, and you were won-
derful. I love the way you sing those songs.
Again my thanks and best to you,
As always,[12]

In 1987 Tony Bennett would record an entire album of Irving
Berlin songs, *Bennett/Berlin*. Along with Fred Astaire, Ella Fitzgerald, and Frank Sinatra, he remains one of the great singers
of Berlin.

*   *   *

Berlin's postretirement correspondence with his friends
shows a far more easygoing side of him than that seen by intru-
sive strangers. He even grew more relaxed about his painting,
to which he seems to have returned with diminished expectations. He liked to give the oils to friends and family as gifts,
often with his tongue slightly in cheek. In September 1971 he
wrote to Astaire:

Dear Fred:
I had no idea that this painting would turn out the way it did.
I started out doing a bird and for some reason, which I can't
explain, I thought of you, so I gave it a top hat and a white tie.
I hope you like it.
With love to you from Ellin and me,
   As always,[13]

Though Astaire always seemed on the verge of retirement,
he kept working through the 1970s, now as a straight actor
rather than a singer and dancer, in a business that felt increasingly alien to him. In December 1970 Berlin sent him another
painting—apparently one more picture of Astaire in top hat,
white tie, and tails—as a Christmas gift. Ten days later Astaire
wrote back, in longhand:

Dear Irving—
   Again I must express my appreciation for your painting!
I think its terrific and it sure means a lot to me. That's a

<u>pretty</u> <u>graceful</u> <u>step</u> you've got me doing there with the fly-
ing tails! Love it—love it!

I do hope I'll see you this year. It'll be fun to talk about
the <u>present</u> <u>day</u> <u>screwed</u> up <u>nudie</u> <u>rudie</u> foul show business.
It's so overloaded with crummy crap I just wont go to see
anything anymore. Neither will my youngsters.

Best love to Ellin—

As ever—

Fred[14]

Berlin would not have told the prudish Astaire about a late-
1972 expedition he made with Abe Berman and Harold Arlen
to see *Last Tango in Paris*. Afterward he gave Mary Ellin his verdict: "Very long, very dirty, Brando brilliant."[15]

* * *

Harold Arlen, born Chaim Arluck in 1905, had been a good
friend of Berlin's since the early thirties: the two men shared a
mutual esteem, a fondness for things Yiddish, and a naughty
sense of humor. They had other things in common as well—
like Berlin, Arlen was the son of a cantor, and, perhaps to an
even greater extent than Berlin, was a deeply melancholy man.
Hebrew chants and, by extension, the blues saturated some of
his most famous melodies (Arlen wrote music only): "Stormy
Weather," "That Old Black Magic," "Blues in the Night," "One
for My Baby (and One More for the Road)," and "The Man
That Got Away," among many others. But he had also composed a number of more upbeat tunes, such as "Ac-Cent-Tchu-
Ate the Positive," "I've Got the World on a String," "Let's Fall
in Love," and, with E. Y. "Yip" Harburg, the score for *The
Wizard of Oz* (though "Over the Rainbow" is one of the most
bittersweet songs in the American songbook).

Misfortune began overtaking Arlen in the early fifties, when
his wife, the former fashion model Anya Taranda, suffered a
mental breakdown and was institutionalized. His friendship with

Berlin was one of the few bright spots in his life. For several years, Arlen, a skilled pianist and singer, would write and record a birthday song for Berlin and send the recording to Beekman Place; Berlin would respond with a funny note or a few lines of verse. Berlin also began sending his friend paintings, as this note from 1966 attests:

> Dear Hymie:
> I thought you would like this reproduction of my latest masterpiece.
> In the original, the eye wanders all over the place which causes much gelechter.[16]
> Love to you and Anya,[17]

On Arlen's birthday in 1968—the year of Berlin's eightieth—Berlin wrote:

> Dear Harold:
> I understand that today is your 63rd birthday. Many happy returns.
> In the Tennessee mountains, I could be your father.
> If you take care of yourself and stop smoking those stinking small black cigars, you may live to a ripe old age and in seventeen years from now you'll be eligible for the Sullivan Show. I won't be around, but I'm sure Sullivan will.
> With my best to you,
> As always,[18]

In 1970 Anya died of a brain tumor at fifty-five; Arlen became gravely depressed and withdrawn. But amazingly, two months after his wife's death he sent Berlin another birthday song. Berlin wrote back the next day:

> Dear Harold:
>
> I swear to heaven
> Till May eleven

I didn't sneak even a tiny little peek
At your birthday song
But now that I've seen it
I've got to say
That the Arlen music is quite okay,
But your lyrics
Have me in hysterics
As a lyric writer
I think that you
Are almost as good
As you know who
Your lyrics Mr. Music Man
Are simply for the birds
Ac-cent-u-ate the melody
Don't mess around with the words
But I thank you for your kindness
Regardless of your rhyme
And I hope when you
Reach eighty-two
You're as big a shmuck as I'm.

As ever,[19]

A late upsurge in testosterone seems to have inspired a series of birthday greetings by Berlin in the seventies. On February 15, 1972, a telegram:

DEAR HAROLD: HAPPY 67TH. TWO MORE YEARS AND YOU
SHALL BE A MAN.
          IZZY[20]

Two years later:

Dear Hymie:
Happy 69th.
That's a wonderful number but how do we celebrate? Do we drink a toast to the famous American regiment or the well-known popular indoor sport?

Not from your lawyer
Not from your brother
Zei mir gezunt[21]

From one shmuck to another.
    Love,

And on February 15, 1976:

SEVENTY-ONE

CAN BE FUN

IF YOU STILL HAVE BULLETS

IN YOUR GUN

Zei mir gezunt,[22]

Berlin continued to read the newspapers faithfully, and continued to be outraged by the general decline in moral standards and patriotism. That November, Yip Harburg, an inveterate left-winger, published a book of verse that contained the following lines:

Build Pentagons and armories
From Boston to La Jolla
There is no fortress strong enough
To placate paranoia.[23]

Berlin the inveterate patriot immediately fired off a letter to Arlen:

Dear Harold:
I saw one of the verses from Yipper's new book in the Times, which I'm enclosing, where he complains that the Pentagon is spending too much of his taxes for defense.
I thought you might be amused by the following four lines:

There's a big atomic submarine
Manned by a Russian skipper
Bound for Martha's Vineyard
Coming to get Yipper.

My best,

As always,[24]

*   *   *

In 1971, the *New York Times*'s Mel Gussow interviewed Berlin on the occasion of the Music Box Theater's fiftieth anniversary. The theater was still going strong—Anthony Shaffer's *Sleuth*, the most profitable show ever to play there, was doing sellout business—even if its cofounder wasn't. Berlin discussed the idea he'd had for an anniversary edition of the *Music Box Revue*, but then had to admit he'd been unable to bring it off: "I have song writer's stomach, and at 83 it makes you worry," he said. "I worried so about the anniversary show." He also had to confess that he'd turned aside the talk of an all-star celebration for the theater and Berlin—"I'm not up to it," he said, simply.[25]

It was his last interview.

He made his last public appearance in the spring of 1973, leading the singing of "God Bless America" at a White House benefit for returning Vietnam POWs and momentarily distracting President Nixon from Watergate.

Through the seventies, writes Mary Ellin Barrett, her father suffered a series of losses, the "last pals who got him out of the house going, one by one." In 1971, Irving Hoffman, the friend Berlin depended upon most, died. In 1975, Abe Berman. The following year, Harold Arlen developed Parkinson's disease. The amusing correspondence tailed off. Berlin stayed in touch with him by telephone for the remaining decade of Arlen's life.

In January 1978 Berlin lost his last remaining sibling, Gussie. Of the eight Balines who had stepped down the gangplank of the S.S. *Rhynland*—bedraggled, bewildered, unwanted—on that September day in 1893, he alone, the baby of the family, remained.

*   *   *

The losses of the 1970s were counterbalanced by family: nine grandchildren by 1972, his three daughters and their broods stopping by Beekman Place or coming up to the Catskills when the weather was warm. Asked what she and her husband did in Lew Beach, Ellin said, "Irving likes to fish. He paints. We walk. We read in the evenings, occasionally watch television. Sometimes the grandchildren come and it's lovely having them and we miss them when they leave but it's nice to be alone."[26]

Now and then he ventured to the typewriter or even the piano. A typed lyric sheet from March 19, 1981 was titled "Fred Astaire":

> Give my regards to Fred Astaire the singer—
> Fred as a singer is a real humdinger.
> So many times have I been in clover,
> For his heart's in the song before his feet take over.

"This song," Robert Kimball writes, "may have had the last Berlin melody. Nothing later is known to survive."[27]

In 1983 Irving and Ellin left the Catskills house for good and "withdrew completely into Beekman Place, closing the door behind them," Barrett writes.

> Even family visits were discouraged and eventually stopped entirely. My aged father took care of my mother, whose health had failed. Little things at first, a bad leg, a broken knee, then more serious symptoms, osteosclerosis, hardening of the arteries. Both had nurses. A doctor came every few days. His own health was terrible from the neck down, my father said, though his head was as clear as a bell.[28]

From time to time Berlin would take a constitutional around the neighborhood, accompanied by a male nurse and, according to Bergreen, presenting "a cranky and forbidding aspect to the world, chasing away children who strayed across his path and refusing to acknowledge the greetings of local residents."[29]

There was plenty to be cranky about. His sole companion, his soul mate of fifty-seven years, was inside, suffering. Yet an East 50s neighbor, a songwriter and cabaret singer named John Wallowitch, encountered a friendlier Berlin. Wallowitch, fifty-ish and a passionate devotee of musical theater, was in the habit of walking his dog around Beekman Place, where now and then he caught a thrilling glimpse of the great man. He was even more thrilled when one day Irving Berlin spoke to him. "I wish I had a dog like that, but my wife won't let me," he told Wallowitch.

Now and then after this they would exchange a few words. One day Wallowitch startled Berlin by asking him about his 1909 composition, "Sadie Salome, Go Home." "How do you know about these songs?" Berlin asked, then teased the younger man: "You must be an old-timer."

Transported by meeting his idol, Wallowitch returned to Beekman Place one Christmas Eve with four friends and sang "White Christmas" to Berlin's darkened townhouse. He began to ask friends to join him in the ritual. After a year or two the band of carolers grew to seventeen.

The night of December 24, 1983, was brutally cold, with winds whipping off the East River and temperatures in the low single digits. After Wallowitch and his crew had sung the song, a friend dared Wallowitch to ring Berlin's doorbell.

"I found myself overcome with fear," he remembered. "After what seemed an eternity I pushed the doorbell, and the house, which [was] usually dark, suddenly lit up like a Christmas tree. On the third floor, a shade was being pulled. We sang 'Always,' repeated 'White Christmas,' and the front door opened."

A maid stood in the doorway. "Mr. Berlin wants to thank you," she said.

"We're here to thank *him*," Wallowitch told her.

To their astonishment, the maid invited them into the kitchen, where the ninety-five-year-old songwriter greeted them.

"He was standing there in his bathrobe and slippers, and it was so touching," Wallowitch recalled. "He kissed all the girls and hugged all the guys and said, 'This is the nicest Christmas present I ever got.'"[30]

* * *

More losses, deep ones. Merman, in February 1984. Arlen, in April 1986. Unable to attend a November memorial service, the ninety-eight-year-old Berlin sent a brief statement:

> Harold Arlen was one of my oldest and best friends. We would talk on the telephone for hours. Never about songs. Conversation would start when one of us would ask, "How did you sleep last night?" This would continue until we were both worn out and too tired to sleep.
> Music by Harold Arlen is,
>> Stormy Weather
>> Over the Rainbow
>> That Old Black Magic
>> Blues in the Night
> and many other songs that will stay around for a long time. He wasn't as well known as some of us, but he was a better songwriter than most of us and he will be missed by all of us.
>> Irving Berlin[31]

Then, in June of 1987, came the death of Fred Astaire. It was a loss, not just of a friend, but of a dream of moonlight and music and love and romance, living on so powerfully in Berlin that it had found its way into his paintings fifty years after he wrote the songs.

Inconceivably, his centennial was on the way.

* * *

His final lyric is dated September 2, 1987, eight months before his hundredth birthday. It ends:

> Just hope that heaven above
> Will send you someone to love

Who'll keep the blues away
While you're growing gray.[32]

No music is known to survive.

* * *

Shortly before midnight on May 10, 1988, John Wallowitch and some of his customary crew gathered outside 17 Beekman Place; soon, out of curiosity, others joined them, and their numbers swelled to forty or more: "actors and bag ladies, people walking dogs in the pleasant night, a few pedestrians attracted by the crowd," Patricia O'Haire wrote in the *Daily News*. "They stood quietly, whispering to each other, clutching the music, watching the clock."

When the clock reached twelve, the crowd sang "Happy Birthday" to Berlin. Meanwhile, "the house was as silent as the Williamsburg Bridge. Every shade was drawn, but there were lights on behind them, and several windows open on the top floor."

Then a shade fluttered. "[A] light went out, the shade was raised, someone looked out," O'Haire wrote. "But who? No one knew."

Wallowitch and company went into "Always," then sang a reprise of "Happy Birthday."

A voice called from above: "He's coming down."

The crowd waited, hushed. And waited. Then, at length, the voice again: "Sorry. He looked out and decided it was too cold. But he thanks you very much."[33]

On the evening of the great day, Carnegie Hall—itself a mere ninety-seven years old—hosted a sold-out, star-jammed tribute to Berlin, to be televised on CBS later in the month. Irving and Ellin elected to stay at home and have dinner on trays in the library, surrounded by floral tributes from family and well-wishers such as Bob and Dolores Hope, Kitty Hart, Rosemary Clooney, and Frank Sinatra.

Sinatra was also on hand at Carnegie Hall, to sing "When I Lost You" and "Always," though even he couldn't dominate an event emceed by Walter Cronkite and featuring performances by Tony Bennett ("Let's Face the Music and Dance"), Leonard Bernstein (for inexplicable reasons, a composition of his own called "Twelve-Tone Lullaby"), Nell Carter ("Alexander's Ragtime Band"), Ray Charles ("How Deep Is the Ocean?"), Clooney ("White Christmas"), Michael Feinstein ("I Love a Piano"), Marilyn Horne ("God Bless America"), Willie Nelson ("Blue Skies"), Tommy Tune ("Puttin' on the Ritz"), and Garrison Keillor, reciting rather than singing the lyrics to "All Alone."

The highlight of the evening, hands down, was Madeline Kahn's gloriously dirty rendition of "You'd Be Surprised," from the *Ziegfeld Follies of 1919*. It pierced the general air of devoutness and got to the New York pith of who Berlin really was:

> At a party or at a ball,
> I've got to admit, he's nothing at all,
> But in an easy chair,
> You'd be surprised . . .[34]

About a week later, Barrett recalled,

With an infection and a fever, on top of a bad reaction to his birthday, my father had had what his nurse called "an episode." He wanted to see me, to tell me something, she said, but must warn me that he was confused as to where he was. "He thinks he is in a hotel somewhere," she whispered.

In actuality, he was sitting in his red-leather bedroom chair, in a pair of blue pajamas, wrapped in a cashmere blanket. A small, very small, man whose narrow face, pale olive, curiously smooth, nose pared to the bone, had the look of a carving, except for the live steel-gray hair and defiantly dark brows. In his liquid-eyed youth he looked Italian; now he was a very Jewish looking, very old man, reunited with his forebears.

She knew he could barely see her because of his cataracts. Still, he seemed to be looking straight at her,

> seeing me with sunken but still intense eyes. And though confused, he was, within his confusion, firm-voiced and precise. "I want you to tell your mother everything is fine," he said. "I'm still out of town on this business matter. Explain to her. It's nothing for her to worry about, just a business thing. I'll be home in a few days." "Of course," I said. "And give her my love, he added, "Be sure to give her my love." "Oh, I will." And again to the nurse, "Be sure to give Mrs. Berlin my love."

There had been so many hotels over the decades, so many overnight work marathons out of town, in Atlantic City, in New Haven and Boston and London. He had traveled so many thousands of miles; now, in place, he was still traveling, on the edge of an even greater voyage.

Mary Ellin and the nurse went downstairs to Ellin. "I just saw Daddy," Mary Ellin said. Her mother asked how he was; she'd been told he was under the weather. "He's fine," her daughter said—and then the nurse broke in. "He wanted me to be sure to give you his love," she said.

"At that," Mary Ellin Barrett recalled, "my mother got that look, a raised-eyebrow look, you might say, a 'really?' look. The look with which she had silenced three living generations.

"'I *know* I have that,' she said slowly and firmly."[35]

Some two months later, on July 29, Mary Ellin and Elizabeth —Linda hadn't yet arrived from Paris—stood by their father's bedside and told him that their mother, his Ellin, had died during the night.

* * *

On the day after Christmas, Berlin had a stroke and sank into a coma; his doctor said he wouldn't wake up. "There was no need to move him to the hospital," Barrett writes. "Everything could be done at home, which was where he had said he wanted to die." But a week later he startled everyone by opening his eyes and saying he felt cold. It was, Linda Emmet said, like that eight-year-old newsboy who should have drowned but didn't and was recovered from the East River, still clutching the pennies he had earned that day.[36]

The great engine that had produced so many words had now nearly halted. Just a few syllables were left: *good*, when he heard that his second great-grandchild had been born, and that "Mr. Monotony" had finally made it into a show (*Jerome Robbins' Broadway*); *okay*, pointedly, when one of his bedside visitors had taxed him with too much talk. And most important, *I love you*, in return for the same sentiment.

On Thursday, September 21, 1989, Mary Ellin stopped by with two pieces of good news: that Berlin's two-year-old great-grandson liked dancing to "Alexander's Ragtime Band," and that his friend the producer David Brown thought that *A Few Good Men*, the play set to open at the Music Box in November, was going to be a hit.

"Good," Berlin said, barely audibly, to both pieces of news. "Good."[37]

Late the following afternoon—warm, windy, and rainy in Manhattan, another summer about to turn to fall—he breathed his last.

Word got out, and spread quickly. An Associated Press reporter calling Beekman Place reached Elizabeth's husband, Alton Peters, who confirmed that Irving Berlin had died, at around five-thirty.

"Was he ill?" the reporter asked.

"No," Peters said. "He was a hundred and one years old. He just fell asleep."[38]

Page 336 is blank

Quotations from Berlin songs in Preface are from Linda Berlin Emmet and Robert Kimball, *The Complete Lyrics of Irving Berlin* (Alfred A. Knopf, 2001), 236 ("The Monkey Doodle Doo"), and 18 ("Oh, How That German Could Love").

1. The Fugitive

1. Although a number of sources list Israel's middle name as Isidore, the Berlin family has no record that he was ever so dubbed.

2. One Beilin son stayed in Belorussia, and a married daughter emigrated separately with her husband.

3. It is the contention of Berlin's daughter Linda Berlin Emmet, however, that since there were no pogroms in Siberia or the part of the Pale of Settlement occupied by the family before emigration, her father may have imagined the incident.

4. The Beilins' exodus, like those of thousands of their compatriots, was partly or largely funded by the Alliance Israélite Universelle, underwritten by the Baron Maurice de Hirsch.

NOTES TO PAGES 000–000

5. Two of Berlin's daughters have, in my hearing, pronounced the name those two ways. In addition, the first English rendering of the family name was Beilin—a spelling that survives among distant relatives.

6. Most Berlin biographies list the address as 330 Cherry Street, surely an error stemming from Alexander Woollcott's colorful, highly imaginative 1925 life, *The Story of Irving Berlin* (1925; Da Capo, 1983).

7. The 1900 U.S. Census, dated June 5, lists Israel Baline's birth date as May 1887, not 1888, as family history sometimes (but not always) maintains. I will stick with the later date.

8. Leo Rosten, *The Joys of Yiddish* (Pocket Books, 1968), 50.

9. Woollcott, *Story*, 13.

10. *New York Sun*, February 24, 1947.

11. Edouard Emmet, interview by author (July 22, 2011).

12. Many years later, polishing his bio, he would tell a reporter, "I didn't have much education in anything. I had to leave school after the second grade." *New York Times*, May 11, 1966.

13. Woollcott, *Story*, 20–21.

14. Mary Ellin Barrett, interview by author (May 18, 2011).

15. Edward Jablonski, *Irving Berlin: American Troubadour* (Henry Holt, 1999), 21.

2. I Have Discovered a Great Kid

1. *New York Sun*, February 24, 1947.

2. Edward Jablonski, *Irving Berlin: American Troubadour* (Henry Holt, 1999), 22.

3. Because at one point he shortened his last name to Gumm, it has been stated authoritatively in at least two Irving Berlin biographies that Von Tilzer was the uncle of Judy Garland, born Frances Gumm. He was not. Garland's (Christian) paternal roots went back to Tennessee in the early nineteenth century, where the family name had always been spelled Gumm or Gum.

4. *Lowell Sun*, December 3, 1910.

5. The nickname, so offensive to the modern ear (or any sensitive ear, for that matter), was, in a less enlightened era, commonly

bestowed on Jews who happened to have features deemed African. In *A Renegade History of the United States* (Free Press, 2010), 171, Thaddeus Russell astonishingly maintains that the appellation represented "Jewish identification with African Americans." The nickname also seems to have carried admiring macho overtones. Examples abounded, especially among Jewish gangsters such as "Yoski Nigger" of the Yiddish Black Hand, "Nigger Benny" Snyder of the Greaser Gang, and Harry "Nig" Rosen of Philadelphia's 69th Street Gang.

6. Philip Furia, *Irving Berlin: A Life in Song* (Schirmer, 1998), 18.

7. Calomel and jalap were the key ingredients: this particular variety of Mickey Finn, rather than rendering its victim unconscious, brought on the instant and volcanic need to defecate.

It was at Olliffe's—which had been in continuous operation since the Jefferson administration, and was also the neighborhood purveyor of opium—that Baline befriended the coproprietors, Joe and Nick Schenck, ages twenty-six and twenty-two. The Schenck (pronounced *Skenk*) brothers, who would soon put aside the drugstore business for the amusement-park business, and subsequently put aside the amusement-park business for the motion-picture business, were to become major powers in Hollywood, Joe as the president of United Artists and then the chairman of 20th Century–Fox, and Nick as president of MGM. Joe Schenck would remain one of Irving Berlin's closest friends until the movie magnate's death in 1961.

8. Irving Berlin Collection, Library of Congress.

9. Charles Hamm, *Irving Berlin: Songs from the Melting Pot: The Formative Years, 1907–1914* (Oxford University Press, 1997), viii.

10. Linda Berlin Emmet and Robert Kimball, *The Complete Lyrics of Irving Berlin* (Alfred A. Knopf, 2001), 4.

11. Jablonski, *American Troubadour*, 29.

12. Alexander Woollcott, *The Story of Irving Berlin* (1925; Da Capo, 1983), 68.

13. Furia, *A Life in Song*, 23.

14. Woollcott, *Story*, 70.

3. You Can Never Tell Your Finish When You Start

1. Alexander Woollcott, *The Story of Irving Berlin* (1925; Da Capo, 1983), 64–65.

2. "When his hair wasn't slicked down, as most people think of him, he was very, very curly," Berlin's daughter Mary Ellin Barrett remembered. "Sometimes, he could almost look like Charlie Chaplin, with the eyebrows and the curly hair. There was something comical about it." Barrett, interview by author (May 18, 2011).

3. Barbara W. Grossman, *Funny Woman: The Life and Times of Fanny Brice* (Indiana University Press, 1992), 14.

4. Linda Berlin Emmet and Robert Kimball, *The Complete Lyrics of Irving Berlin* (Alfred A. Knopf, 2001), 4.

5. Ibid.

6. Ibid., 5.

7. Woollcott, *Story*, 72.

8. Philip Furia, *Irving Berlin: A Life in Song* (Schirmer, 1998), 27.

9. Emmet and Kimball, *Complete Lyrics*, 7.

10. Ibid. Whiting would go on to write the lyrics to Walter Donaldson's melody for the 1927 hit "My Blue Heaven."

11. *American Magazine*, October 1920.

12. Emmet and Kimball, *Complete Lyrics*, 8.

13. Fingers, plural. Though the legend later arose that Berlin was strictly a one-finger player, he heard chords from the beginning, and his hands sought them out. Furia, *A Life in Song*, endnotes.

14. *Theatre*, February 1915.

15. Woollcott, *Story*, 74.

16. Emmet and Kimball, *Complete Lyrics*, 13.

17. Ibid., 14.

4. I Sweat Blood

1. The census lists Berlin as twenty-two; see Chapter 1.

2. An intriguing case in point is July 9's "Oh, That Beautiful Rag," an enthusiastic but undistinguished "coon song," with lyrics as unmemorable as its music except for two arresting bits: some

verbiage in the verse ("Honey, that leader man / Leads like a leader can") that will soon come up again in a significant way; and the beginning of the chorus ("Oh! Oh! Oh! Oh! / Oh! That beautiful rag . . ."), which will find an eerie echo a dozen years hence in T. S. Eliot's *The Waste Land.*

3. Linda Berlin Emmet and Robert Kimball, *The Complete Lyrics of Irving Berlin* (Alfred A. Knopf, 2001), 20.

4. Charles Hamm, *Irving Berlin: Songs from the Melting Pot: The Formative Years, 1907–1914* (Oxford University Press, 1997), 115.

5. Rennold Wolf, "The Boy Who Revived Ragtime," *Green Book*, August 1913.

6. *Theatre*, February 1915. Cf. the writer Gene Fowler (1890–1960): "Writing is easy. All you do is stare at a blank sheet of paper until drops of blood form on your forehead." And Hemingway: "There is nothing to writing. All you do is sit down at a typewriter and bleed."

7. Alexander Woollcott, *The Story of Irving Berlin* (1925; Da Capo, 1983), 112.

8. Emmet and Kimball, *Complete Lyrics*, 21.

9. Though it had been a dozen years since the breakout success of Scott Joplin's 1899 "Maple Leaf Rag," ragtime was still all the rage in the slower-moving popular culture of the early twentieth century.

10. Hamm, *Songs from the Melting Pot*, 103.

11. *American Magazine*, July–December 1920.

12. Edward Jablonski, *Irving Berlin: American Troubadour* (Henry Holt and Co., Inc., 1999), 47.

13. Hamm, *Songs from the Melting Pot*, 133.

14. Irving Berlin Collection, Library of Congress (hereafter IB LOC).

15. Woollcott, *Story*, 92–93.

16. *Variety*, September 11, 1911.

17. Laurence Bergreen, *As Thousands Cheer: The Life of Irving Berlin* (Da Capo, 1996), 114.

18. Hamm, *Songs from the Melting Pot*, 107, quoting *Green Book*, April 1916.

19. Lawrence T. Carter, *Eubie Blake: Keys of Memory* (Balamp, 1979), 53.

5. At the Devil's Ball

1. *Variety*, January 4, 1912.
2. Linda Berlin Emmet and Robert Kimball, *The Complete Lyrics of Irving Berlin* (Alfred A. Knopf, 2001), 37.
3. Ibid., 40.
4. Laurence Bergreen, *As Thousands Cheer: The Life of Irving Berlin* (Da Capo, 1996), 79.
5. Alexander Woollcott, *The Story of Irving Berlin* (1925; Da Capo, 1983), 103.
6. Emmet and Kimball, *Complete Lyrics*, 60.
7. Ibid.
8. Jeffrey Magee, *Irving Berlin's American Musical Theater* (Oxford University Press, 2012), 19.
9. Ibid.
10. Amos Oz and Fania Oz-Salzberger, *Jews and Words* (Yale University Press, 2012), 28.
11. Mary Ellin Barrett, interview by author (December 16, 2011).
12. Edward Jablonski, *Irving Berlin: American Troubadour* (Henry Holt, 1999), 52.
13. It continues to be recorded. Maude Maggart included "When I Lost You" on an all-Berlin CD in 2005; in 1962, Frank Sinatra sang it on his all-waltz album *All Alone;* and in 1987, Tony Bennett did a beautiful a cappella version on *Bennett/Berlin.*
14. Woollcott, *Story*, 104.
15. Alec Wilder, *American Popular Song: The Great Innovators, 1900–1950* (Oxford University Press, 1972), 96.
16. George S. Kaufman, *New Yorker,* June 11, 1960.
17. Emmet and Kimball, *Complete Lyrics*, 59.
18. See "Bob Dylan's Dream," "Talkin' World War III Blues," and "Bob Dylan's 115th Dream."
19. Emmet and Kimball, *Complete Lyrics*, 62.
20. Ibid., xvi.
21. Ibid., xvi–xvii.

22. Magee, *American Musical Theater*, 9.

23. Jablonski, *American Troubadour*, 54.

24. Ibid.

25. Bergreen, *As Thousands Cheer*, 93.

26. Ibid., 90.

27. Emmet and Kimball, *Complete Lyrics*, 80; Woollcott, *Story*, 95.

6. Play a Simple Melody

1. Edward Jablonski, *Irving Berlin: American Troubadour* (Henry Holt, 1999), 56.

2. Philip Furia, *Irving Berlin: A Life in Song* (Schirmer, 1998), 69.

3. Jeffrey Magee, *Irving Berlin's American Musical Theater* (Oxford University Press, 2012), 311.

4. Ibid., 78.

5. Furia, *A Life in Song*, 58.

6. Magee, *American Musical Theater*, 47.

7. Ibid.

8. Harry B. Smith, *First Nights and First Editions* (Little, Brown, 1931), 280–81.

9. Magee, *American Musical Theater*, 47.

10. Linda Berlin Emmet and Robert Kimball, *The Complete Lyrics of Irving Berlin* (Alfred A. Knopf, 2001), 119.

11. Laurence Bergreen, *As Thousands Cheer: The Life of Irving Berlin* (Da Capo, 1996), 107.

12. Ibid., 108.

13. Ibid.

14. Ibid.

15. *New York Times*, December 9, 1914.

16. Castle would die in a plane crash, a training accident, in early 1918.

17. Emmet and Kimball, *Complete Lyrics*, 133.

18. Bergreen, *As Thousands Cheer*, 133.

19. Emmet and Kimball, *Complete Lyrics*, 135.

20. Ibid., 155.

7. I Wasn't Much of a Soldier

1. Edward Jablonski, *Irving Berlin: American Troubadour* (Henry Holt, 1999), 71.

2. Laurence Bergreen, *As Thousands Cheer: The Life of Irving Berlin* (Da Capo, 1996), 135–36.

3. Michael Freedland, *Irving Berlin* (Stein and Day, 1978), 51.

4. As incontrovertible proof, a lead sheet for the 1931 "Soft Lights and Sweet Music," handwritten by the songwriter, resides in the Irving Berlin Collection of the Music Division of the Library of Congress.

5. Mary Ellin Barrett, interview by author (January 16, 2012). A TV clip from the 1950s (https://www.youtube.com/watch?v=bO8VZoRw214) proves the point: as Dinah Shore and Tony Martin look on, Berlin plays "Call Me Up Some Rainy Afternoon" on his "Buick" with marvelous two-handed suppleness.

6. Alexander Woollcott, *New York Times*, November 7, 1916.

7. *Variety*, November 7, 1916.

8. Linda Berlin Emmet and Robert Kimball, *The Complete Lyrics of Irving Berlin* (Alfred A. Knopf, 2001), 92.

9. In later years, Groucho Marx used to enjoy tweaking his now ultrapatriotic pal Berlin by breaking into the song in public. "Every time I see him," Berlin said, "I stick my hand in my pocket and ask him, 'How much if you don't sing it?'" *New York Times*, May 11, 1958. In 1915 Al Piantadosi—whose 1906 "My Mariuccia Take a Steamboat" indirectly resulted in Berlin's becoming a songwriter—had a million seller in a similar vein with "I Didn't Raise My Boy to be a Soldier."

10. Emmet and Kimball, *Complete Lyrics*, 154.

11. Jablonski, *American Troubadour*, 74.

12. Alexander Woollcott, *The Story of Irving Berlin* (1925; Da Capo, 1983), 112.

13. Jablonski, *American Troubadour*, 76.

14. *American Heritage*, August 1967.

15. Irving Berlin Collection, Library of Congress (hereafter IB LOC).

16. Emmet and Kimball, *Complete Lyrics*, 169.

17. Max Wilk, *They're Playing Our Song: Conversations with America's Classic Songwriters* (Easton Studio Press, 2008), 275.

18. Ibid.

19. Emmet and Kimball, *Complete Lyrics*, 171.

20. Sime Silverman, *Variety*, August 23, 1918.

21. *New York Times*, August 20, 1918.

22. *Theatre*, October 1918.

23. Emmet and Kimball, *Complete Lyrics*, 172; Nancy Furstinger, *Say It with Music: The Story of Irving Berlin* (Morgan Reynolds, 2003), 44.

24. IB LOC.

25. Wilk, *They're Playing Our Song*, 353.

26. *American Heritage*, August 1967.

8. Work for Yourself!

1. Linda Berlin Emmet and Robert Kimball, *The Complete Lyrics of Irving Berlin* (Alfred A. Knopf, 2001), 174.

2. Edward Jablonski, *Irving Berlin: American Troubadour* (Henry HoltX, 1999), 85.

3. Robert Kimball and Alfred Simon, *The Gershwins* (Atheneum, 1973), 20.

4. Jablonski, *American Troubadour*, 92.

5. Ibid.

6. Ibid., 93.

7. Laurence Bergreen, *As Thousands Cheer: The Life of Irving Berlin* (Da Capo, 1996), 179.

8. Jablonski, *American Troubadour*, 94.

9. *American Magazine*, October 1920. The other eight rules: 1) "The melody must musically be within the range of the *average voice* of the average public singer"; 2) "The title, which must be simple and easily remembered, must be '*planted*' effectively in the song"; 3) "A popular song should be *sexless*, that is, the ideas and the wording must be of a kind that can be logically voiced by either a male or a female singer"; 4) "The song should contain *heart interest*, even if it is a comic song"; 5) "The song must be *original* in ideas, words, and music"; 6) "Your lyric must have to do with ideas, emotions, or

objects known to everyone"; 7) "The lyric must be *euphonious*— written in easily singable words and phrases in which there are many open vowels"; and 8) "Your song must be perfectly *simple*. Simplicity is achieved only after much hard work, but you must attain it."

10. Emmet and Kimball, *Complete Lyrics*, 194.

11. Alexander Woollcott, *The Story of Irving Berlin* (1925; Da Capo, 1983), 192–93.

12. "The Music Box is everybody's dream of a theatre," Moss Hart would write in his 1959 memoir *Act One*. "Except for the Haymarket Theatre in London, I know of no other that possesses so strong an atmosphere of its own, as living and as personal, as the Music Box" (264).

13. Jablonski, *American Troubadour*, 94.

14. Woollcott, *Story*, 181–82.

15. Ibid., 186–87.

16. John Lahr, *Show and Tell: New Yorker Profiles* (University of California Press, 2000), 149.

17. Philip Furia, *Irving Berlin: A Life in Song* (Schirmer, 1998), 89.

18. Woollcott, *Story*, 183.

19. Bergreen, *As Thousands Cheer*, 182.

20. Woollcott, *Story*, 183–84.

21. Emmet and Kimball, *Complete Lyrics*, 194.

22. Ibid., 198.

23. The middle of whom, Josephine—aka Bobbe—would live until 1999, when she died at age ninety-seven, having outlived her eleven-years-younger second husband, the songwriter Edward Chester Babcock—aka Jimmy Van Heusen—by nine years.

24. Emmet and Kimball, *Complete Lyrics*, 199.

25. Jeffrey Magee, *Irving Berlin's American Musical Theater* (Oxford University Press, 2012), 129. In a 1957 lyric, Berlin wrote of the song: "I don't mean to boast, / But it was played from coast to coast, / And I really think / 'Twas the connecting link / Between ragtime and jazz." Emmet and Kimball, *Complete Lyrics*, 457.

26. Magee, *American Musical Theater*, 140.

27. Emmet and Kimball, *Complete Lyrics*, 203.

9. What Shall I Do?

1. P. G. Wodehouse, *Bring on the Girls!* (Everyman, 2014), 179.

2. Mary Ellin Barrett, *Irving Berlin: A Daughter's Memoir* (Simon and Schuster, 1994), 14–15.

3. Max Wilk, *They're Playing Our Song: Conversations with America's Classic Songwriters* (Easton Studio, 2008), 356.

4. Ibid.

5. Marion Meade, *Dorothy Parker: What Fresh Hell Is This?* (Penguin, 1989), 80.

6. Brian Gallagher, *Anything Goes: The Jazz Age Adventures of Neysa McMein and Her Extravagant Circle of Friends* (Times Books, 1987), 13.

7. Linda Berlin Emmet and Robert Kimball, *The Complete Lyrics of Irving Berlin* (Alfred A. Knopf, 2001), 225.

8. Edward Jablonski, *Irving Berlin: American Troubadour* (Henry Holt, 1999), 99.

9. Emmet and Kimball, *Complete Lyrics*, 225.

10. Philip Furia, *Irving Berlin: A Life in Song* (Schirmer, 1998), 101.

11. Emmet and Kimball, *Complete Lyrics*, 225.

12. Furia, *A Life in Song*, 101.

13. Emmet and Kimball, *Complete Lyrics*, 220.

14. Laurence Bergreen, *As Thousands Cheer: The Life of Irving Berlin* (Da Capo, 1996), 200.

15. Ibid., 205.

16. Saul Bellow, *Ravelstein* (Viking, 2000), 8.

17. Meade, *Dorothy Parker*, 59.

18. Dorothy Herrmann, *With Malice toward All: The Quips, Lives and Loves of Some Celebrated 20th-Century American Wits* (G. P. Putnam's Sons, 1982), 85.

19. Richard Meryman, *Mank: The Wit, World, and Life of Herman Mankiewicz* (William Morrow, 1978), 97.

20. Barrett, *A Daughter's Memoir*, 18.

21. *New York Herald*, January 4, 1924.

22. Jablonski, *American Troubadour*, 103.

23. Barrett, *A Daughter's Memoir*, 21.

24. Ibid.

10. Always

1. Mary Ellin Barrett, *Irving Berlin: A Daughter's Memoir* (Simon and Schuster, 1994), 28.

2. Irving Berlin Collection, Library of Congress (hereafter IB LOC).

3. Ibid.

4. Linda Berlin Emmet and Robert Kimball, *The Complete Lyrics of Irving Berlin* (Alfred A. Knopf, 2001), 215, 217.

5. Ibid., 226.

6. Ibid., 228.

7. Ibid.

8. Ibid.

9. Barrett, *A Daughter's Memoir*, 40–41.

10. *New York Times*, April 16, 1925.

11. A fifth brother, Gummo (Milton), left the act soon after the Great War and was replaced by Zeppo.

12. Harpo Marx and Rowland Barber, *Harpo Speaks* (Limelight, 2004), 186.

13. Edward Jablonski, *Irving Berlin: American Troubadour* (Henry Holt, 1999), 115.

14. George S. Kaufman, *New Yorker*, June 11, 1960.

15. IB LOC.

16. Kaufman, *New Yorker*.

17. IB LOC.

18. Irving Berlin, *Leader*, October 5, 1946.

19. Emmet and Kimball, *Complete Lyrics*, 235.

20. Barrett, *A Daughter's Memoir*, 40.

21. Ibid., 41.

22. Laurence Bergreen, *As Thousands Cheer: The Life of Irving Berlin* (Da Capo, 1996), 250.

23. Ellin Mackay, *New Yorker*, November 28, 1925.

24. Barrett, *A Daughter's Memoir*, 42–43.

25. Bergreen, *As Thousands Cheer*, 253.

26. Mary Ellin Barrett email to author, August 10, 2016.

27. Ibid.

28. *New York Times*, January 6, 1926.

29. *New York Times*, January 5, 1926.

30. *New York Times*, January 6, 1926.

31. Michael Freedland, *Irving Berlin* (Stein and Day, 1974), 84.

32. Jablonski, *American Troubadour*, 125.

33. Bergreen, *As Thousands Cheer*, 268.

34. IB LOC.

11. Never Saw the Sun Shining So Bright

1. Mary Ellin Barrett, *Irving Berlin: A Daughter's Memoir* (Simon and Schuster, 1994), 49.

2. Ibid., 55.

3. Philip Furia, *Irving Berlin: A Life in Song* (Schirmer, 1998), 120.

4. Max Wilk, *They're Playing Our Song: Conversations with America's Classic Songwriters* (Easton Studio Press, 2008), 281–82.

5. Linda Berlin Emmet and Robert Kimball, *The Complete Lyrics of Irving Berlin* (Alfred A. Knopf, 2001), 231.

6. Wilk, *They're Playing Our Song*, 282.

7. Richard Rodgers, *Musical Stages: An Autobiography* (Da Capo, 2002), 96.

8. The most memorable from Jolson, just before he breaks into "Toot, Toot, Tootsie, Goodbye": "Wait a minute! Wait a minute! You ain't heard nothin' yet . . ."

9. Emmet and Kimball, *Complete Lyrics*, 231.

10. Barrett, *A Daughter's Memoir*, 76.

11. Conversation with Robert Kimball (September 14, 2013). Berlin would name his second daughter after Porter's wife, Linda.

12. The song also bears a mildly uncomfortable rhythmic, melodic, and titular resemblance—surely coincidence?—to the Gershwins' 1925 "Kickin' the Clouds Away."

13. Irving Berlin Collection, Library of Congress (hereafter IB LOC).

14. Ibid.

15. Barrett, *A Daughter's Memoir,* 71.

16. Rob Nixon, TCM website, http://www.tcm.com/this-month /article/87777%7C0/The-Cocoanuts.html.

17. John Mosher, *New Yorker,* June 1, 1929.

18. IB LOC.

19. Emmet and Kimball, *Complete Lyrics,* 262. In 1946 Berlin would rewrite the lyric, changing the song's locale to Park Avenue, for Fred Astaire to sing in the Paramount film *Blue Skies.* It was a rare instance of an update that was also a substantial improvement: without it, the world would never have had "Come let's mix where Rockefellers/Walk with sticks or umbrellas/In their mitts/Puttin' on the Ritz."

20. IB LOC.

21. In his biography of Berlin, Laurence Bergreen flatly asserts as fact what had circulated as a rumor for years: "Berlin," he writes, "extended the olive branch of charity to his financially humbled father-in-law by giving the old man a million dollars to make him comfortable in his declining years." *As Thousands Cheer: The Life of Irving Berlin* (Da Capo, 1996), 299. But in conversation with the author, Mary Ellin Barrett flatly denied this—"It's a myth," she said. Mary Ellin Barrett, interview by author (September 24, 2012).

22. Jared Brown, *Moss Hart, a Prince of the Theatre: A Biography in Three Acts* (Back Stage, 2006), 37.

23. Edward Jablonski, *Irving Berlin: American Troubadour* (Henry Holt, 1999), 145.

12. Good God, Another Revue!

1. Legend has it that around this time a wag from Lindy's, the Broadway restaurant and show-biz hangout Berlin frequented, stopped him on the street and said, "What's the matter, Irving, has the little colored boy been sick?" "No," Berlin snapped. "He's dead." Max Wilk, *They're Playing Our Song: Conversations with America's Classic Songwriters* (Easton Studio Press, 2008), 386.

2. Robert Rusie, Broadway 101: The History of the Great White Way, http://www.talkinbroadway.com/bway101/5.html.

3. Jared Brown, *Moss Hart, a Prince of the Theatre: A Biography in Three Acts* (Back Stage Books, 2006), 75.

4. Ibid.

5. Ibid.

6. *Stage* magazine, August 1936.

7. *New York Herald Tribune*, February 23, 1932.

8. *Stage*, August 1936.

9. Linda Berlin Emmet and Robert Kimball, *The Complete Lyrics of Irving Berlin* (Alfred A. Knopf, 2001), 273.

10. Ibid., 273–74.

11. Irving Berlin Collection, Library of Congress (hereafter IB LOC).

12. Mary Ellin Barrett, *Irving Berlin: A Daughter's Memoir* (Simon and Schuster, 1994), 107; Laurence Bergreen, *As Thousands Cheer: The Life of Irving Berlin* (Da Capo, 1996), 313.

13. IB LOC.

14. Associated Press, September 2, 1932.

15. Emmet and Kimball, *Complete Lyrics*, 298. The lines were: "How much does she love me? / I'll tell you no lie: / How deep is the ocean? / How high is the sky?"

16. *New York Times*, October 8, 1933.

17. Steven Bach, *Dazzler: The Life and Times of Moss Hart* (Da Capo, 2002), 104.

18. Barrett, *A Daughter's Memoir,* 115.

19. Edward Jablonski, *Irving Berlin: American Troubadour* (Henry Holt, 1999), 157.

20. Emmet and Kimball, *Complete Lyrics*, 287.

21. Philip Furia and Michael Lasser, *America's Songs: The Stories behind the Songs of Broadway, Hollywood, and Tin Pan Alley* (Taylor and Francis, 2006), 107.

22. Ethel Waters, *His Eye Is on the Sparrow: An Autobiography* (Da Capo, 1992), 220. Barrett also writes that Berlin's deep and long-lasting friendship with Harold Arlen began when they met at the Cotton Club that spring. *A Daughter's Memoir,* 137.

23. Waters, *His Eye Is on the Sparrow*, 222.

24. Jeffrey Magee, *Irving Berlin's American Musical Theater* (Oxford University Press, 2012), 191.

25. Jablonski, *American Troubadour*, 160–61.

26. Magee, *American Musical Theater*, 190.

27. *New Yorker*, October 7, 1933.

28. *New York Times*, October 2, 1933.

29. On her Sunday-night radio show with the Jack Denny Orchestra, the sponsor (Amoco) compelled Waters to bowdlerize the lyric to the nonsensical "By letting her *feet* wave" [italics mine]. *New Yorker*, December 23, 1933.

30. Emmet and Kimball, *Complete Lyrics*, 284.

31. IB LOC.

13. Before They Ask Us to Pay the Bill

1. As the show's coproducer Berlin received forty percent of profits; as coowner of the Music Box he also received a percentage of ticket sales; additionally, he earned royalties as composer and lyricist, and as the publisher of the show's songs, made further profits from the sale of sheet music.

2. Mary Ellin Barrett, *Irving Berlin: A Daughter's Memoir* (Simon and Schuster, 1994), 124.

3. Mary Ellin Barrett, interview by author (December 16, 2011). It may have been more than a suggestion: Ellin's cousin Alice Duer Miller told her early on, "My dear, if you don't stop nagging, I don't give this marriage a year." Barrett, *A Daughter's Memoir*, 138.

4. Laurence Bergreen, *As Thousands Cheer: The Life of Irving Berlin* (Da Capo, 1996), 333.

5. Barrett, *A Daughter's Memoir*, 126.

6. Ibid., 126–27.

7. Linda Berlin Emmet and Robert Kimball, *The Complete Lyrics of Irving Berlin* (Alfred A. Knopf, 2001), 293.

8. Alexander Woollcott, *The Story of Irving Berlin* (1925; Da Capo, 1983), 214.

9. *Time*, May 28, 1934.z

10. Emmet and Kimball, *Complete Lyrics*, 300.

11. Although the moviegoing public had loved them together in supporting roles in 1933's *Flying Down to Rio*.

12. William McBrien, *Cole Porter: A Biography* (Alfred A. Knopf, 1998), 149–50.

13. *New York Times*, November 29, 1976.

14. Edward Jablonski, *Irving Berlin: American Troubadour* (Henry Holt, 1999), 164.

15. Barrett, *A Daughter's Memoir*, 142.

16. Philip Furia, *Irving Berlin: A Life in Song* (Schirmer, 1998), 176.

17. Ibid.

18. Jablonski, *American Troubadour*, 170; Arlene Croce, *The Fred Astaire and Ginger Rogers Book* (Galahad, 1972), 67. Borne claimed to have invented the musical refrain "dah-dah-dee" that punctuates the phrase "Heaven,/I'm in heaven."

19. Bob Thomas, *I Got Rhythm: The Ethel Merman Story* (Putnam Adult, 1985), 111.

20. Bergreen, *As Thousands Cheer*, 345.

21. Barrett, *A Daughter's Memoir*, 142.

22. Barrett, notes on October 1990 conversation with Samuel Goldwyn, Jr.

23. Bergreen, *As Thousands Cheer*, 346–47.

24. And thanks to a deal that now looked prescient, earning Berlin a whopping $320,000—the equivalent of some $5.8 million in today's dollars.

25. Thomas, *I Got Rhythm*, 114–16.

26. Ethan Mordden, *When Broadway Went to Hollywood* (Oxford University Press, 2016), 64.

27. Barrett, *A Daughter's Memoir*, 145.

28. Ibid., 146.

29. Art is difficult: after the weighted sleeve of Rogers's gown accidentally smacked Astaire in the face as the two swept through a turn, Sandrich reshot the scene twenty more times. In the end, the first take stayed in the picture.

30. Emmet and Kimball, *Complete Lyrics*, 307.

14. Write Hits Like Irving Berlin

1. Mary Ellin Barrett, *Irving Berlin: A Daughter's Memoir* (Simon and Schuster, 1994), 143. The eighth Academy Awards, on March 5, 1936, was the first time the golden statuette was called Oscar.

2. Michael Freedland, *Irving Berlin* (Stein and Day, 1974), 130.

3. Benjamin Sears, ed., *The Irving Berlin Reader* (Oxford University Press, 2012), 186.

4. *Variety*, January 21, 1936.

5. Laurence Bergreen, *As Thousands Cheer: The Life of Irving Berlin* (Da Capo, 1996), 359.

6. Ibid., 359–60; 20th Century–Fox Archives at University of Southern California.

7. 20th Century–Fox Archives.

8. Walter Rimler, *George Gershwin: An Intimate Portrait* (University of Illinois Press, 2009), 126.

9. Ibid.

10. Ibid., 156.

11. In whose verse Ira put a couplet that pays tribute to Berlin: "The song is over, but as the songwriter wrote / The melody lingers on."

12. Barrett, *A Daughter's Memoir*, 155.

13. Sears, *Irving Berlin Reader*, 186–87.

14. Ibid., 187. The account confirms that by his fiftieth year, Irving had become a competent player of nontransposing pianos.

15. Barrett, *A Daughter's Memoir*, 157.

16. *Variety*, March 11, 1938.

17. Gary Giddins, *Bing Crosby: A Pocketful of Dreams, The Early Years, 1903–1940* (Back Bay Books, 2002), 483.

18. *Variety*, April 29, 1938.

19. But gorgeously sung by Tony Bennett on his exquisite *Bennett/Berlin* album.

20. *Life*, September 5, 1938. The picture's success spawned a string of songwriter biopics: in short order Hollywood would churn out movies professing to chronicle the lives of Cole Porter, George

Gershwin, and most successfully, George M. Cohan (Warner's 1942 *Yankee Doodle Dandy*).

21. *New York Times*, August 6, 1938.

22. Ibid.

23. Philip Furia, *Irving Berlin: A Life in Song* (Schirmer, 1998), 186.

24. Irving Berlin Collection, Library of Congress.

25. Linda Berlin Emmet and Robert Kimball, *The Complete Lyrics of Irving Berlin* (Alfred A. Knopf, 2001), 317.

26. Alec Wilder, *American Popular Song: The Great Innovators, 1900–1950* (Oxford University Press, 1972), p. 109.

27. New York *Journal-American*, September 4, 1938.

15. While the Storm Clouds Gather

1. Irving Berlin Collection, Library of Congress (hereafter IB LOC).

2. CBS transcript in public domain.

3. Mary Ellin Barrett, *Irving Berlin: A Daughter's Memoir* (Simon and Schuster, 1994), 163.

4. Associated Press report, December 9, 1938.

5. Barrett, *A Daughter's Memoir*, 165.

6. Ibid., 166.

7. Linda Berlin Emmet and Robert Kimball, *The Complete Lyrics of Irving Berlin* (Alfred A. Knopf, 2001), 225.

8. Lindy's was a Times Square deli/restaurant, famed for its cheesecake and beloved by Broadway denizens high and low, including Berlin. The original location closed in 1957.

9. Barrett, *A Daughter's Memoir*, 171.

10. *Variety*, May 16, 1939.

11. *National Road Traveler*, October 24, 1941.

12. Edward Jablonski, *Irving Berlin: American Troubadour* (Henry Holt, 1999), 193.

13. *New York Times*, July 14, 1940.

14. Mason City (Iowa) *Globe-Gazette*, June 17, 1939.

15. August 16, 1943, letter to Dale Carnegie. IB LOC.

16. Philip Furia, *Irving Berlin: A Life in Song* (Schirmer, 1998), 195.

17. *New York Times*, July 29, 1940.

18. United Press report, February 21, 1939.

19. Philip Roth, *The Plot against America* (Vintage International, 2004), 15–16.

20. *New York Times*, May 29, 1940.

21. *New York Times*, June 21, 1996.

22. IB LOC.

23. Emmet and Kimball, *Complete Lyrics*, 337.

24. Ibid.

25. Alec Wilder, *American Popular Song: The Great Innovators, 1900–1950* (Oxford University Press, 1972), 114.

26. Emmet and Kimball, *Complete Lyrics*, 339.

27. Barrett, *A Daughter's Memoir*, 186.

28. National Editorial Association story, July 30, 1940.

29. Ibid.

30. Ibid.

31. Associated Press dispatch, July 11, 1940.

32. Barrett, *A Daughter's Memoir*, 173.

33. David A. Banks, "The Lost and Found ASCAP 'Cavalcade of Music' Recordings," http://www.sfmuseum.org/hist5/cavalcade.html.

16. What Is a War Song?

1. Jody Rosen, *White Christmas: The Story of an American Song* (Scribner, 2002), 61.

2. Frank Capra, *The Name Above the Title: An Autobiography* (Da Capo, 1997), 280.

3. Rosen, *White Christmas*, 61.

4. Linda Berlin Emmet and Robert Kimball, *The Complete Lyrics of Irving Berlin* (Alfred A. Knopf, 2001), 350; *Los Angeles Mirror*, December 21, 1954.

5. Emmet and Kimball, *Complete Lyrics*, 351.

6. Laurence Bergreen, *As Thousands Cheer: The Life of Irving Berlin* (Da Capo, 1996), 386.

7. *Jamaica* (Long Island) *Press*, September 24, 1954.

8. Rosen, *White Christmas*, 32.

9. *Los Angeles Examiner,* December 14, 1954.

10. Rosen, *White Christmas*, 61.

11. Irving Berlin Collection, Library of Congress (hereafter IB LOC).

12. *Variety*, December 4, 1940.

13. IB LOC.

14. Associated Press report, January 20, 1941.

15. IB LOC.

16. Ibid.

17. Ibid.

18. *Variety*, August 11, 1941.

19. *Los Angeles Mirror,* December 21, 1954.

20. Rosen, *White Christmas*, 108.

21. Ibid.

22. Ibid., 110.

23. Emmet and Kimball, *Complete Lyrics*, 373.

24. Robert M. Yoder, "Sure Sign That Christmas Is Coming," *Saturday Evening Post*, November 17, 1951.

25. "The Christmas I Can't Forget," *Washington Post*, December 19, 1954.

26. Philip Roth, *Operation Shylock: A Confession* (Vintage International, 1994), 157.

27. Rosen, *White Christmas*, 13–14.

28. Alec Wilder, *American Popular Song: The Great Innovators, 1900–1950* (Oxford University Press, 1972), 94.

29. Philip Furia, *Irving Berlin: A Life in Song* (Schirmer, 1998), 204.

30. Carl Sandburg, *Chicago Times*, December 6, 1942.

31. Rosen, *White Christmas*, 128.

17. This Is the Army, Mr. Jones

1. Irving Berlin Collection, Library of Congress (hereafter IB LOC).

2. Linda Berlin Emmet and Robert Kimball, *The Complete Lyrics of Irving Berlin* (Alfred A. Knopf, 2001), 357.

3. Edward Jablonski, *Irving Berlin: American Troubadour* (Henry Holt, 1999), 208.

4. Ibid., 207–8.

5. Emmet and Kimball, *Complete Lyrics*, 358.

6. *New York Times*, May 17, 1942.

7. Laurence Bergreen, *As Thousands Cheer: The Life of Irving Berlin* (Da Capo, 1996), 395.

8. Ibid., 397. Snapshots from the overseas portion of the tour, after Stone had left the troupe, show that the "Mandy" skit, a holdover from *Yip! Yip! Yaphank*, was done in blackface. Max Showalter journals.

9. *Time*, November 23, 1942. Most modern telecasts of *Holiday Inn* cut the "Abraham" scene entirely.

10. Bergreen, *As Thousands Cheer*, 398.

11. Ibid., 400.

12. Ibid., 400–401.

13. Joshua Logan, *Josh: My Up and Down, In and Out Life* (Delacorte, 1976), 190.

14. Ibid.

15. Mary Ellin Barrett, *Irving Berlin: A Daughter's Memoir* (Simon and Schuster, 1994), 201–2.

16. Emmet and Kimball, *Complete Lyrics*, 360.

17. Barrett, *A Daughter's Memoir*, 203.

18. Jablonski, *American Troubadour*, 216.

19. Ibid.

20. Jody Rosen, *White Christmas: The Story of an American Song* (Scribner, 2002), 132.

21. Edith L. Graham column, *Charleston* (West Virginia) *Gazette*, October 4, 1942.

22. Rosen, *White Christmas*, 132.

23. Bergreen, *As Thousands Cheer*, 407.

24. Emmet and Kimball, *Complete Lyrics*, 353.

25. Jablonski, *American Troubadour*, 217.

26. Rosen, *White Christmas*, 134.

27. Ibid., 135–36.

28. *Time*, November 23, 1942. The sentence should have read

"first big *American* sentimental song hit of World War II"—Lale Andersen's recording of "Lili Marleen" had first become wildly popular with German soldiers in late 1941, and soon caught on with Allied forces as well.

29. Jablonski, *American Troubadour,* 217.

30. IB LOC.

31. Ibid.

32. Letter from Alan Anderson to Mary Ellin Barrett, December 6, 1999.

33. Ibid.

34. Alan Anderson, *The Songwriter Goes to War: The Story of Irving Berlin's World War II All-Army Production of "This Is the Army"* (Limelight, 2004), 98.

35. Philip Furia, *Irving Berlin: A Life in Song* (Schirmer, 1998), 211.

36. *Variety,* August 4, 1943.

37. And its effacement of things Jewish nearly complete. Green's review made a dark but elliptical reference to Oshins's and Ezra Stone's performances' largely winding up on the cutting-room floor, due to "photogenic restrictions." Ibid.

38. Ibid.

18. To War

1. *Holiday Inn* brought in $3,750,000 in domestic box-office receipts; Berlin's ten percent of the gross, $375,000, translates to more than $5 million in today's dollars. On "White Christmas" sales, Jody Rosen, *White Christmas: The Story of an American Song* (Scribner, 2002), 145.

2. For all the hit songs Berlin wrote for the movies, this was the only Oscar he would ever win.

3. Laurence Bergreen, *As Thousands Cheer: The Life of Irving Berlin* (Da Capo, 1996), 426.

4. Edward Jablonski, *Irving Berlin: American Troubadour* (Henry Holt, 1999), 222.

5. Linda Berlin Emmet and Robert Kimball, *The Complete Lyrics of Irving Berlin* (Alfred A. Knopf, 2001), 364.

6. Ibid., 365.

7. Associated Press story, November 11, 1943.

8. Max Showalter journals.

9. Jablonski, *American Troubadour*, 222. The song would not be performed again after the British tour.

10. Irving Berlin Collection, Library of Congress (hereafter IB LOC).

11. Showalter journals. Showalter was the only young actor in *This Is the Army* who went on to forge a successful career in movies and television, often billed as Casey Adams. For access to the detailed and charming journals (in six handwritten volumes) of his wartime travels with the show, I am grateful to John Brady, Joshua S. Ritter of the Scherer Library of Musical Theatre, East Haddam, Connecticut, and the Max Showalter Trust.

12. Bergreen, *As Thousands Cheer*, 432.

13. IB LOC.

14. Bergreen, *As Thousands Cheer*, 335–36.

15. IB LOC.

16. Bergreen, *As Thousands Cheer*, 433.

17. Showalter journals.

18. Emmet and Kimball, *Complete Lyrics*, 367.

19. *New York Times*, May 28, 1944.

20. IB LOC.

21. Ibid.

22. Jablonski, *American Troubadour*, 224.

23. Showalter journals.

24. *New York Times*, August 20, 1944.

25. Mary Ellin Barrett, *Irving Berlin: A Daughter's Memoir* (Simon and Schuster, 1994), 215.

26. IB LOC.

27. Showalter journals.

19. And Back

1. Mary Ellin Barrett, *Irving Berlin: A Daughter's Memoir* (Simon and Schuster, 1994), 219.

2. Mary Ellin Barrett, interview by author (September 24, 2012).

3. *Variety*, April 5, 1944.

4. Barrett interview.

5. *Variety*, September 6, 1944; Edward Jablonski, *Irving Berlin: American Troubadour* (Henry Holt, 1999), 226.

6. Jablonski, *American Troubadour*, 226–27.

7. Max Showalter journals.

8. Laurence Bergreen, *As Thousands Cheer: The Life of Irving Berlin* (Da Capo, 1996), 438.

9. Showalter journals.

10. Ibid.

11. Ibid.

12. Irving Berlin Collection, Library of Congress (hereafter IB LOC).

13. Ibid.

14. *Variety*, April 16, 1945.

15. Barrett interview; Barrett, *A Daughter's Memoir*, 227.

16. Barrett, *A Daughter's Memoir*, 232.

17. Ibid., 227–28.

18. IB LOC.

19. Barrett interview; IB LOC.

20. Jablonski, *American Troubadour*, 229.

21. IB LOC.

22. Associated Press report, October 1, 1945.

23. Showalter journals.

24. Linda Berlin Emmet and Robert Kimball, *The Complete Lyrics of Irving Berlin* (Alfred A. Knopf, 2001), 363.

25. *Stars and Stripes*, October 23, 1945.

26. Ibid.

27. Barrett, *A Daughter's Memoir*, 208.

20. There Is America's Folk Song Writer

1. *New York Times*, November 3, 1945.

2. Edward Jablonski, *Irving Berlin: American Troubadour* (Henry Holt, 1999), 236.

3. Max Wilk, *They're Playing Our Song: Conversations with America's Classic Songwriters* (Easton Studio Press, 2008), 366.

4. Ibid., 367.

5. Richard Rodgers, *Musical Stages: An Autobiography* (Da Capo Press, 2002), 247.

6. Wilk, *They're Playing Our Song,* 366.

7. *Variety,* October 10, 1945.

8. Rodgers, *Musical Stages,* 248.

9. Hugh Fordin, *The World of Entertainment: Hollywood's Greatest Musicals* (Doubleday, 1975), 243.

10. Ibid., 243–44.

11. Jablonski, *American Troubadour,* 236.

12. Irving Berlin Collection, Library of Congress (hereafter IB LOC).

13. Jeffrey Magee, *Irving Berlin's American Musical Theater* (Oxford University Press, 2012), 229.

14. Her father's testimony notwithstanding, Mary Ellin Barrett claims, "he came back [from Atlantic City] with no less than three, maybe five, songs"—though perhaps not all were finished to Berlin's satisfaction. *Irving Berlin: A Daughter's Memoir* (Simon and Schuster, 1994), 235.

15. Jablonski, *American Troubadour,* 237.

16. Fordin, *World of Entertainment,* 244.

17. Jablonski, *American Troubadour,* 237.

18. IB LOC.

19. *New York Times,* May 11, 1958.

20. Philip Furia, *Irving Berlin: A Life in Song* (Schirmer, 1998), 220.

21. Jay Blackton, interview by Mary Ellin Barrett (April 1993).

22. Linda Berlin Emmet and Robert Kimball, *The Complete Lyrics of Irving Berlin* (Alfred A. Knopf, 2001), 385.

23. Magee, *American Musical Theater,* 229.

24. Fordin, *World of Entertainment,* 244–45.

25. IB LOC.

26. The remark has been attributed to the vaudeville comedian Joe Frisco.

27. Wilk, *They're Playing Our Song*, 367; Joshua Logan, *Josh: My Up and Down, In and Out Life* (Delacorte, 1976), 182.

28. Jesse Green, "Irving Berlin's Snow Business," *New York Times*, November 25, 2008.

29. Laurence Bergreen, *As Thousands Cheer: The Life of Irving Berlin* (Da Capo, 1996), 452–53.

30. Logan, *Josh*, 182–83.

31. Bergreen, *As Thousands Cheer*, 453.

32. Wilk, *They're Playing Our Song*, 368–69.

33. Logan, *Josh*, 184.

34. Furia, *A Life in Song*, 225.

35. Alec Wilder, *American Popular Song: The Great Innovators, 1900–1950* (Oxford University Press, 1972), 115.

36. Ibid., 116.

37. *New York Herald Tribune*, June 4, 1962.

38. *New York Daily News*, May 17, 1946.

39. Barrett, *A Daughter's Memoir*, 237.

40. Jablonski, *American Troubadour*, 243.

41. IB LOC.

42. I am grateful to the New York Public Library for the Performing Arts, Dorothy & Lewis B. Cullman Center, where I was able to read Herbert and Dorothy Fields's superb original libretto for *Annie Oakley*.

43. Fordin, *World of Entertainment*, 244.

44. Jablonski, *American Troubadour*, 239.

45. Radie Harris, *Variety*, September 4, 1946.

46. IB LOC.

21. I've Never Been in a Tougher Spot

1. Benjamin Sears, ed., *The Irving Berlin Reader* (Oxford University Press, 2012), 9–15; *New York Sun*, February 24, 1947.

2. *New York Times*, May 11, 1958.

3. Ibid.; Edward Jablonski, *Irving Berlin: American Troubadour* (Henry Holt, 1999), 249.

4. *New York Times*, May 11, 1958.

5. *Variety*, February 27, 1947.

6. Jablonski, *American Troubadour*, 252.

7. Gerald Clarke, *Get Happy: The Life of Judy Garland* (Random House, 2000), p. 238.

8. Linda Berlin Emmet and Robert Kimball, *The Complete Lyrics of Irving Berlin* (Alfred A. Knopf), 402.

9. Hugh Fordin, *The World of Entertainment: Hollywood's Greatest Musicals* (Doubleday, 1975), 233.

10. Jablonski, *American Troubadour*, 254.

11. Mary Ellin Barrett, *Irving Berlin: A Daughter's Memoir* (Simon and Schuster, 1994), 247.

12. Fordin, *World of Entertainment*, 225.

13. Barrett, *A Daughter's Memoir*, 250.

14. *Time*, April 28, 1952.

15. Jablonski, *American Troubadour*, 258; Philip Furia, *Irving Berlin: A Life in Song* (Schirmer, 1998), 238.

16. *New York Times*, June 5, 1949.

17. Jablonski, *American Troubadour*, 258–59; Furia, *A Life in Song*, 239.

18. Furia, *A Life in Song*, 239.

19. Laurence Bergreen, *As Thousands Cheer: The Life of Irving Berlin* (Da Capo, 1996), 490. The anecdote is from a written reminiscence given by Jenkins to James T. Maher, the editor of Alec Wilder's *American Popular Song*.

20. Jared Brown, *Moss Hart, a Prince of the Theatre: A Biography in Three Acts* (Back Stage, 2006), 291.

21. Bergreen, *As Thousands Cheer*, 488.

22. Brown, *Moss Hart*, 291.

23. Barrett, *A Daughter's Memoir*, 252.

24. *New York Times*, July 16, 1949.

25. *Variety*, July 20, 1949.

26. *Kiss Me Kate* would win the first Tony for Best Musical in 1949; the following year, *South Pacific* would win *ten* Tonys, as well as the Pulitzer Prize for drama, only the second musical since the Gershwins' *Of Thee I Sing* to do so.

27. Brown, *Moss Hart*, 292.

28. Furia, *A Life in Song*, 238; *St. Louis Star-Times*, December 20, 1942.

29. Barrett, *A Daughter's Memoir*, 252.

22. We'll Never Get Off the Stage

1. *Variety*, September 21, 1949.

2. Mary Ellin Barrett, interview by author (September 24, 2012).

3. Philip Furia, *Irving Berlin: A Life in Song* (Schirmer, 1998), 244–45; *Boston Post*, September 24, 1950.

4. Furia, *A Life in Song*, 245; *Boston Post*, September 24, 1950.

5. Jay Blackton, interview by Mary Ellin Barrett (April 1993).

6. Mary Ellin Barrett, *Irving Berlin: A Daughter's Memoir* (Simon and Schuster, 1994), 262.

7. Linda Berlin Emmet and Robert Kimball, *The Complete Lyrics of Irving Berlin* (Alfred A. Knopf, 2001), 426.

8. Edward Jablonski, *Irving Berlin: American Troubadour* (Henry Holt, 1999), 266; *Variety*, July 5, 1950.

9. *New York Times*, May 8, 1988.

10. Bob Thomas, *I Got Rhythm: The Ethel Merman Story* (Putnam Adult, 1985), 110.

11. Emmet and Kimball, *Complete Lyrics*, 435.

12. Ibid., 434–35.

13. Ibid., 435.

14. Brian Kellow, *Ethel Merman: A Life* (Penguin, 2007), 130.

15. *New York World-Telegram and Sun*, October 13, 1950.

16. *Variety*, October 13, 1950.

17. *New York Times*, October 15, 1950.

18. *New York Times*, October 22, 1950.

19. Irving Berlin Collection, Library of Congress (hereafter IB LOC).

20. Barrett, *A Daughter's Memoir*, 271–72.

21. *Variety*, January 24, 1951.

22. IB LOC.

23. *New York Times*, May 8, 1988.

24. *New York Times*, February 11, 1952; Emmet and Kimball, *Complete Lyrics*, 433.

25. *Variety*, May 28, 1952.
26. Linda Emmet, interview by author (July 22, 2011).
27. Emmet and Kimball, *Complete Lyrics*, 445.
28. IB LOC.
29. Emmet and Kimball, *Complete Lyrics*, 440.

23. A Worried Old Man on the Hill

1. Mary Ellin Barrett, *Irving Berlin: A Daughter's Memoir* (Simon and Schuster, 1994), 280.
2. *Time*, March 23, 1953.
3. Walter Winchell, syndicated column, April 21, 1953.
4. Associated Press item, May 12, 1953.
5. Winchell column, July 24, 1953.
6. Henry Ephron, *We Thought We Could Do Anything* (W. W. Norton, 1977), 123–24.
7. *Variety*, February 11, 1953.
8. Philip Furia, *Irving Berlin: A Life in Song* (Schirmer, 1998), 250.
9. *New York Times*, October 18, 1953.
10. United Press report, February 13, 1954.
11. Louella Parsons, *Los Angeles Examiner*, February 2, 1954.
12. Bosley Crowther, *New York Times*, October 24, 1954.
13. New York *Herald Tribune*, October 17, 1954.
14. Furia, *A Life in Song*, 254.
15. *New York Daily News*, March 27, 1956.
16. Graham Payn, with Barry Day, *My Life with Noël Coward* (Applause, 1994), 99.
17. Edward Jablonski, *Irving Berlin: American Troubadour* (Henry Holt, 1999), 283.
18. Associated Press report, February 18, 1955.
19. *New York Times*, November 29, 1955.
20. Irving Berlin Collection, Library of Congress (hereafter IB LOC).
21. Linda Berlin Emmet and Robert Kimball, *The Complete Lyrics of Irving Berlin* (Alfred A. Knopf, 2001), 450.
22. Jablonski, *American Troubadour*, 285.

23. Emmet and Kimball, *Complete Lyrics*, 454.

24. Barrett, *A Daughter's Memoir*, 285.

25. Mary Ellin Barrett, interview by author (September 24, 2012).

26. *London Daily Express*, September 13, 1963; Whitney Bolton, syndicated column, August 26, 1966.

27. Emmet and Kimball, *Complete Lyrics*, 464–65.

28. Barrett, *A Daughter's Memoir*, 285–86.

29. Gilbert Millstein, *New York Times*, May 11, 1958.

30. IB LOC.

31. Edouard Emmet, letter to Mary Ellin Barrett (June 1990).

32. *Life*, May 3, 1963.

24. What Have You Written Lately?

1. *New York Times*, October 14, 1962.

2. The proposals included George Bernard Shaw's *Pygmalion*, which in the hands of Alan Jay Lerner and Frederick Loewe became 1956's *My Fair Lady*.

3. *Saturday Evening Post*, October 20, 1962.

4. Ibid.

5. *New York Times*, October 14, 1962.

6. Linda Berlin Emmet and Robert Kimball, *The Complete Lyrics of Irving Berlin* (Alfred A. Knopf, 2001), 470.

7. Edward Jablonski, *Irving Berlin: American Troubadour* (Henry Holt, 1999), 291.

8. Sam Zolotow, *New York Times*, September 1, 1961.

9. Edouard Emmet, letter to Mary Ellin Barrett (June 1990).

10. *Saturday Evening Post*, October 20, 1962.

11. John Crosby, *New York Herald Tribune*, June 11, 1962.

12. Ibid.

13. *Saturday Evening Post*, October 20, 1962.

14. Emmet and Kimball, *Complete Lyrics*, 468.

15. *Saturday Evening Post*, October 20, 1962.

16. Laurence Bergreen, *As Thousands Cheer: The Life of Irving Berlin* (Da Capo, 1996), 538–39.

17. Jeffrey Magee, *Irving Berlin's American Musical Theater* (Oxford University Press, 2012), 298.

18. Mary Ellin Barrett, *Irving Berlin: A Daughter's Memoir* (Simon and Schuster, 1994), 289.

19. Marjorie Hunter, *New York Times*, September 26, 1962.

20. Ibid.

21. Jablonski, *American Troubadour*, 300.

22. President Henderson: "Well, what did you think of the conversation with Charles de Gaulle? He's got a mind like a steel trap." First Lady: "Yes, and it snapped shut years ago." Bergreen, *As Thousands Cheer*, 543.

23. Ibid., 544.

24. Barrett, *A Daughter's Memoir*, 289.

25. Bergreen, *As Thousands Cheer*, 545.

26. Quoted in *Variety*, September 27, 1962.

27. *New York Times*, October 14, 1962.

28. Ibid.

29. The actual lyrics are: "It gets lonely in the White House/ When you've been attacked/By the loyal opposition/Getting in the act . . ." Emmet and Kimball, *Complete Lyrics*, 471.

30. Walter Kerr, *New York Herald Tribune*, October 22, 1962.

31. Bergreen, *As Thousands Cheer*, 546.

32. Emmet and Kimball, *Complete Lyrics*, 476.

33. Emmet letter to Barrett.

34. Barrett, *A Daughter's Memoir*, 290.

35. Herbert Kretzmer, *London Daily Express*, September 13, 1963.

36. Irving Berlin Collection, Library of Congress.

37. Emmet and Kimball, *Complete Lyrics*, 396.

38. Jablonski, *American Troubadour*, 310.

39. *New York Times*, June 1, 1966.

40. *Billboard*, December 10, 1966.

41. Peter Hay, *Broadway Anecdotes* (Oxford University Press, 1990), 250.

42. Emmet and Kimball, *Complete Lyrics*, 485.

43. Mark Griffin, *A Hundred or More Hidden Things: The Life and Films of Vincente Minnelli* (Da Capo, 2010), 265.

44. *Los Angeles Times*, January 22, 1968.

45. George Gent, *New York Times*, May 6, 1968. Berlin's actual song output was closer to fifteen hundred.

46. Ibid.

47. *New York Times*, May 12, 1968.

Diminuendo and Coda

1. Mary Ellin Barrett, *Irving Berlin: A Daughter's Memoir* (Simon and Schuster, 1994), 294–95.

2. Linda Berlin Emmet and Robert Kimball, *The Complete Lyrics of Irving Berlin* (Alfred A. Knopf, 2001), xix.

3. Ibid., 491.

4. Ibid.

5. Irving Berlin Collection, Library of Congress (hereafter IB LOC).

6. Edward Jablonski, *Irving Berlin: American Troubadour* (Henry Holt, 1999), 322.

7. Emmet and Kimball, *Complete Lyrics*, xix.

8. Barrett, *A Daughter's Memoir*, 293.

9. Laurence Bergreen, *As Thousands Cheer: The Life of Irving Berlin* (Da Capo, 1996), 562–63.

10. Barrett, *A Daughter's Memoir*, 294.

11. Emmet and Kimball, *Complete Lyrics*, xviii.

12. IB LOC.

13. Ibid.

14. Ibid.

15. Barrett, *A Daughter's Memoir*, 292.

16. Yiddish for laughter.

17. IB LOC.

18. Ibid.

19. Ibid.

20. Ibid.

21. Roughly: good health to you from me.

22. IB LOC.

23. E. Y. "Yip" Harburg, *At This Point in Rhyme: E. Y. Harburg's Poems* (Crown, 1976), 64.

24. IB LOC.

25. Mel Gussow, *New York Times*, September 23, 1971.

26. Barrett, *A Daughter's Memoir*, 295.

27. Emmet and Kimball, *Complete Lyrics*, 499.

28. Barrett, *A Daughter's Memoir*, 296.

29. Bergreen, *As Thousands Cheer*, 574–75.

30. Ibid., 573–74; *New York Times*, December 23, 2005.

31. IB LOC.

32. Emmet and Kimball, *Complete Lyrics*, 501.

33. Jablonski, *American Troubadour*, 329.

34. Emmet and Kimball, *Complete Lyrics*, 187; https://www.you tube.com/watch?v=DVtT8it5EoU.

35. Barrett, *A Daughter's Memoir*, 297–98.

36. Ibid., 298–99.

37. Ibid., 299.

38. Associated Press report, September 23, 1989.

ACKNOWLEDGMENTS

THIS BOOK would have barely got going without the generous cooperation and encouragement of Irving and Ellin Berlin's eldest daughter, the dedicatee of "Blue Skies" and sterling memoirist Mary Ellin Berlin Barrett. Yet from the beginning there were no conditions. Throughout my work, Mary Ellin served as an invaluable source and sounding board, her chief concern never whether the book showed her father in a positive light but whether it was accurate.

I am also lastingly grateful to Mary Ellin's sister Linda Berlin Emmet and her husband, Edouard, for an unforgettable lunch in Paris and for their many memories of Berlin in the City of Light, with which he instantly fell in love on his first visit in 1911.

But the great unspoken gift both Berlin sisters gave me (to my regret, I never had the chance to meet the youngest daughter, Elizabeth) was their *presence*, the vivid embodiment of the qualities of their remarkable parents, qualities I needed to try and summon in my narrative.

My deep thanks, as always, go to my wife, Karen Cumbus, for her incisive psychological insights and her steady forbearance with the grumpy obsessive in the attic.

My late brother Peter, who so passionately loved Irving Berlin—both his music and his Jewish, gum-chewing, wisecracking, Manhattan-ese essence—was my initial inspiration, both for falling deeply into the Great American Songbook (a phrase he hated) way back when, and for beginning this project, some ten years ago. My late mother, Roberta Wennik Kaplan, who played Berlin on her Steinway and sang along, bringing the plangent greatness of "How Deep Is the Ocean" alive, gifted me with her passion for music. And my dear friend Peter Bogdanovich saved me from foundering many times, reading each chapter as I finished it and cheering me on, an essential ally in bringing my ship into port.

I'm once again profoundly grateful to my longtime literary agent and ally Joy Harris. And, once more, to Adam Reed in Joy's office.

I am indebted to Ileene Smith, who did me the honor of commissioning this book for the Yale University Press Jewish Lives series, and edited it with a sharp eye and a growing sense of discovery—exciting to both of us—of the greatness of Berlin.

I'm equally beholden to my keen-eyed manuscript editor Dan Heaton, who brought great enthusiasm for the subject, infused our work together with wit and fun, and saved me from more gaffes and infelicities than I'd like to admit.

My sincere thanks also go to Heather Gold, the in-house coordinator for the Jewish Lives series, and to the rest of the team at Yale University Press.

And crucially, I'm grateful to the Leon D. Black Foundation for underwriting the Jewish Lives Series.

My thanks as well to the following: George Avakian, John Brady, Tim Brooks; Ted Chapin, Nicole Harman, David Loughner, and Zachary Reiser at the Rodgers & Hammerstein Organization; Mark Cyzyk, David Reynolds, and James Stimpert at the Sheridan Libraries of Johns Hopkins University; Erin Dickenson of Concord Music; Michael Feinstein, Bert Fink, Norm Hirschy;

Mark Eden Horowitz and the rest of the staff at the Music Division of the Library of Congress; W. Campbell Hudson, Robert Kimball, Gary Marmorstein, Ted Panken; Joshua S. Ritter and the staff of the Scherer Library of Musical Theatre; Mark Saltzman, Jonathan Schwartz, Andy Senior, and the Max Showalter Trust.

Page 374 is blank

CREDITS

JEWISH LIVES is a prizewinning series of interpretative biography designed to explore the many facets of Jewish identity. Individual volumes illuminate the imprint of Jewish figures upon literature, religion, philosophy, politics, cultural and economic life, and the arts and sciences. Subjects are paired with authors to elicit lively, deeply informed books that explore the range and depth of the Jewish experience from antiquity to the present.

Jewish Lives is a partnership of Yale University Press and the Leon D. Black Foundation. Ileene Smith is editorial director. Anita Shapira and Steven J. Zipperstein are series editors.